All of London exploded on the night of 18 May 1900, in the biggest West End party ever seen. The mix of media manipulation, patriotism, and class, race, and gender politics that produced the "spontaneous" festivities of Mafeking Night begins this analysis of the cultural politics of late-Victorian imperialism. Paula M. Krebs examines "the last of the gentlemen's wars" – the Boer War of 1899–1902 – and the struggles to maintain an imperialist hegemony in a twentieth-century world, through the war writings of Arthur Conan Doyle, Olive Schreiner, H. Rider Haggard, and Rudyard Kipling, as well as contemporary journalism, propaganda, and other forms of public discourse. Her feminist analysis of such matters as the sexual honor of the British soldier at war, the deaths of thousands of women and children in "concentration camps," and new concepts of race in South Africa marks this book as a significant contribution to British imperial studies.

Paula M. Krebs is Associate Professor of English at Wheaton College, Massachusetts. She is co-editor of *The Feminist Teacher Anthology: Pedagogies and Classroom Strategies* (1998) and has published articles in *Victorian Studies*, *History Workshop Journal*, and *Victorian Literature and Culture*.

CAMBRIDGE STUDIES IN NINETEENTH-CENTURY
LITERATURE AND CULTURE 23

GENDER, RACE, AND THE
WRITING OF EMPIRE

CAMBRIDGE STUDIES IN NINETEENTH-CENTURY
LITERATURE AND CULTURE

General editor
Gillian Beer, *University of Cambridge*

Nineteenth-century British literature and culture have been rich fields for interdisciplinary studies. Since the turn of the twentieth century, scholars and critics have tracked the intersections and tensions between Victorian literature and the visual arts, politics, social organization, economic life, technical innovations, scientific thought – in short, culture in its broadest sense. In recent years, theoretical challenges and historiographical shifts have unsettled the assumptions of previous scholarly syntheses and called into question the terms of older debates. Whereas the tendency in much past literary critical interpretation was to use the metaphor of culture as "background," feminist, Foucauldian, and other analyses have employed more dynamic models that raise questions of power and of circulation. Such developments have reanimated the field.

This series aims to accommodate and promote the most interesting work being undertaken on the frontiers of the field of nineteenth-century literary studies: work which intersects fruitfully with other fields of study such as history, or literary theory, or the history of science. Comparative as well as interdisciplinary approaches are welcomed.

A complete list of titles published will be found at the end of the book.

GENDER, RACE, AND THE WRITING OF EMPIRE

Public Discourse and the Boer War

PAULA M. KREBS

Wheaton College, Massachusetts

CAMBRIDGE
UNIVERSITY PRESS

PUBLISHED BY THE PRESS SYNDICATE OF THE UNIVERSITY OF CAMBRIDGE
The Pitt Building, Trumpington Street, Cambridge CB2 IRP, United Kingdom

CAMBRIDGE UNIVERSITY PRESS
The Edinburgh Building, Cambridge, CB2 2RU, UK http://www.cup.cam.ac.uk
40 West 20th Street, New York, NY 10011-4211, USA http://www.cup.org
10 Stamford Road, Oakleigh, Melbourne 3166, Australia

First published 1999

Printed in the United Kingdom at the University Press, Cambridge

Typeset in Baskerville 11/12.5pt [VN]

A catalogue record for this book is available from the British Library

Library of Congress Cataloguing in Publication data

Krebs, Paula M.
Gender, race, and the writing of empire: public discourse and the
Boer War / Paula M. Krebs.
p. cm. – (Cambridge studies in nineteenth-century literature
and culture: 23)
Includes bibliographical references and index.
ISBN 0 521 65322 3 hardback
1. South African War, 1899–1902 – Literature and the war. 2. South
African War, 1899–1902 – Foreign public opinion, British. 3. English
literature – 20th century – History and criticism. 4. English
literature – 19th century – History and criticism. 5. South Africa –
Foreign relations – Great Britain. 6. Great Britain – Foreign
relations – South Africa. 7. South Africa – Foreign public opinion,
British. 8. South Africa – In literature. 9. Imperialism in
literature. 10. Sex role in literature. 11. Race in literature.
I. Title. II. Series.
PR129.S6K74 1999
820.9'358 – dc21 98–47072 CIP

ISBN 0 521 65322 3 hardback

To my mother, Dorothy M. Krebs, and to the memory of
my father, George F. Krebs, who knew war and
knew not to glamorize it.

Contents

Acknowledgments

The research for this book was carried out with the generous assistance of many individuals and institutions. I have for many years benefited enormously from the resources of the University of London's Institute of Commonwealth Studies. I am especially grateful to the Institute for the Henry Charles Chapman Fellowship, which I held for eight months in 1994. The Institute's seminars on *Societies of Southern Africa in the Nineteenth and Twentieth Centuries* and *Gender, Commonwealth, and Empire* have been exciting and challenging venues at which to offer my own work and equally important places at which to learn from the work of others. Wheaton College provided a semester of research leave under the generous terms of the Hewlett-Mellon Research Award program and an additional semester of unpaid leave, in addition to the travel funds necessary for the research to complete this book. The Graduate School at Indiana University awarded funds for travel to collections, and the Indiana University Victorian Studies Program funded the important first year of my research. The Charlotte W. Newcombe Fellowship, from the Woodrow Wilson Foundation in Princeton, New Jersey, enabled me to finish the doctoral dissertation that was the first stage of this book.

I would like to thank the Trustees of Indiana University for permission to reprint material that appeared in *Victorian Studies* and the Editorial Collective of *History Workshop Journal* for permission to reprint material from that publication. For permission to quote from the Joseph Chamberlain Papers, I thank the University of Birmingham library. Lord Milner's correspondence is quoted by permission of the Warden and Fellows, New College Oxford. For permission to use the cover illustration, I thank the John Hay Library at Brown University and Peter Harrington, curator of the Anne S. K. Brown Military Collection. I am grateful to the librarians at the British Library and the British Library Newspaper Library at Colindale, the Public Record Office at

Kew, the University of York's Centre for Southern African Studies, the Indiana University library, the library of the London School of Economics and Political Science, the Bodleian Library at Oxford University, the National Army Museum, the Madeline Clark Wallace Library at Wheaton College – especially Martha Mitchell, the library of the University of London's School of Oriental and African Studies, David Doughan and the Fawcett Library, the Royal Commonwealth Society, and David Blake and his staff at the Institute of Commonwealth Studies.

Tricia Lootens, Carolyn Burdett, Donald Gray, Regenia Gagnier, Patrick Brantlinger, Paul Zietlow, G. Cleveland Wilhoit, and Susan Gubar read and commented on chapters of this work, and I have benefited tremendously from their help. I would also like to thank the anonymous readers for *Victorian Studies* and *History Workshop Journal*, and, especially, the extremely helpful readers for Cambridge University Press. Thanks also to my wonderful editor at CUP, Linda Bree. Friends and colleagues who have heard me present aspects of the argument at seminars and in lectures and who have provided valuable feedback include Kate Darien-Smith, Shula Marks, Deborah Gaitskell, Hilary Sapire, Shaun Milton, Chee Heng Leng, Annie Coombes, Lynda Nead, Dian Kriz, John Miller, Travis Crosby, and Kathryn Tomasek. I am extremely grateful as well for the useful advice of Sue Wiseman, Tim Armstrong, Joe Bristow, Wendy Kolmar, Nicola Bown, Beverly Clark, Richard Pearce, and Sue Lafky. My undergraduate research assistant, the late Sam Maltese, helped with the Kipling material; he would have contributed much to the field of literary and cultural studies. I offer a sincere thank you to Marilyn Todesco and to my indexer, Jessica Benjamin. My intellectual debt to Patrick Brantlinger will be obvious in the pages that follow, and I thank him very much. Tricia Lootens has been my partner in Victorian Studies for many years – my best friend, collaborator, mentor. Claire Buck made this book possible, always making the time to read and discuss drafts, and always asking the toughest questions. Her intellectual, practical, and emotional support have made all the difference.

CHAPTER I

The war at home

In the 1939 Shirley Temple film of the classic children's story *A Little Princess*, young Sara Crewe rousts all the slumbering residents of Miss Minchin's Female Seminary from their beds with the cry of "Mafeking is relieved! Mafeking is relieved!" Sara patriotically drags her schoolmates and teachers into the wild London street celebrations marking the end of the Boer War siege that she and the rest of England had been following in the newspapers for months. This particular scene in the film seems a bit odd to those familiar with Frances Hodgson Burnett's novel (1905), however, because the novel never mentions the Boer War – Sara's father is posted in India, not South Africa. But in 1939, it was better to send Captain Crewe to Mafeking. With Britain at war and the United States weighing its options, fellow-feeling for the British was important. If a film was to inspire transatlantic loyalties, to remind American audiences of the kind of stuff those Brits were made of, then Mafeking Night was a perfect image to use. Mafeking, in the early part of the century, still meant wartime hope, British pluck, and home-front patriotism. Using Mafeking Night as its centerpiece, *The Little Princess* (the film's title) was a kind of *Mrs. Miniver* for children.

Mafeking Night must have been an irresistible choice for the makers of *The Little Princess* – it had military glory, class-mixing, and rowdiness in the gaslit streets of nostalgia-laden Victorian London. The scene had been truly unprecedented.[1] When news of the relief of Mafeking reached London at 9:17 p.m. on Friday 18 May 1900, thanks to a Reuters News Agency telegram, central London exploded. Thousands danced, drank, kissed, and created general uproar. In what has been seen as perhaps the premier expression of crude public support of late-Victorian imperialism, Liverpool, Newcastle, Birmingham, York, and Glasgow rioted with fireworks, brass bands, and blasts on factory sirens. This celebration of empire was made possible by the new halfpenny press that spread the daily news to thousands of households

that had never before read a newspaper daily. The most significant
spontaneous public eruption in London since the 1886 Trafalgar Square
riots, Mafeking Night could hardly have been more different in character from those protests of unemployment. Economic theorist J. A.
Hobson, and V. I. Lenin, whose *Imperialism: The Highest Stage of Capitalism*
(1916) grew directly from Hobson's writings, argued that imperialism
distracted the British working classes from their economic problems by
promising payoffs from afar in imperial trade as well as by replacing
class consciousness with nationalism and pride in the empire. Mafeking
Night has come down to us as a central symbol of such distraction – the
premier image of late-Victorian mass support for nationalism, patriotism, and imperial capitalism.

This chapter argues that the events of Mafeking Night must be read
differently. The events that led to the "spontaneous" riots of Mafeking
Night show that the celebrations in fact say less about British support for
imperialism than they do about the power of the press to tease the
British public into a frenzy of anticipation and then to release that
tension in a rush of carefully-directed enthusiasm. Mafeking Night
symbolizes what J. A. Hobson saw as the dangerous power of the
popular press in creating imperial sentiment in the service of capitalism.
It is a compilation of the power of some other very important symbols
that were at work in support of imperialism – symbols of British
masculinity, class structure, and patronage of "lower races." Each of
these symbols is at work in the making of Mafeking Night, and each
holds some profound contradictions in the period of the Boer War,
which is why Mafeking Night itself is such a highly ambiguous symbol of
Victorian support for imperialism.

Mafeking Night made jingoism safe for the middle classes by blurring
the distinction between jingoism, which had been seen as working-class
over-enthusiasm for the empire, and patriotism, that middle-class virtue
of support for one's country against foreign opposition. Mafeking Night
defused the threat that had been posed by mass action in London, such
as the bloody Trafalgar Square riots of just fourteen years before. Anne
McClintock points out the fear of the "crowd" in late-Victorian London: "In the last decades of the nineteenth century, the urban crowd
became a recurring fetish for ruling-class fears of social unrest and
underclass militancy. Lurking in the resplendent metropolis, the crowd
embodied a 'savage' and dangerous underclass waiting to spring upon
the propertied classes" (*Imperial Leather* 118–19). The nineteenth-century
study of crowd psychology, which began with examinations of the

French Revolution and the Paris Commune, focused on fear, as J. S. McClelland points out in *The Crowd and the Mob* (200). By the publication of Gustave Le Bon's book on the crowd (published in English in 1899 as *The Psychology of Peoples*), "crowd psychology had long been chipping away at the sense of distance which ordinary, civilized, law-abiding men had always felt when they looked at crowds" (McClelland *The Crowd and the Mob* 200), and Le Bon's elitism encouraged a middle-class fear of being subsumed into an underclass crowd. Mafeking Night was a mass action in the streets, but it was neither produced nor controlled by the working classes. Young Sara Crewe would have been perfectly safe in the 18 and 19 May outdoor revels in the West End of London, for they had nothing at all in common with working-class protests of unemployment or with the worker unrest that had terrified the ruling classes earlier in the century. In the newspaper versions of the event, Mafeking Night was a middle-class party (with some working-class guests). The date had been set and invitations issued by lower-middle-class media – the popular press.

In a Victorian Britain where masses in the streets had always meant strikes and riots, there had been no precedent for large-scale public celebration – even the public celebrations of victory over Napoleon had been relatively small and sedate. But the British people surged into the twentieth century when they poured into the West End to celebrate the relief of Mafeking. Newspapers and journals touted the mixed-class nature of the Mafeking festivities: costermongers mingled with gentlemen. The rioters were not working-class radicals, threatening the political or social order. In the language the press used to describe Mafeking Night and the following day, they were "everyone" and "London" and even "England." They were created as a group by the newspapers, and this chapter examines the mechanism of their creation and the function of them as a group representing "public opinion."

After the demise of the eighteenth-century coffeehouse culture around which Jürgen Habermas formed his concept of the "public sphere," the arena through which governments heard feedback from elite social groups about public policies, the equivalent forum for public exchange of ideas became the periodicals – the reviews and even the magazines.[2] But by the end of the Victorian period, the periodicals, though still prestigious as public forums, were losing their pride of place in public opinion formation to the newspapers. With the spread of literacy after the Education Act of 1870 and the emergence of the new popular press, some political debates, including questions about South

Africa, shifted to the newspapers. As "public" took on new meanings in the nineteenth century, as new publics were being created that included women and the lower-middle and working classes, the quality and the popular press, daily and weekly, became the "public sphere," and public discourse of many kinds became important in the creation of government and even military policy.

The Reform Acts of 1832 and 1870 had begun to create a new relationship between the government and the "public" in Britain. Historians of public opinion, such as J.A.W. Gunn and Dror Wahrman, recognize the significance of newspapers in public opinion, even if they rarely resolve whether the press shapes or reflects public opinion. But the eighteenth-century newspaper, and even the 1830s newspaper, was a qualitatively and quantitatively different thing from the daily of 1899, and the publics reached by the end-of-century newspapers were very different indeed from earlier ones. After the establishment of the *Daily Mail* in 1896, as tabloid journalism emerged coincident with the New Imperialism, public opinion about the Boer War became quite directly dependent on newspapers. With the New Journalism, the newspaper-reading public was a far wider collection of people in 1899 than it had been during any previous British war. But while the popular press thrived on the daily drama of war reporting from South Africa and benefited in circulation figures and influence from the war, the government's colonial and war policies benefited just as much from the success of the halfpenny papers, especially the *Daily Mail*.

To consider terms such as public discourse, public sphere, and public opinion as useful analytical tools for an examination of imperial ideology, we must first understand turn-of-the-century creation of "the public." As Mary Poovey ("Abortion Question"), Judith Butler ("Contingent Foundations"), and other feminist theorists have shown, discourses that presuppose a unified, universal subject, such as arguments that rely on a language of "rights," are implicated in the creation of that subject. The subject, Poovey argues, is a gendered, mythical construction that is deemed to have "personhood" based on an inner essence that must pre-exist it ("Abortion Question" 240). The creation of the "public" by late-nineteenth-century newspapers and political officials can be considered similarly to the ways Poovey and Butler consider the construction of the liberal individual political subject – the system ends up constructing the very subject whose existence it thinks it is acknowledging. In the events of Mafeking Night we see the emergence of a British public that observers had been assuming existed all the while that they were creating it. The newspapers were considering "what the public wants" while teaching it what to want, and the celebrations of Mafeking Night served as both evidence that there was one "public" in ritain and as example of the effectiveness of the press, in consultation with the military and the Colonial Office, in the creation of that public out of many separate and distinct publics.

WAR AND THE PUBLIC

The Boer War marked an important turning point for imperial Britain. The war, fought by two white armies for control over a land where whites were far outnumbered by indigenous Africans, pitted the British Empire against the farmers (the literal translation of "Boers") of Dutch descent who lived in the two South African republics. In Britain, the Boers were seen as backward, petty tyrants who sought to exploit British settlers in the gold-mining districts of the Witwatersrand. When war was declared in October 1899, it was general knowledge in Britain that the ragged bands ("commandos") of untrained Boer soldiers riding ponies could never mount a credible attack on the British army, and the war would be over by Christmas. But, as Oscar Wilde had said, wars are never over by Christmas, and this one dragged on for almost three years, as British fighting methods, horses, supplies, and health all proved inadequate to the task. Although few British statesmen came out fully against the war, by the war's end the rest of Europe vehemently denounced the British cause and fighting methods, and conflict about the methods employed by the British army resulted in a split in the already divided Liberal party and in public opinion throughout Britain.

From the newspaper coverage of the war in popular and quality dailies to the private correspondence of public figures, writings about the war reveal splits in public opinion and serious new concerns about British imperialism. Concern about British aims in southern Africa had been stirred in late 1895, when entrepreneur Cecil Rhodes' ally Leander Starr Jameson had led an abortive raid against the Boer government of the Transvaal. Jameson had been trying to stir up rebellion among the "uitlanders," the mostly-British foreigners working in the mining district, so Britain could justify annexing the region, and it was easy to portray the Boer War that came three years later as a government-led attempt to achieve what Rhodes had been unable to achieve with the Jameson Raid – a Transvaal in the political control of the British rather than the Boer farmers.

In looking at Mafeking Night, this chapter problematizes the concept of public opinion and its relation to late-Victorian imperialism, examining the assumptions about, for example, race, gender, evolution, and economics under which the ideology of imperialism was operating. It all starts with Mafeking Night – the celebrations that marked that event point to the issues that characterized the rest of the war. The Mafeking Night celebrations have been portrayed as spontaneous, unproblematically patriotic, and at the same time nationally uncharacteristic. That is, they were distinctly un-British: Kipling wrote to William Alexander Fraser shortly after Mafeking Night, "You've seen something that I never suspected lay in the national character – the nation letting itself go."[3] But that hitherto hidden side of the national character was not as spontaneously revealed as Kipling implied: Carrie Kipling noted in her diary on Mafeking Night that it was her husband himself who was responsible for the celebrations at Rottingdean, where he had roused the "inhabitants to celebrate" the relief of Mafeking (quoted in Pinney *Letters* 18).

The events surrounding the relief of Mafeking prove characteristic of both the New Imperialism and the New Journalism. The interlocking of these two developments allowed the Anglo-Boer to be what one soldier called "the last of the gentlemen's wars,"[4] with all the gender, race, and class-based associations inherent in the phrase, but made it also the first of the sensation-mongers' wars. And the sensation journalism that supported the New Imperialism called into question some of the central assumptions behind the concept of the British gentleman.

The press had, since the eighteenth century, been seen as an important influence on "public opinion," as it was defined by government and opposition. But, with the Reform Acts and the Education Act of 1870 creating an expanded and more literate electorate, the late-Victorian press had come to assume an even more significant role in the determination of public opinion. Critics such as J. A. Hobson attributed much power to the press in creating and sustaining mass support for imperialism. But Hobson's critique of imperialism has a strong anti-working-class bias: the public he sees as deluded into supporting imperialism is the workers. Hobson was right to the extent that the new popular press was not aimed at the constituency thought to make up public opinion earlier in the century. The *Daily Mail*, the newspaper Salisbury is reported to have said was "written by office boys for office boys" (quoted in Ensor *England* 313), sought a different public than such venerable organs as *The Times*. It was not until the New Journalism that newspapers could be said to reach readers who were not at least upper-middle class. The penny dailies (and the threepenny *Times*) aimed at political influence and sought it in the traditional readership of the daily press. But the new halfpennies, starting with the *Daily Mail*, sought huge circulations and the profits that accompanied them. While "public opinion" from the early eighteenth-century origin of the term seems to have meant the opinion of that part of the public that constituted the electorate, public opinion by the time of the Boer War was not so easily defined. The new variety in the press paralleled a new variety of publics: a large, literate electorate and even some of the non-enfranchised – women. (The *Daily Mail* ran regular features directed at its female readers, including fiction and fashion articles.) The Mafeking Night celebrations were the product of the new newspapers' relationships with the new British publics they were creating, and the celebrations, while they would seem to demonstrate "common sense,"[5] natural support for imperialism in turn-of-the-century Britain, actually reveal that such support was carefully manufactured through the press by a careful manipulation of public opinion(s) to create a very temporary spasm of jingoism.

The jingoism/patriotism of Mafeking Night helped to rally national and, indeed, imperial sentiment behind a war that had not been going well. Because of a series of British setbacks early in the war, it had become important that something potent emerge to bring Britons together in support of the conflict. A symbol would need to evoke sentiments that could unite Britons, whether or not they supported Joseph Chamberlain in the Colonial Office, the embattled War Office, or the war itself. The million-circulation *Daily Mail* and its allies in the new popular journalism of the late 1890s handed the British government the answer: The siege of Mafeking, with its strong, masculine hero in Colonel Robert Baden-Powell, its plucky British civilians (including the elegant Lady Sarah Wilson) making the best of a bad lot, and its loyal African population rallying behind the Union Jack, was a war publicist's dream. The popular press beat the drum for Britain, and, while it did not succeed in converting the nation wholesale into jingoes, it managed nevertheless to produce in Mafeking Night itself a spectacle of English enthusiasm for empire that united class with class and provided an image of imperial solidarity to inspire much-needed support for the war.

By the 1899 start of the Boer War, imperialism had entered British public discourse in countless ways; John MacKenzie's work on propaganda and empire points to the myriad symbols of empire in everyday

life by the turn of the century. Everything from biscuit tins to advertisements to schoolbooks, as Kathryn Castle shows, reminded Britons of
"their" empire. Edward Said talks of the place of imperialism in the
works of "Ruskin, Tennyson, Meredith, Dickens, Arnold, Thackeray,
George Eliot, Carlyle, Mill – in short, the full roster of significant
Victorian writers" (*Culture* 126), and of the ways the British imperial
identity affected the world view of such figures as they came to "identify
themselves with this power" (*Culture* 127) that was imperialism. Literature played a significant part in the development of an imperial imaginary – images and myths about the empire working in conjunction with
"facts" coming from the empire – that was necessary to sustain British
public support for the economic project of empire.[6] The final chapter of
this book takes up the issue of literary figures and their relation to
imperialism during the Boer War. For the purposes of this first chapter,
however, I would like to examine the ways the average newspaper-
reading public came to "identify [itself] with this power" of imperialism. Rather than tracing imperial themes in literature, as many excellent recent studies have done, this volume examines assumptions about
British imperialism and what sustained it in public discourse about the
Boer War as well as analyzing the ways various kinds of public discourse
functioned to support and critique that imperialism.

MAFEKING MYTH

Despite or perhaps because of the strategic unimportance of the town,
the siege of Mafeking became a myth almost as soon as the town was
encircled by Boer troops in October 1899. The importance of the myth
of Mafeking has been noted, especially in Brian Gardner's study of
Mafeking: A Victorian Legend. The present chapter seeks to trace the myth's
origins in the contemporary press treatments of the siege and to examine the importance of the myth-making function of the popular press
within the New Imperialism of the late nineteenth century. Much
cultural studies work on the ideology of imperialism has underplayed
the importance of newspapers or seen their role in image-making as
relatively straightforward. Anne McClintock, for example, in *Imperial
Leather*'s insightful analysis of newspaper photographs, advertisements,
and illustrations, devotes almost no attention to the text that surrounded
much of the visual material. When she quotes newspapers, it is as
historical evidence. But even during the Boer War, commentators were
already formulating analyses of the ideological function of the news-

papers, the music halls, the schools, and the pulpits. An examination of such contemporary critiques reveals a complicated picture of how imperialism functioned culturally in turn-of-the-century Britain. J. A. Hobson, W. T. Stead, Olive Schreiner, and other anti-war writers, as well as those writing on the other side, recognized popular culture, including the press, as essential to the war effort. Starting with an examination of Mafeking Night and then moving to more detailed analyses of aspects of writing about the South African War, this volume seeks to shift cultural studies' approach to the late-Victorian empire. As McClintock, Preben Kaarsholm, and others have pointed out, late-Victorian imperialism was not a cultural monolith: support for the empire coexisted with critiques of aspects of the capitalism that helped to drive it; working-class jingoism sat uneasily with patriotic Britons from other classes who might or might not support the war; the rights of Africans were invoked on the pro- and anti-war sides, with equally vain results. The complexity of the ideologies of imperialism during the Boer War is borne out by this study of a range of texts and authors, all of which were elements in a culture in which empire was assumed and yet critiqued, was understood and yet always needed to be explained, was far away and yet appeared at the breakfast table every morning.

During the last decades of Victoria's reign, as John MacKenzie's work has shown, images of empire abounded in advertising, popular literature and theater, exhibitions, and other cultural spaces. But being inundated with evidence of empire is not the same as supporting the economic or political ideal of British imperialism. Such imperial advocates as H. Rider Haggard bemoaned through the 1880s and 1890s the British public's lack of interest in its own empire. Occasional periodical articles addressed imperial issues, but even the Zulu War and the first conflict with the Boers failed to rouse the British from cozy domestic concerns. The Anglo-Boer War of 1899–1902, however, was different. It was a long, large-scale war with another white nation, it cost millions of pounds of public money, and it couldn't help but catch the interest of the British public very decisively. The press followed the events of the war in such detail that Haggard decided by the end of the war to give up the idea of writing a series of articles on South Africa for the *Daily Express* – people were sick and tired of constantly reading about South Africa, he said. The key factor in igniting public interest in this imperial conflict was the new popular press of the late 1890s, the cheap, sensation-oriented jingoist reporting and editing that was already known as the New Journalism. The New Imperialism of the late nineteenth century, which included the direct acquisition by the British government of African land, was generally supported by jingo papers that grew out of the New Journalism. The New Journalism was able to build that support by creating a new sense of the Great British Public, and the buildup to and reporting about Mafeking Night illustrates how it was done.

To begin this exploration of the connections between New Imperialism and New Journalism, we return to the night of 18 May 1900 and the events that led up to it. T. Wemyss Reid, of the *Leeds Mercury*, wrote a monthly column in the *Nineteenth Century* called "The Newspapers," in which he kept a daily journal of the significant stories in the papers and the public events and trends behind them. Reid was a self-proclaimed "old journalist" and complained regularly about the excesses of the new popular press. We can trace the factors that led up to Mafeking Night through Reid's chronicle of war coverage after the crushing British defeats of Black Week in December 1899. The setbacks of that week, Reid warned, should:

open the eyes of our Jingo journalists to some of the risks which a great Empire runs when it enters upon a serious military expedition. Hitherto they have seen only the picturesque side of war . . . (January 1900, 164)

Jingo journalists are a new breed during the Boer War, an important part of the style of the New Journalism. Jingo did not mean patriotic – all major British dailies would have considered themselves patriotic, even the very few who opposed the war. Jingo was, rather, a class-inflected concept. The jingo journalist, with screaming headlines and rah-rah attitude, was the press equivalent of the music hall song-and-dance act, as compared to the solid Shakespearians of *The Times* and its fellow "quality" papers. Grumblings about jingoism were coded complaints about the likes of the *Daily Mail*'s pandering to the working classes.

Wemyss Reid's analysis combines resentment of censorship, a problem throughout the war, with his objections to the popular press: "the news, as we know, is very meagre. Either because of the severity of the censorship, or for some other reason, we have an entire absence of the brilliant descriptive writing we have been accustomed to get in former campaigns. The descriptive element is supplied, indeed, by the sub-editors with their sensational head-lines and inflammatory placards" (January 1900, 165). Reid sees the "descriptive writing" of earlier wars, the colorful, often poignant sketches of the scene of war as well as the battles themselves, as being replaced by two-column headlines and half-truths on placards. This is the doing of the new journalists, for whom sensation replaces analysis. The *Daily Mail* was indeed exaggerating every cabled bit of news from South Africa into a headline. The surest way to attract customers, the *Daily Mail*'s Alfred Harmsworth appeared to believe, was to cheer for the British army as if it were a national football team. According to Reid, knee-jerk jingoism was the central characteristic of the new approach to journalism. Jingoism was, of course, one of the most significant excesses of the *Daily Mail*, but it was by no means its only difference from the quality papers. The older, more respectable newspapers such as *The Times*, the *Daily Telegraph*, the *Daily News*, or the *Manchester Guardian* were still, in 1900, devoting more attention to parliamentary reporting and political speeches and news than to human-interest stories, crime, and fashion tips.

We can see through Reid how government censorship combined with sensationalism to produce the climate for Mafeking. Reid records the tension around General Buller's ill-fated effort to capture Spion Kop hill (the British walked into a trap and suffered massive casualties). On 15 January 1900, Reid records in his press diary:

> Again we are enduring the heavy strain of suspense. The silence that is maintained with regard to General Buller's movements is borne with ill-concealed impatience by the public, as the fluctuating crowds which thronged the portals of the War Office yesterday from morning till late at night proved. Wild rumours ran through the streets and the clubs. Newsboys shouted hoarsely in all our thoroughfares and squares. We were told of defeat, of victory, of great battles at that moment raging . . . But when the silence of night fell upon us, we were still without authentic news. (February 1900, 358–59)

Newspapers tried to sell copies by pretending to have news, telling the public conflicting stories of battles that never happened. But what the papers were selling was not what Reid could call "news." He lays out a contradictory picture of the public: first the "public" is the "fluctuating crowd" thronging the War Office, with no indication of class. But then Reid reveals that there are in fact two kinds of publics in question, those in "the streets" and those in "the clubs." We see a map of central London, its "thoroughfares and squares," its legitimate public spaces. Those to whom the newsboys hawked their illegitimate news, the victims of wild rumor, were "we." But which was the "we"? The people whose domain was the streets or those who dwelt in the clubs?

Two days later Reid complains about the evening jingo journals. Although no morning paper had yet joined the *Daily Mail* in its assault on the journalistic approach of *The Times* and others, the evening papers were closer in kind to the popular appeal of the Harmsworth paper. Reid resents the new sensation-seeking (and circulation-seeking) of the evening journals' war news: "If only the scandal of the evening news-papers could be repressed, people would begin to be cheerful again; but this afternoon these prints have surpassed themselves in sensationalism and exaggeration" (February 1900, 360). Reid now attributes the mood of the "people" entirely to the New Journalism. He is worried about the mood of the lower-middle-class readers of such papers. The "we" of his earlier account no longer includes him. *His* mood is fine. It's the "people" who are not cheerful. But Reid will go to great lengths to avoid directly mentioning the class associations of the papers with which he quarrels. On 12 February, he finds that "there is much depression to-day" about the siege of Ladysmith (March 1900, 532), and "the general mood to-day is one of depression – undue depression, it seems to me" (March 1900, 533). Here the "general mood" definitely excludes Reid – public depression is unjustified, as it will prove to be shortly thereafter, when Ladysmith is relieved. For Reid, the people who are the public, whose opinion and mood he records, seem to be the readers of the sensationalist papers. But that will change with Mafeking.

THE NATIONAL JOY

From the Spion Kop debacle in February until May, the papers were lacking in any major war news, and other news dominated both the newspapers and Reid's column in the *Nineteenth Century*. On 14 May, Reid records:

Once more the attention of the country is riveted upon the war ... Much more engrossing for most people than the question of a possible dissolution is the prospect of the early relief of Mafeking. The nerves of the public, which now takes the war so quietly – possibly, indeed, in the opinion of superficial observers so apathetically – have got into the "jumpy" state in which they were before the relief of Ladysmith, and every day a new story that the beleaguered village has at last been relieved is started and accepted with pathetic eagerness. When the good news comes at last it seems at least probable that we shall witness a repetition of the outbreak of joy that greeted the succour of Sir George White and his brave comrades, and the idea that the calmness which now distinguishes the public has anything of callous indifference in it will be effectually dispelled. (June 1900, 1044–45)

The public Reid is defending against charges of apathy and "callous indifference" to the war takes on a different character when the news of Mafeking's relief finally arrives in London. Now, for Reid, the public has come to include him:

[T]o such a night – or rather such a night and day, for I write at the close of this memorable Saturday – none of us can recall a parallel. The news of the relief of Mafeking came unexpectedly in the end. For two days everybody had been inquiring almost hourly for the news so eagerly awaited. When it had not arrived by dinner time yesterday most of us prepared to wait with such patience as we could command for another night. And then, just as we were reconciling ourselves to the fact that the 18th of May was not to witness the realization of the promise made by Lord Roberts, the news came that the promise was most brilliantly fulfilled. (June 1900, 1046–47)

The "people" and the "public" have become "us" and "we" with the relief of Mafeking by the 18 May deadline set by the commander-in-chief. The resulting huge, leaderless crowd in central London is safe for the middle class, even includes the middle class. The idea of the jingo mob that has come down to us is a working-class, flag-waving, slogan-shouting crowd, and Reid confirms that in every respect but the most crucial:

It was in the thoroughfares of the West End ... that the most wonderful sight was seen. Here the streets were blocked by a shouting, singing, cheering multitude, composed of both sexes and all classes – a multitude that seemed literally to have gone mad with joy... Every vehicle in the streets and a majority of the passers-by have borne [flags] – it was almost dangerous, indeed, to be seen without some emblem of the national joy. (June 1900, 1047–48)

A loud, boisterous multitude gone mad, but one that posed no threat to the middle class because it included "all classes." This is, of course, a far cry from 1886 in Trafalgar Square; after all, this crowd is happy. Mafeking Night was an unruly gathering of a size unprecedented in London. For Reid, however, it is not a mob; it is "London." And for the commentators in the daily papers, the crowd represented something larger still. The *Westminster Gazette* of 19 May declared, under a headline of "London Relieved!/The Empire's Rejoicing/Fervid Cheers for Mafeking and 'B.-P.,'" "That section of London which was not at home was delirious last night, and to-day is far on the way to proving the liveliest day ever experienced by the Capital. If for 'London' we read not merely 'Country,' but 'Empire,' the case is not put too high" (6). The enthusiasm of the British press at the relief of Mafeking is perhaps most concretely demonstrated by the first-ever use of an across-the-page headline by a London newspaper, by the *Daily Express* in its announcement of the end of the siege (Lake *British Newspapers* 111).

Tracing the implications of Mafeking Night illustrates changes in the concept of public opinion. Wemyss Reid blames the placard-producing press for creating moods of despair or anticipation in the lead-up to Mafeking Night, but he does not in turn credit that press for the events of the night. The rather gullible public that he sees as manipulated by the popular press throughout the war suddenly disappears for Reid on Mafeking Night. The crowd becomes one with him in celebrating an event that transcends gender and class. Even this most virulent anti-tabloid press critic falls into the mood created by that very press when the mood represents "the national joy."

How did Wemyss Reid and the rest of London (not to mention cities throughout the empire) get drawn into the melodrama of the siege of Mafeking? A siege makes for good long-term drama for a newspaper, almost as good as serial fiction for winning reader loyalty. It takes no great military mind to follow the details of a siege, and the situation itself – dwindling supplies and ammunition, no relief in sight – inspires concern. Mafeking was a more interesting siege than the other major Boer War sieges (Kimberley and Ladysmith) because of its isolated location, its last-minute relief, and its makeshift defending force. The tiny frontier town inspired concern in Britain from even before the start of the siege, so ripe was it for Boer picking. And the *Daily Mail*, through stories carried out of town by African runners, kept Mafeking in the news throughout the siege, updating readers on the occasional sorties from the town, the food stocks, and the mood of the garrison. The tactics of the *Daily Mail* captured the attention of the nation; the newspaper dramatized the situation of the town by emphasizing the danger that it might have to surrender and by stressing the inhabitants' heroic good cheer and the ingenuity of the garrison's leader, Baden-Powell.

"B.-P."

Although the halfpennies led the way in dramatizing Mafeking's plight, the qualities were not slow to pick up on the tactics of their lesser brethren. Press historian Stephen Koss cites *The Times* editors writing to their war correspondent Leo Amery, encouraging him to focus on individuals rather than on "abstract theories" (Koss *Rise and Fall* 419). The focus on personality came directly from the popular press: Moberly Bell wrote to Amery, "whatever your Harmsworths and Pearsons don't know they do know the public" (quoted in Koss *Rise and Fall* 419). The Victorian cult of personality had moved into the press by the turn of the century, and the military version of the focus on individuals at the expense of issues, already in place by Gordon's death,[7] shifted into high gear in the Boer War. In the early days of the war, the *Daily Mail* ran regular features on the officers it predicted would be important, including Baden-Powell.[8] In his work on the empire, John MacKenzie connects military hero-worship to late-Victorian racial ideology, and we can trace that connection through an examination of the Boer War's biggest hero. MacKenzie notes that:

Concepts of race were closely related in popular literature to the imperative of conflict between cultures, and the evidence of superiority it provided. Colonial heroes became the prime exemplars of a master people, and this enhanced their position in the military cult of personality. Their fame enabled them to exert great influence in leading service and conscription associations and youth organisations, in travelling extensively on speaking visits to schools or in public lectures in civic halls, as well as participating in ceremonial throughout the country. (*Propaganda and Empire* 7)

Of course the foremost Victorian military figure to lead a youth organization was the founder of the Scouts. Throughout the siege of Mafeking, Baden-Powell had grown larger and larger in British public estimation, holding off the besiegers who so outnumbered his makeshift assembly of troops. "The Wolf That Does Not Sleep" managed to keep the town inhabitants alive with the scarce food available, mounted occasional sneak attacks on the besiegers, and performed in town entertainments designed to keep spirits up. He represented British pluck at its pluckiest. The creation of the public image of Baden-Powell was a group effort by the Victorian press, but it was solidified by the *Daily Mail* and its special Mafeking correspondent Lady Sarah Wilson.

At the start of the war, Lady Sarah, the athletic, adventurous sister of the late Lord Randolph Churchill and wife of a captain in the Royal Horse Guards who joined Baden-Powell's troops at Mafeking, had taken refuge at the farm of an English friend near Vryburg, down the rail line. Chafing at her inactivity, she sent by carrier pigeon to Baden-Powell with an offer to spy on the Boers; unfortunately, the Boers shot the pigeon down, discovered the offer, and imprisoned her at the farm. She decided to get to Mafeking, and, knowing that one of the *Daily Mail* reporters had been captured by the Boers and sent to Pretoria, she offered to serve as Mafeking correspondent for that paper. She managed to persuade her guards to take her to the general commanding the siege, who offered to exchange her for a Boer prisoner in Mafeking.[9]

Sarah Wilson's letters and telegrams to the *Daily Mail* from Mafeking focused on the everyday life of the siege – food shortages, boredom, details of the bombardment. But it was her descriptions of Baden-Powell himself that the *Daily Mail* played up most. "The Two B.-P.'s/Sketched from Life by Lady Sarah Wilson" (20 April 1900, 4), for example, was a long article about the conditions of the siege, only the last third of which discussed Baden-Powell, despite its headline.

The detail about Baden-Powell provided by Lady Sarah supplemented the feature stories on his record that the *Daily Mail* had put together. In its leading articles, too, the paper located hopes for Mafeking, and indeed for the war, in Baden-Powell. On 24 March 1900, for example, the paper's leader opined that:

The repulse – for such we fear it must be accounted – of Colonel Plumer's column near Lobatsi, followed, as it has been, by a retreat to Crocodile Pools, would be an incident of infinitesimal importance in the great campaign now proceeding, were it not the case that upon it may hinge the fate of gallant little Mafeking... The British public do not consider its surrender from the military standpoint. They remember the protracted, the heroic defence which the tiny garrison has made under that splendid officer Colonel Baden-Powell, and they hope and believe that the place will yet be snatched from its Boer besiegers at the eleventh hour.

It is strange to reflect how a man whose very name six months ago was almost unknown to the British public has now secured the confidence of the whole Empire, so that it firmly believes that no situation, however desperate, will prove too much for his resourcefulness and courage. But for our implicit trust in Colonel Baden-Powell, our hopes for Mafeking's safety would be indeed feeble ... ("Devoted Mafeking" 4)

But it was the details provided by Sarah Wilson that gave the hero a personality for the readers. Lady Sarah had access to a Baden-Powell whom few other correspondents could have known; in her bomb-proof shelter she had a direct telephone to the colonel's headquarters, and her sex and class standing meant that her quarters were the site of the most civilized of social gatherings of officers in Mafeking, including the 1899 Christmas dinner for Baden-Powell and his staff. Wilson's description of "the two B.-P.'s" fed into the public's growing sense of Baden-Powell as an extraordinary *person* as well as military leader:

At five o'clock we had a most successful concert, when really great talent was displayed, considering we are in a besieged town; but Colonel Baden-Powell on the stage is simply inimitable; in his quite extempore sketches he held the hall entranced or convulsed with laughter, and no one would have thought he had another idea in his mind beyond the nonsense he was talking. He certainly, by so thoroughly amusing them, put everyone on good terms with themselves.

A few hours afterwards there was an alarm of a night attack: firing suddenly commenced all round the town – a most unusual occurrence on a Sunday night, and the bullets rattled freely all over the roofs.

There was the same man, under a totally different aspect. One who was with him told me he could not help marveling at the change.

Quiet, composed, and far-seeing, in a second he had anticipated every contingency and laid his plans ... (4)

Her praise of the Colonel's stage antics only serves as a contrast to highlight his composure and level-headedness as a military leader. Wilson does not actually describe what Baden-Powell does on stage – the point is how his sketches "put everyone on good terms with themselves," that is, kept people from what he himself referred to as "grousing."

MacKenzie's assertion that Victorian military hero-worship was connected to racial ideology is useful in an analysis of Baden-Powell's Mafeking publicity, but in a different way than MacKenzie would seem to suggest. Baden-Powell's superiority was not evidence of the "imperative of conflict between cultures" of black and white, since the Boer War was a war between white nations. His success was evidence of the superiority of the British over the Boer "race" rather than over Africans. But his public position as strategic genius did depend on his racial position in relation to Africans as well – Baden-Powell had to keep white people fed and relatively happy and keep loyal Africans alive on a very limited supply of food. Lady Sarah's articles as well as those of other siege correspondents had the ticklish job of portraying as humanitarian a leader who decreed an entirely unequal distribution of rations between whites and blacks that resulted in starvation of Africans while whites were still allotted meat to eat.

STARVING (THE) AFRICANS

We can see an example of the public image problem with which the *Daily Mail* was wrestling in the 10 April 1900 coverage of the Mafeking siege. The *Mail*'s efforts to create drama about Mafeking resulted in some fancy footwork. Headlines that day read "Lady Sarah Wilson Says 'Failure Quite Possible' ... Famished Mafeking/Rumours about the Southern Relief Column/Plumer's Advance Causes No Relaxation/The Garrison Aware His Failure Is Possible," and readers were invited to picture the worst fate for the gallant garrison. At the same time, the town had to be shown as doing its best: Lady Sarah's story pointed out that "Although the white population here is on a very restricted diet, every measure has been taken to alleviate distress, the numerous soup kitchens being able to feed all applicants" (5). Lady Sarah and the other

Daily Mail correspondent consistently discuss the food troubles of whites and blacks in Mafeking separately, making clear that the Africans were worse off. How would it be possible to show Baden-Powell as humanitarian and as a good provider for his besieged dependents, black and white, while making clear that white people were not being asked to waste away on the same rations as Africans were? Lady Sarah follows up her mention of the whites' "restricted diet" by saying, "No native need starve if he will but walk a short distance to the soup kitchen in his particular district." There is no mention in even the most dismal of the *Daily Mail* correspondents' Mafeking reports of the possibility of white people actually starving. The inference is that the garrison would be forced to surrender if Baden-Powell's loaves-and-fishes act gave out before help arrived. But Africans are often referred to in terms of starving: they are forced to try to escape from Mafeking to look for food, or they starve in Mafeking "needlessly," by refusing to eat horseflesh because it is against their custom.

Barolong inhabitants of Mafikeng, the "native stadt" included by Baden-Powell within the borders of Mafeking for purposes of the siege, were sold food along with whites and were allotted rations as well, once rationing began in March. But, as Sol Plaatje, then a court translator at Mafeking and later a founder of the South African Native National Congress, explains, food stores were closed to the refugee populations of Africans, "the blackish races of this continent – mostly Zulus and Zambesians," in February, and these populations had to make do on what they could scrounge until the establishment of the soup kitchens in April. The understanding was that the refugees would leave Mafeking and cease to be a drain on the town's stores, although Plaatje points out that many of them remained, begged, and starved (*Mafeking Diary* 124–25). Plaatje's version of the feeding of Africans during the siege is not nearly as critical as the versions in other books about the siege. *The Times* correspondent, Angus Hamilton, was scathing about British policy towards the Africans in the siege. He pointed out that Africans were driven by hunger out of Mafeking, trekking to the camp of Colonel Plumer, who had been stocked up to feed the refugees: "The natives here, who are already so reduced that they are dying from sheer inanition, having successfully accomplished the journey, which is one of ninety miles, may feed to their hearts' content – provided that they are able to pay for the rations which are so generously distributed to them" (*Siege* 249). Hamilton criticized Baden-Powell as well, for charging Africans for the horsemeat soup served out in the Mafeking soup kitchens.

"[T]here can be no doubt that the drastic principles of economy which Colonel Baden-Powell has been practicing in these later days are opposed to and altogether at variance with the dignity of the liberalism which we profess," (249) he wrote on 3 March in the diary he later published as *The Siege of Mafeking*. Edward Ross, a Mafeking resident whose siege diary was published by Brian Willan in 1980, recorded on 9 March that "[t]he lower class of natives are beginning to suffer the pangs of starvation very severely," then on 10 March, "It does seem rather hard that we can go and buy food-stuffs whilst the natives are in such straights (sic) to keep body and soul together" (*Diary* 179). The residents of Mafeking, in their reply to Baden-Powell's report on the siege submitted in March of 1902, noted among their complaints that Baden-Powell's Commissariat Department made "sales at a profit to starving natives" (241). Even B.-P.'s defenders, such as *Pall Mall Gazette* correspondent J. Emerson Neilly, described in detail the "black spectres and living skeletons"(*Besieged* 227) that the Africans had become by March – those who were still alive. "Probably hundreds died from starvation or the diseases that always accompany famine," wrote Neilly (*Besieged with B.-P.* 227). But he complained about "grousing" critics in the town who would "have the Colonel kill our very few ill-fed beeves and give them to the blacks and allow them to have a daily share of the white rations." If such a policy had been carried out, declared Neilly, "we would either have died of starvation in the works [the fortifications] or surrendered and been marched as prisoners of war to Pretoria" (*Besieged* 231). Clearly the "we" in his analysis meant the white inhabitants of Mafeking.

The very thought of the white inhabitants of Mafeking being marched to Pretoria was enough to chill the blood, Neilly assumes. And, indeed, it was just that spectacle that Baden-Powell was working so hard to prevent. To that end, he exploited the African population of Mafeking in different ways throughout the siege. He employed Africans extensively in building the defense works for the town and, with his famous "Cape Boys" and "Black Watch," as troops as well. Baden-Powell was quite judicious in his use of news about Africans in his accounts of the siege. For example, the *Westminster Gazette* of 3 May 1900, under the headline "Incidents at Mafeking/Cheerful Report from Baden-Powell," included a Baden-Powell despatch:

Party of thirteen native women tried to get away on night of 15th. Enemy opened fire on them; killed nine, wounded two, who got back and reported. I wrote to Snyman pointing out that he shelled native stadt, which is full of women and children; and that when they were trying to escape from Mafeking by day Boers flogged and sent them back, and that they by night shot them down, pretending to mistake them for night attacks. He has not replied, proportion of killed and wounded above speaking for itself. (7)

This despatch comes from the man whose policy was to starve Africans into escaping from Mafeking through the Boer lines.

Mentions of Africans in Mafeking despatches and news stories fall into two categories, the first of which is exemplified by Baden-Powell's despatch: blame African hardships on the Boers (even Sol Plaatje blames African refugee starvation on the Boers rather than on Baden-Powell). This reinforces British notions of Boer inhumanity toward Africans, the pro-war argument of the "negrophilists." The other category into which mentions of Africans fall is praise of the loyalty of the Cape Boys and the Black Watch, the Africans who fought in defense of the town. But this category was played up more by the war correspondents than by Baden-Powell, who consistently denied credit to the fighting Africans in his efforts to keep public perception of the war as a "white man's war." Africans as loyal subjects of the Queen and Africans as victims of the cruel Boers – these were the possibilities in British public versions of the siege. Brian Willan points out that Baden-Powell prevented the town newspaper from printing the true account of the role of the Barolong in fending off the final assault of the Boers (*Sol Plaatje* 89). Not until the publication of Plaatje's diary in 1973 did a version of the siege emerge in which Africans were portrayed as economic and social beings with families, homes, and relationships, money troubles, and job concerns.

Baden-Powell survived the public relations problems inherent in his situation to become the symbol not only for Mafeking but for British pluck in general and for the war effort as a whole. Headline writers of all kinds of papers could count on their readers knowing who "B.-P." was (after the siege, Baden-Powell told of a letter addressed simply to "B.-P." that was delivered to him by the Royal Mail). And the celebrations of the relief, as the *Illustrated London News* made clear, were celebrations of Baden-Powell:

[T]he heart of the public manifestly went out to the extraordinarily skilful and resourceful commander, who for seven long and anxious months held Mafeking against the Boer besiegers. "B.-P." richly deserved every word of praise bestowed upon him ... Colonel Robert Stephenson Smyth Baden-Powell's gallant defense of Mafeking won for him the warmest admiration of the Queen and the whole Empire. He has worked nobly, and eminently deserves promotion to the rank of Major-General. As the War in South Africa progressed, the calm, heroic figure of the ever vigilant and patient defender of Mafeking became the chief centre of interest. The thoroughness with which he threw himself with characteristic versatility into the entertainments got up to distract the attention of the beleaguered townsfolk from the belt of iron that environed them, and vied with the liveliest in song and dance, was of a piece with his devotion to his exacting military duties. ("War Reviewed" 2).

As recent biographical studies of Lord Baden-Powell have noted, the commanding officer at Mafeking had some control of the events on the scene and worked the siege to his own advantage.[10] Indeed, "[b]oth Baden-Powell's critics and his supporters seem to agree that he expected, desired, and sought to provoke a siege" in the first place, for reasons of military strategy.[11] Certainly the founder of the Scouts movement made his reputation through the siege. The celebrations of the relief of Mafeking were certainly brought about by the "instruments of popular education" cited by J. A. Hobson – especially the press – but it is important not to ignore the role of the military itself in fashioning its own public image.

B.-P. seemed singlehandedly to have united the classes in London. The *Illustrated London News* emphasizes the class-mixing atmosphere of the celebrations, citing "a vast crowd of butchers sweeping down Piccadilly, all in their blue smocks, many of them with stencil portraits of B-P painted on their backs" and "a huge procession headed by the Kensington Art Students in white smocks, dragging a triumphal car surmounted by a fine bust of the hero of Mafeking, beneath which was a massive model of the British Lion."[12]

The *Illustrated London News* joined the *Nineteenth Century* and the daily newspapers in advertising the cross-class nature of the Mafeking joy. Just as Wemyss Reid had discussed "all classes" celebrating Mafeking's relief, the *ILN* pointed out, "Elderly City gentlemen, usually severe of aspect, seemed to have forgotten all about their dignity, and stood on the pavements tootling benignly with costers from Ratcliffe Highway."[13] Was it the "tootling" that was beneath the gentlemen's dignity or the fact that they stood on the pavements with costers? With the exception of the undignified elderly City gents above, in the *ILN*'s illustrations and the descriptions of the celebrations, the classes seem to party separately. The butchers have their group, the Kensington art students theirs.

Social class was rarely emphasized in the coverage of the siege itself (as opposed to the celebrations of the relief), but the predominant image of the Boers as ignorant, backward peasants was often reinforced by stories about the siege. On one occasion, reported the regular *Daily Mail* Mafeking correspondent, British soldiers played a concertina to lure the simple Boers out of hiding, then picked them off.[14] The story was picked up by the *Westminster Gazette* that evening as an example of the humorous side of the siege. War stories rarely emphasized class unless the officer involved was noble. The anomalous position of Lady Sarah Wilson did attract some notice, but the real issues of class that arise from Mafeking come from the home-front celebrations. Mafeking Night marks the emergence of the benign entity of the middle-class mob: the New Imperialism and the New Journalism had together managed to trans-form the street mob from a violent working-class threat into a cheery middle-class (or, perhaps, classless) party and to transform jingoism from a vulgar working-class sport into a respectable middle-class (or, perhaps, classless) enthusiasm.

J. A. HOBSON'S CRITIQUE

Mafeking Night is the prime example of the late-Victorian press's role in creating a climate of public support for imperialism. But not all Victor-ian press critics succumbed to uncritical enthusiasm about Mafeking and imperialism. The Boer War writing of J. A. Hobson, whose theories of imperialism influenced Lenin and historians throughout this century, provides the terms in which some of the most important challenges to jingoism were framed during the war. Although Hobson's economic critiques of imperialism are the basis for his reputation with imperial historians – he is often cited as the originator of the economic theory of imperialism – Hobson was equally insightful about the cultural factors in imperialism, and this section will treat Hobson as a cultural critic of the late-Victorian empire. Hobson's theory of imperialism grew out of his experience as a journalist in the Boer War, and the significance of that experience has been ignored or underplayed by historians. John Allett, in *New Liberalism: The Political Economy of J.A. Hobson*, denies the importance of Hobson's South African experience to his theorizing about imperialism (26, 131). Although Allett is correct in saying that Hobson's interest in imperialism predated the Boer War, it was the Boer War that led Hobson fully to formulate his theory of imperialism. Bernard Porter, in *Critics of Empire*, takes pains to show that Hobson developed his economic theory of imperialism based on Britain's China experience. Nevertheless, for an exploration of Hobson's insights into the cultural conditions necessary to sustain imperialism, we must look to the Boer War – the place where Hobson learned first-hand about culture and imperialism and the necessity of ideological control for imperial hegemony. Mafeking Night is the event from which to begin an examination of the Boer War and the British public, and Hobson's *The Psychology of Jingoism* is certainly the context in which such an event must initially be seen. The key to Hobson's analysis of the causes and operations of imperialism is his examination, in *Imperialism: A Study* (1902), *The Psychology of Jingoism* (1901), and *The War in South Africa: Its Causes and Effects* (1900), of the newspaper press and its role in popular culture.

Going to South Africa had not been Hobson's idea. By the summer of 1899, C. P. Scott, editor of the *Manchester Guardian*, knew he'd better get somebody over to South Africa soon. War was brewing between Briton and Boer, and Scott didn't want to have to rely on news agency reports for information from the Cape. Leonard T. Hobhouse, then a leader writer for Scott, recommended that the newspaper send Hobson as a special correspondent, based on Hobson's 1898 article about imperialism in the *Contemporary Review*. Scott agreed, and Hobson sailed for South Africa in July. Through the late summer and early autumn, he traversed the Cape Colony and the Boer Republics, interviewing English and Dutch South Africans, investigating the growing discontent of the largely British "Uitlanders" in the mining district of the Witwatersrand. Hobson was still in South Africa at the collapse of negotiations between the British and the Boers, which culminated in the Boer ultimatum of 9 October, which demanded that Britain agree to arbitration, remove its troops from the Transvaal borders, withdraw its new reinforcements from South Africa, and not land any more troops (Pakenham *Boer War* 104).

Robin Winks, who calls Hobson the "most important critic of imperial expansion from an economic viewpoint" (*Historiography* 4), points out that Hobson has remained the central figure with whom theorists of imperialism must engage, chiefly because he did not confine his analysis of imperialism to economic factors. Before Hobson's analysis of British imperialism, few people had attempted critical examinations of the phenomenon in its political, economic, and social dimensions. To be sure, imperialism had not been without its critics in the nineteenth century: Richard Cobden and John Bright, for example, maintained that British imperialism was a bad idea because it was a financial and military burden. But Hobson's analysis in *Imperialism* cut to the heart of the imperialist impulse itself, laying bare the interplay of economic and

ideological factors that went into producing an imperial state. Nevertheless, Hobson's *Guardian* articles, and his collection of them and his
articles from the *Speaker* in *The War in South Africa: Its Causes and Effects*,
reflect his early, rather sloppy analysis of the South African situation.
The *Guardian* series, which was titled "The Truth about the Transvaal,"
tried to expose the economic machinations behind the drive for war in
South Africa; but, as Stephen Koss (*The Pro-Boers*) and others have
pointed out, these early pieces reek of anti-Semitism, blaming "a small
group of international financiers, chiefly German in origin and Jewish in
race" for the war push, despite a half-hearted prefatory disclaimer that
he did not want to seem "to appeal to the ignominious passion of
Judenhetze" (*War* 189). Hobson could not see that he himself was
succumbing to "Judenhetze," even as he analyzed the "moral and
ethical" factors that went into the creation of imperialism.[15]

Hobson's *Guardian* articles were key sources of information to anti-
war activists early in the conflict, and he remained an important voice
during the course of the war. In *The War in South Africa*, published shortly
after the outbreak of the war, Hobson examines the maneuverings of
capitalists in the conduct of imperialism, but he also emphasizes the
importance of "popular passion" (*War* 306) for maintaining a war effort
on the home front. He sees that neither government policy nor the
initiative of capitalists alone could bring about or sustain a war such as
the Boer War. Both of those forces would need the support of public
opinion. And public opinion, Hobson asserts, is formed through a
complex process involving the press, popular entertainment, the
church, education, and other cultural factors. Hobson's analysis of the
importance of the press in stirring public opinion about the war is
divided between a strong focus on the press in South Africa and its effect
on war sentiment there and attention to the press back in England. One
of the most significant points he makes in analyzing the maintenance of
a culture of imperialism in Britain is his revelation of the ways British
dailies depended on the gold mining interests for their South African
news: the South African pro-British press was inextricably tied to Rand
capitalists, and the London dailies depended absolutely on war cable-
grams from those same South African organs. Both *The Psychology of
Jingoism* and *The War in South Africa* include extensive detail about the
ownership of various South African newspapers – the leading interests
of mine-owners Rhodes, Eckstein, and Barnato in the *Cape Argus*, *Johannesburg Star*, *Bulawayo Chronicle*, *Rhodesia Herald*, and *African Review*, for
example (*War* 207).

In *The War in South Africa* Hobson develops his concept of the "chartered press" as the central agent in "the interplay of political and economic motives in Imperialism" (*Confessions* 60). Pro-Boer outcry against the press, Hobson notes, had been focusing on the "less reputable organs," the sensation-mongering of the Yellow Press in its efforts, for example, to stir up people to disrupt anti-war meetings. But after his South African experience for the *Guardian*, Hobson saw that the danger came not from the halfpennies but from the quality press, whose South African coverage was, for the most part, under the control of the mining companies. These capitalist-controlled newspapers, he explains, reached all the way to London in their efforts to stir up anti-Boer sentiment:

What I am describing is nothing else than an elaborate factory of misrepresentations for the purpose of stimulating British action. To those unacquainted with the mechanism it may seem incredible that with modern means of communication it has been possible to poison the conscience and intelligence of England. But when it is understood that the great London press receives its information almost exclusively from the offices of the kept press of South Africa, the mystery is solved. (*War* 216)

Hobson avoids blaming the London press directly for its one-sided coverage of the war: Fleet Street was manipulated by the English-language press in South Africa.

"One of the chief general cable services, widely used by the most important London newspapers, was fed from Johannesburg by a prominent member of the Executive of the South African League [an anti-Boer English South African group]," Hobson explained:

The London "Liberal" paper whose perversion from the true path of Liberalism has inflicted the heaviest blow upon the cause of truth and honesty in England [the *Daily News*], was fully and constantly inspired by the editor of the *Cape Times* [controlled by Rutherford Harris, director of the Chartered Company], upon which office, I am informed, no fewer than three other important London dailies relied for their Cape Town intelligence. The *Cape Times* and the *Argus* [Rhodes, Eckstein and Barnato-controlled] offices also supplied two great general channels of cable information to the English press. (*War* 217)

Over and over again in *The War in South Africa* and *The Psychology of Jingoism*, Hobson expresses his disappointment with the London press, Liberal and Conservative, for allowing itself to be thus manipulated by the Rand capitalists. "For practical purposes," he laments, "there no longer exists a free press in England, affording full security for adequate discussion of the vital issues of politics" (*Psychology* 119). Hobson's Liberal politics led him to believe that a "free press" would necessarily check abuses of power in a democracy. The problem with the London press, he asserts, is that its sources in South Africa are not "independent" and so "the authority they exercised" is not "legitimate" (*Psychology* 109). Not that the pro-Boer side should be the only one presented; both sides should be presented to the British public, who would then be able to make an informed decision about the merits of the war. Neither newspapers nor magazines would print "pro-Boer" articles: "Even the genius of Olive Schreiner could not get a hearing for what she most cared to say in any important English magazine," and Messrs. Smith and Son, booksellers, when asked "But surely you keep books dealing with both sides of the South African question?" had replied, "there is only one side for us – that of our country" (*Psychology* 118–19).

MODERN WAR-SPIRIT

The Psychology of Jingoism, also contemporary with the publication of Hobson's Boer War book and the composition of *Imperialism*, examines in more detail than was possible in his newspaper articles the psychological and cultural factors involved in creating a public ideology of imperialism. Based largely upon Gustave Le Bon's study of crowd psychology, *The Psychology of Jingoism* explores in depth the influence of the pulpit, the music hall, and, most importantly, the press in forming a climate of public opinion favorable to war. Hobson saw *The Psychology of Jingoism* as "an analysis of the modern war-spirit" and said that the work "dwelt upon the mixture of national arrogance and folly at the disposal of the imperialists and business men who were the working partners in the preparation and production of modern wars" (*Confessions* 62–3). While *The War in South Africa* approached the particulars of the Boer War with the eye of a journalist, concerned with the specifics on the spot, such as the role of the Boer police in the Witwatersrand or the analysis of the parts played by specific South African politicians, *The Psychology of Jingoism* took a more general approach, treating the war as a case study in crowd identity-formation and blind obedience to the prevailing sentiment of the day.

The public, according to Hobson, formed its views from music-hall ballads and the testimony of friends of friends, but, most importantly, from the opinions offered in the newspapers, which were controlled by capitalists and the Chamberlain interests in government. Hobson saw public opinion at the turn of the century as a qualitatively new phenomenon, as "a community of thought, language, and action which was hitherto unknown" (*Psychology* 18). This new tendency to form community opinion was, as he saw it, inseparable from the new (in nineteenth-century Britain) tendency to mass behavior such as the Mafeking riots. And both the mass opinion-formation and the rioting, Hobson contended, were prompted by the press: "What the orator does for his audience the press has done for the nation," Hobson argued in *The Psychology of Jingoism*: "The British nation became a great crowd, and exposed its crowd-mind to the suggestions of the press" (18, 19). Hobson's assessment includes all of British society in its indictment, from working-class men, to members of upper-class men's clubs, to middle-class women, and his analysis of crowd conduct relies on conceptions of crowd behavior as "savage," carrying an undercurrent of fear of the masses.

As Richard Price notes, the phenomenon of mafficking made certain middle-class social commentators, including Hobson, very nervous. Another contemporary analyst of the emergence of jingoism, C. F. G. Masterman, feared that the working class had "crept into daylight . . . it is straightening itself and learning to gambol with heavy and grotesque antics in the sunshine" (quoted in Price *An Imperial War* 134). The working classes were living in towns that, according to Hobson, bred nervousness and susceptibility to ideas like jingoism. Hobson's jingo crowd is certainly a working-class crowd:

A large population, singularly destitute of intellectual curiosity, and with a low valuation for things of the mind, has during the last few decades been instructed in the art of reading printed words, without acquiring an adequate supply of information or any training in the reasoning faculties such as would enable them to give a proper value to the words they read. A huge press has come into being for the purpose of supplying to this uneducated people . . . statements, true or false, designed to give passing satisfaction to . . . some lust of animalism. (*Psychology* 9–10)

Hobson's analysis of jingoism vacillates between blaming the "lust of animalism" of the working classes and blaming the naive middle classes for believing everything they're told. In the above passage, his fear of the mob is palpable, and his contempt obvious, but it is capitalists (and especially Jews) who are to be blamed, he argues, for the mass jingo hysteria of Mafeking.

In *Imperialism*, Hobson extended beyond South Africa his analysis of the power of the press and of other noneconomic factors, such as religion, in shaping public opinion in favor of imperialism. Hobson saw that the "verbal armoury of Imperialism" was as important as any physical armory (207). In *Imperialism* he revealed how the British government released information about the war to the public through the press. He cited, for example, the "shifts of detailed mendacity and curious invention" necessary for the British government to be able to convince the public first that the Boers were so tiny a nation that it was ridiculously insolent of them to start a war with "the greatest Empire of the world" and simultaneously that "we were contending with a Power as large, numerically, as ourselves," when it came time to rejoice over a victory. Hobson pointed to:

how the numbers alternately and automatically expanded and contracted according as it was sought to impress upon the nation the necessity of voting large supplies of troops and money, or else to represent the war as 'nearly over' and having lapsed into a trifling guerrilla struggle. (*Imperialism* 210)

Hobson went on to examine the workings of the "small, able, and well-organized groups in a nation" who "secure the active co-operation of statesmen and of political cliques," and who appeal to the "conservative instincts of members of the possessing classes, whose vested interest and class dominance are best preserved by diverting the currents of political energy from domestic on to foreign politics" (*Imperialism* 212). These power elites work most effectively on the public mind, Hobson explained, through "the four chief instruments of popular education" – the church, the press, the schools and colleges, and the political machine (*Imperialism* 216).

As Hobson pointed out, the domination of the imperial idea in Britain arose not simply from the ruling class persuading the working class of the importance of imperialism and of the Boer War for the nation. Rather, the South African mine-owners and British government officials such as Colonial Secretary Joseph Chamberlain and South African High Commissioner Alfred Milner were able to achieve hegemony over the rest of Britain, including the "educated classes" who should, Hobson pointed out, have known better. "Our educated classes are usually scornful of the man who believes everything he reads in the newspapers," said Hobson. "Yet the majority of these cultured persons have submitted their intelligence to the dominion of popular prejudice and passion as subserviently as the man in the street, whom they despise" (*Psychology* 21). The reason why the man in the street and the cultured person have surrendered to the "strange amalgam of race feeling, animal pugnacity, rapacity, and sporting zest, which they dignify by the name of patriotism" is plain. People "allow their minds to be swayed by the unanimity of the British testimony from South Africa, as presented by this press and by the politicians who have got their information from the same factory of falsehood" (*Psychology* 21, 22). Iain Smith points out the significance of Hobson's analysis of the role of the South African press in swinging public opinion in Britain in favor of war, noting as well that recent research has shown how important the mine-owners in 1898–99 felt the role of English newspapers in the Transvaal to be (399). But the primary significance of Hobson's work on the war remains his legacy in asserting the importance of such ideological factors as the press, the churches, and the schools in creating and maintaining public support for a government policy. He recognized "psychology" as essential to jingoism and jingoism as essential to capitalism.

NEW IMPERIALISM, NEW JOURNALISM, NEW PUBLICS

The nation, patriotic or not, celebrated the relief of Mafeking because it had been prompted to do so. Even such critics of the press as Wemyss Reid, who reviewed the newspapers every day, were persuaded that the relief of Mafeking was important for the war and that the celebrations of that relief were a spontaneous outpouring of patriotism rather than an orchestrated public event in service of what Hobson called a capitalist-inspired war. The events of Mafeking Night serve as an especially effective case study in which to examine both the role of the press in the formation of public opinion about imperialism and the role of the press in the formation of the concept of public opinion itself. Mafeking Night marks the powerful beginning of the New Journalism at the same time as it marks the beginning of the end of the New Imperialism. The coincidence of these occasions arises from the nature of the South African War. J. A. Hobson argued that public support is necessary for the New Imperialism; but that support seems to have become necessary only at the time of the Boer War. New Imperialism got along fine without mass support through most of the latter third of the nineteenth century because the Scramble for Africa was more a phenomenon of international capital than a governmental policy of military acquisition. Large-scale public support for British imperialism became necessary only when the British embarked on a colonial war, fought largely with volunteers, against a white nation.

The concept of public opinion is the missing piece in cultural studies analysis of the public (and private) discourse of Victorian imperialism. A concept understood by press, politicians, and publics alike throughout the nineteenth century, public opinion is nevertheless impossible to pin down. Since the first Gallup polls in the United States and Britain in the 1930s, public opinion has come to mean something very specific and, most importantly, quantifiable (Worcester *British Public Opinion* 3). But the Victorians operated under a notion of public opinion that was perhaps equally specific but not at all quantifiable. That is, public opinion was a matter of concern on public policy issues, but the public whose opinion mattered was not a random or representative cross-section of the population. Those whose opinions affected policy were upper-middle-class and higher, and almost certainly male. To gauge public opinion one read the letters in *The Times*. By the time of the Boer War, the concept of public opinion was shifting, as class dynamics changed, as the franchise was extended, and as access to education expanded. The most concrete example of the shift in ways of accounting for public opinion is the flowering of, and the attention paid to, the popular press. Historians and literary critics have tended to employ the concept of public opinion uncritically in analysis of the nineteenth century, seeing public opinion as the political views of what communications theorists call agenda-setters, the people whose class standing and influence means that they have the ear of the policymakers. If the concept of public opinion is to work as an analytical tool for understanding late-Victorian imperialism, then we must consider whose voices were heard in public debate by the time of the Boer War, who set the agendas on which the "public" held opinions, and which public discourse was being aimed at which segment of the public. This volume agrees with John MacKenzie that there was an "imperial world view" established by an extensive network of cultural propaganda by 1900, but it asserts the importance of looking at particular components of that world view individually. In examining the supporting ideologies that functioned within imperialism at the end of the nineteenth century – chivalry, paternalistic models of race relations, evolutionary thinking – the chapters that follow demonstrate that while imperialism itself was seldom seen by Victorian elites as debatable, issues that were important to the maintenance of consensus on imperialism were very much contested. Newspapers, periodicals, and propaganda of the Boer War addressed varying publics, only some of whose opinions counted in the press and politicians' notion of public opinion. By focusing on the publics addressed in different situations and the assumptions being made about those publics, we arrive at a clearer understanding of imperial ideology's dependence on hierarchies of race, sex, and class and of the ways in which, hand in hand, the New Imperialism and the New Journalism brought Britain into the twentieth century.

CHAPTER 2

The concentration camps controversy and the press

Still reeling from the series of setbacks in December 1899 that came to be known as Black Week, the British army by March 1900 had settled on a new strategy to try to finish the war in South Africa – the war that General Lord Roberts had said would be over by Christmas. Searching for a way to cut off Boer fighters in the field from food and supplies, the British, under the command of Lord Roberts, began to burn the homes and crops of the South African men who were away on commando duty. The farm-burning policy became systematic under Lord Kitchener, who succeeded Roberts as commander-in-chief of the British forces in South Africa in December 1900. Many African settlements and crops in the Orange Free State and the South African Republic (the Transvaal) were added to the list of what was to be "cleared," and Kitchener was left with the problem of what to do with all the noncombatants thus displaced.

In September of that year General John Maxwell had formed camps for surrendered burghers in Bloemfontein and Pretoria, and on 20 December 1900 Kitchener officially proclaimed a South Africa-wide policy whereby surrendered burghers and their families would be housed and fed in such camps, courtesy of the British military. Separate camps were established for whites and for blacks, and because the British military was unwilling to treat women and children in stationary camps differently from soldiers in temporary camps, problems soon arose with food, fuel, and general health conditions.

In June 1901 a report by Emily Hobhouse, who had been distributing clothing and blankets in the camps for the London-based, anti-war, South African Women and Children's Distress Fund, revealed to Britain the unhealthy conditions in the camps. The British government's own figures for the mortality rates in the camps in late summer and fall that year made the conditions in the camps a national scandal. After Hobhouse's report was published, the government rebutted with its own

"Ladies Commission," led by suffragist Millicent Fawcett, to investigate the camps and initiate reforms. By the end of the war 28,000 whites, mostly women and children, died in the Boer camps – more than twice the number of men on both sides killed in the fighting of the war (Spies *Methods* 265). An additional 14,000 Africans died, although there were many fewer camps for them. The rates at which Africans died were even higher than the death rates in the white camps; the African camps did not benefit from publicity (Warwick *Black People* 145).

The camps controversy was the biggest scandal of the South African War, and newspapers on different sides of the war issue handled it very differently, reflecting not only the political differences among the papers but also the changes the New Journalism was causing in the way war made news. The venerable *Times*, supporter of the Conservative-Unionist government headed by Lord Salisbury, backed War Office policy in South Africa and trusted the good intentions of the Army, refusing to believe in anyone's culpability. The upstart *Daily Mail* of Alfred Harmsworth took what it saw as a populist line, holding that whatever the British did for the women and children in the camps was more than they deserved. The *Daily News* changed horses midstream to oppose the government on the camps issue, while the *Manchester Guardian* went with Liberal party leader Sir Henry Campbell-Bannerman and its editor, C. P. Scott, M.P., in coming out against what Campbell-Bannerman called "methods of barbarism" in South Africa. This chapter examines the development of the concentration camps scandal in the daily press and the relationship between press coverage of the scandal and government policy on the camps. The camps controversy is a good case study through which to examine both the role of the daily press in imperialism during the Boer War and the place of gender and race ideology within the imperialism of the war. The publics that were created by the press before Mafeking Night were the same publics that reacted to the news of the death rates in the camps. But the War Office that had colluded in the creation of the jingo frenzy of Mafeking Night had not counted on the same sentimentalism and belief in British traditions and values working against government policy when it came to a very different kind of war news.

As we have seen, J. A. Hobson was the first important figure in a long line of theorists to attribute to the press a good deal of power in shaping the conditions necessary for imperialism, including home-front support. Hobson's experience as a correspondent for the *Manchester Guardian* during the Anglo-Boer War helped to convince him of the importance for imperialism of ideological factors such as the press. Most histories of the press show newspapers as either shaping or reflecting "public opinion" and see the concept as did the American social critic Walter Lippman, who, writing in 1965, called public opinion the "manufacture of consent," managed by governments and newspaper proprietors (*Public Opinion* 158). Stephen Koss argued that the press of the late nineteenth century "did not so much lead as follow public opinion . . . Once chiefly used to communicate ministerial views to the nation (as it was then narrowly defined), newspapers now began to function less predictably as the agencies through which mass enthusiasms were conveyed to Parliamentary leaders" (*Rise and Fall* 215). But what constitutes a "mass enthusiasm"? Who are these nebulous masses that through the press were affecting policymakers in parliament? Using the detailed examinations of the workings of the press that journalism historians such as Koss, Lucy Brown, and Alan Lee provide, we can examine the camps controversy as a case study of the management of a publicly sanctioned imperial enthusiasm in the late nineteenth century. Although individual papers challenged the government's line on the war itself, none challenged the underlying ideologies of race and gender that played key roles in sustaining the policy of imperialism.

One problem with works that examine such "mass enthusiasms" as imperialism has been press historians' limiting of their analysis to the concept of public opinion. It is possible to assess the role of the press in imperialism only if we recognize the existence of more than one kind of public opinion. Most assessments of the press and public opinion have been concerned with a paper's influence on the electorate when it comes to public policy issues: public opinion manifested itself in mass meetings, letters to the editor, arguments on street corners. But public opinion on imperialism was being formed in the age of the New Journalism. We cannot talk simply about the press and public opinion during the Boer War, or we run the risk of creating monolithic structures: if not the press, then at least the party press, or the individual newspaper as a consistent factor in the creation of public opinion. Nevertheless, we cannot refuse entirely the notion of a public opinion, not least because newspaper editors, proprietors, and policymakers believed in it. These public figures operated on the assumption that newspapers could influence the course of events by stirring to action either the political elite or the electorate en masse.

Imperialism in the Boer War was moving from being an ideological issue, situated in the realm of Antonio Gramsci's "common sense," to being a matter of public opinion, political controversy open to debate. As information on the camps surfaced in Britain, members of the British policymaking elite and of the Great British Public began to become aware of what were beginning to seem like contradictions in British imperialism. It slowly became apparent that a political machine, with its own aims, was driving Britain's imperial efforts. This new awareness of the machinations behind British imperialism, in which the press coverage of the concentration camps played a great part, helped to initiate what would become the twentieth-century reevaluation of Britain's imperial mission.

If we look at the role of the press in the ideology of imperialism, both as a producer of ideology and as a subscriber to it, we can see contradictions within the institution of the press and within individual newspapers, contradictions that reflect rifts in British society during this period, the heart of the "crisis of liberalism." Stuart Hall and Bill Schwartz point to the crisis of liberalism as a far-reaching one not simply of the relationship between the state and civil society, but "rather of the very *ideas* of state and civil society, of public and private." They point out that the 1880–1930 period marked a change in "the very means and modes by which hegemony is exerted in the metropolitan nations" (Hall and Schwartz "Crisis in Liberalism" 99). This change appears clearly in the shift in the British government's presentation of imperialism, which changed from a hegemonic concept intrinsic to British self-definition to a political controversy on which it was possible to hold opposing views. Indeed, in Gramsci's *Prison Notebooks*, written during the 1930s, he formulates the conception of hegemony in relation to the period of the late nineteenth century. The notion of hegemony as a cultural as well as political struggle, constantly negotiated between the hegemonic group and the dominated, allows us to account for the contradictions we see in the press of the Boer War. While many ideas about, for example, gender relations were still hegemonic, such ideas as the right of the British to control Africa seem to have moved from the sphere of ideological hegemony into the openly negotiable realm of public opinion.

The Boer War was a natural locus for these ideological shifts because of its singularity among nineteenth-century British imperial wars. The war was fought for control of a non-European land, against a European people. But the Boers were not simply European. They had been in South Africa for generations, having displaced black African peoples in their treks northward from the Cape of Good Hope. The war in South Africa was a war between a European colonial power and a European-descended people for control of land that had originally been inhabited by African peoples. In the camps crisis, the British had to deal with thousands of white women and children in a land that the British army was fast making uninhabitable. And, because Africans were part of the Afrikaner economy, lived and worked on Boer farms, the British were forced to create policy to accommodate thousands of displaced Africans as well. Never had the British War Office or Colonial Office had to address the needs of such a large civilian population, with the racial, gender, and even class issues that overlay the obvious problems of shelter and food.

THE PRESS AND THE CONCENTRATION CAMPS

Nineteenth-century newspaper historians have examined the press as an agency of social control (Curran "Press as an Agency"), have looked at its structures and ownership (Williams "Press and Popular Culture") and its relationship to political parties (Koss *Rise and Fall*). However, the rather straightforward relationships between political parties and the press found by newspaper historians such as Koss, Brown, and Lee are not so straightforward on the issue of the concentration camps. Rather than being a party political question, the camps controversy touched on factors as diverse as beliefs about the social position of women, about race, and about class as well as economic, military, and political factors. The role of newspapers in the creation and questioning of public support for imperialism involves not only the influence of the press on parliament and parliament on the press but also the more mundane details of editing and sub-editing, of layout and headline-writing, of foreign correspondents with minds of their own, wire services that were not always reliable, placard-writers, gossips in governmental and society circles, friends of reporters, and, especially, readers. This chapter, then, looks at the presentation of information about the camps as much as at the information itself.

Newspapers were the central source of information about the Boer War, for the British public in general and for members of parliament not privy to the daily cables from South Africa received at the War Office. Members of parliament often based questions in the House of Commons on information gleaned from the morning papers.[1] Proprietors and editors of newspapers certainly believed that they were in the business of influencing public opinion, although historians of the press have found few ways of verifying that newspapers' editorial policies actually had any effect on the opinions of their readers (Boyce "Fourth Estate"). To complicate matters further, circulation figures for nineteenth and early twentieth-century newspapers are either unreliable or nonexistent. But daily newspapers were widely bought and read by turn-of-the-century Britons, and political decision-makers, as we shall see, considered newspapers as both reflectors and shapers of public opinion. Londoners bought a particular newspaper for many different reasons that might have had little to do with that paper's editorial policy about the Boer War. But when a paper stepped very far out of line from what its readers were willing to accept, trouble resulted. The *Manchester Guardian*, for example, was an essential purchase for businessmen in London and Manchester who could get the cotton prices from America nowhere else. But the speculators' disgust with the paper's anti-war stance was apparently well known on the commuter trains, as businessmen daily turned to the cotton prices, then ostentatiously crumpled up their *Guardian*s and tossed them on the floor of their compartments.[2]

In the debate about the concentration camps, both sides knew how important newspapers were. After portions of Emily Hobhouse's report were published in the *Manchester Guardian* and the government began to realize the extent of the problems in the camps, camp administration was turned over to the civil authorities. The military gladly washed its hands of the mess. While initially both War Secretary St. John Brodrick and Colonial Secretary Joseph Chamberlain had attributed all anxiety in Britain about the camps to "pro-Boerism," they soon had to face the fact that the camps were becoming a bipartisan issue. Immediately after news of Emily Hobhouse's report appeared in London newspapers in June 1901, Mary Ward wrote to Lord Milner, in London on a brief return from South Africa, with a wish to get involved in helping to improve the camps. Milner replied that he "entirely sympathise[d] with the wish to show that sympathy with women and children – especially children – (for some of the women are among the biggest firebrands) is not confined to sympathisers with the enemy."[3] He told Mrs. Ward to get in touch with Mrs. Alfred Lyttleton and the other women of the Victoria League, "which is Imperialist in the broadest lines." Milner sent a copy of his reply to Chamberlain, explaining that "Mrs. Humphry Ward has written to me saying that there is a general desire to start a strong neutral Committee – not pro-Boer – to relieve the sufferings of people in the Refugee Camps."[4] Even though pro-government newspapers did not give much space to the Hobhouse report, or tried to refute it, readers who supported the war were nevertheless concerned about the camps.[5]

Chamberlain worried about opposition to the concentration camps, and, as the one in London, he had to take the heat Milner didn't feel. The Colonial Secretary wrote to Milner in November 1901 that he needed more information on the camps. "I do not want to add more to your labours," Chamberlain wrote, "but it is of the greatest importance that you should write fully and frequently, and, if possible, in a form in which the information conveyed can be published." The Colonial Secretary complained about waiting for a reply from Milner to a telegram, saying, "I am without even the slightest information of what is going on beyond what I gather from newspaper correspondence. I daresay that this contains everything of importance, but it does not satisfy the public for the Government to say 'We can tell you nothing more than you have learned from the newspaper reports.'"[6] Although Chamberlain believed the newspaper reports contained "everything of importance," he was concerned that he *appear* to know more than the newspapers. Newspapers could and did supply essential information to government ministers, but the public wanted its government to know more than the newspapers did. Chamberlain believed that the public wanted the government to supply information from the spot, not mediated through the newspapers.

When he wanted more information from Milner with which to allay public fears about the camps, on 5 November Chamberlain wrote to Milner:

The mortality in the Concentration Camps has undoubtedly roused deep feeling among people who cannot be classed with the pro-Boers. It does not seem to me altogether a complete answer to say that the aggregation of people who are specially liable to infectious disease has produced a state of things which is inevitable. The natural remark is "Why then did you bring them together." If we say that it was because they would have starved on the veldt we enter on a hypothetical consideration and cannot of course prove that in the alternative the mortality would have been as large. Personally, as you know, I have always doubted the wisdom or necessity of this concentration, but, be that as it may, we ought to give some evidence of exceptional measures when the concentration has the results shown by recent statistics. If, immediately on the outbreak of disease, we could have moved the camps either to the ports in Cape Colony or to some other selected situation we should have had something to say for ourselves, but we seem to have accepted the mortality as natural and many good people are distressed at our apparent indifference.[7]

The letter displays the central concern of Chamberlain as the man in London who was most directly responsible for the camps. He was most concerned that he be able to "give some evidence" of "exceptional measures" taken, that the government should have "something to say for ourselves" about alleviating conditions in the camps. He worries about how the government "seems," at its "apparent" indifference. Of course as Colonial Secretary during a period of public scandal about the camps, he would want to avoid blame. In the House he was obliged to defend the policy of the camps while he privately protested to Milner that he had "always doubted the wisdom or necessity" of the policy. But he did not seek changes in the policy as the death-rates rose – he sought information that he could present to the public to appease the "good people" who were joining with the pro-Boers to oppose the camps.

It was when these "good people" began to come out against the war that Chamberlain and Milner began to get nervous about the "wobble" in public opinion that Milner had feared all along.[8] Milner's immediate reaction was to defend not the government policy on the camps but his own actions as civil, not military authority. He wrote to Chamberlain in early December that:

the black spot – the very black spot, – in the picture is the frightful mortality in the Concentration Camps. I entirely agree with you in thinking, that, while a hundred explanations may be offered and a hundred excuses made, they do not really amount to an adequate defence. I should much prefer to say at once, as far as the Civil authorities are concerned, that we were suddenly confronted with a problem not of our making, with which it was beyond our power to grapple. And no doubt its vastness was not realised soon enough. It was not till six weeks or two months ago that it dawned on me personally (I cannot speak for others) that the enormous mortality was not merely incidental to the first formation of the camps and the sudden inrush of thousands of people already sick and starving, but was going to continue. The fact that it continues, is no doubt condemnation of the Camp system. The whole thing, I think now, has been a mistake. At the same time a sudden reversal of policy would only make matters worse. At the present moment certainly everything we know of is being done, both to improve the camps and to reduce the numbers in them. I believe we shall mitigate the evil, but we shall never get rid of it.

While I say all this, however, I do not think that the mortality would have been less if the people had been left in the veld. I do not think it would. But our great error has been in taking a course which made us responsible, for mischiefs, which ought to have rested on the shoulders of the enemy. But it is easy to be wise after the event. The state of affairs, which led to the formation of the camps, was wholly novel and of unusual difficulty, and I believe no General in the world would not have felt compelled to deal with it in some drastic manner.

If we can get over the Concentration Camps, none of the other attacks upon us alarm me in the least.[9]

This extended analysis of the problems with the camps is entirely motivated by worry about the way the camps were being discussed in England. Once the *Guardian* published Hobhouse's information, the camps became news in all sorts of newspapers. Most of the quality press supported British policy on the camps; almost all the outrage about the camps appeared in "pro-Boer" journals. Yet Milner, Chamberlain, and Brodrick clearly worried about public opinion having turned against them on the camps. The "black spot" of the camps was a genuine problem for Milner. Despite the popular press's denial of British responsibility for the Boer camp deaths, and despite almost universal press support for the camps policy, "public opinion" was perceived as having turned against the government. And the government responded with action – both to ameliorate conditions in the camps and to change public opinion. Milner's concern was at being perceived as responsible for the deaths that had become such a big news story. The way to shift that perception was through the press, both the pro-war and the pro-Boer press, and with the appointment of the Ladies Commission by Brodrick, the process had been set in motion already.

The opponents of the camps, too, worked through the newspapers to make themselves heard by the government who made the decisions about the camps. The correspondence of the members of the South African Women and Children's Distress Fund, the committee under whose auspices Emily Hobhouse traveled to South Africa, reveals the members' keen awareness of the strategies behind the publication of their appeals and of the information about their most notorious member, Emily Hobhouse.

During the row over her report, Hobhouse herself learned the ins and outs of the publication of information in newspapers. When she saw Brodrick about the camps and won certain concessions from him regarding their operations, Hobhouse was told by Lord Ripon, of her committee, not to go straight to the newspapers with the information about the meeting. When she did reveal the information to the press, she wrote to Ripon:

May I send a line to say that the publication in yesterday's papers of Mr. Brodrick's letter to me and my reply was *not* done directly contrary to your advice without reason. But it was because I saw Mr. Brodrick on Thursday and he was *very very* angry with me for not having published it instantly. Of course I promised to do so at once only too gladly, but he was not much appeased because he said the mischief was done it was too late. This plainly shewed that the concessions were entirely made for the public and not at all for the Boer women.

He further told me the Government refused to let me go out again, but when I said I should feel obligated to make that refusal public he turned as white as a sheet and said he would send me a letter in writing.[10]

When Brodrick's letter had not arrived by 25 July, Ripon wrote to Hobhouse's friend and fellow committee-member Kate Courtney to express his concern about how they should proceed. He worried about the advisability of Dr. Richard Spence Watson, of their committee, publishing a letter in the newspapers in which he pretended not to know that Emily Hobhouse had been refused permission to return to the camps. Ripon was shrewd about the timing and strategies that would best use the newspapers to the committee's advantage:

I would recommend that Miss Hobhouse should give Mr. Brodrick a day or two longer to send her his promised precis of his grounds for refusing and if he delays to do so she might then I think allow a paragraph to appear in the newspapers to the effect that she had offered the Govt to go out again, but without saying, unless she had heard from Mr. Brodrick, that she had been refused. Such a paragraph would afford ground for a question in the House of Commons, and it would be important to get it asked by some not extreme person.[11]

People of the social standing of Ripon and Kate Courtney (sister of Beatrice Webb and wife of Leonard Courtney, M.P.) could rely on getting what they wanted printed in newspapers in London, at least in the form of letters. The newspapers in question were, of course, *The Times*, the paper of record, and the *Manchester Guardian*, the leading anti-war journal. When Brodrick, Ripon, or Hobhouse spoke of "the newspapers," they were not referring to the jingo halfpennies such as the *Daily Mail*. On an issue such as the camps, the newspapers taken seriously as indices and shapers of public opinion were still the qualities.

The *Daily Mail*'s chief South African War correspondent was Edgar Wallace. Later, in his fiction, Wallace recognized the place of the newspaper in political debates and the uses of the newspaper for politicians and lobbyists alike. The work that brought him fame as a novelist, *The Four Just Men*, published shortly after he left the *Daily Mail* in 1902, centers on a government minister, who takes the step of "making ... public through the press" (17) the threats to his life over his support of a bill. Wallace emphasizes the role of the press, especially the tabloid *Daily Megaphone*, in publicizing for the public good the threats and the progress of the case. The government, police on two continents, and the criminals react to the stories in the *Megaphone*. And, of course, the public acts on what it reads in the newspapers – the threats become the main topic of conversation in London, and people begin to cheer the threatened minister when he walks in public.

But newspapers, according to this newspaperman and novelist, not only inform and influence readers. They also reflect the views of those readers:

> "What are the people thinking about?" asked the Commissioner.
> "You've seen the papers?"
> Mr. Commissioner's shrug was uncomplimentary to British journalism.
> "The papers! Who in Heaven's name is going to take the slightest notice of what is in the papers?" he said petulantly.
> "I am, for one," replied the calm detective; "newspapers are more often than not led by the public; and it seems to me the idea of running a newspaper in a nutshell is to write so that the public will say, 'That's smart – it's what I've said all along.'" (*Four Just Men* 28)

Wallace, the star correspondent of the war by virtue of some key scoops, had come of age under Harmsworth, who worked the above formula into a circulation of nearly a million a day during the war.

PRO-WAR

The granddaddy of London dailies, *The Times*, and Edgar Wallace's employer, the *Daily Mail*, were far apart in their approaches to journalism, but similar in their rallying behind Britain in its war with the South African republics. The *Daily Mail*, full of crime news, tales of tragedy, and scandal, nevertheless prided itself on its foreign news, using the same wire services and War Office releases as *The Times* did in its pages of more sober, traditional reporting, and hiring some of the best foreign correspondents available (Palmer "British Press and International News" 217). Despite claims of non-partisanship, both papers supported the Salisbury government, though the *Daily Mail*'s conservatism was populist and *The Times*'s elitist (Koss *Rise and Fall* 360, 370). This resulted in the *Daily Mail* supporting the war the government had led the country into and *The Times* supporting the government that had drawn the country into war.

When it came to editorial stands on the war these two pro-war papers were very different, as was reflected in the nature and amount of coverage they devoted to the concentration camps. *The Times*, as had been the tradition of London newspapers, took its cues from parliament. "Momentous events might inconveniently occur in distant places, but their impact was fully registered only when they were debated in

Parliament and appraised by the leader-writers of the London press," writes Stephen Koss (*Rise and Fall* 23). But did the leader-writers of the London press ever bother to appraise those distant, momentous events until parliament had pointed them out? First, let us examine how the papers treated information that did come from parliament.

Like *The Times*, the young *Daily Mail* took note of what went on at Westminster. But the *Daily Mail* was the most vigorous proponent of a new trend in British journalism at the end of Victoria's reign – the move away from column after column of verbatim reporting of parliamentary debates and speeches. While *The Times* might present its reader more than a full page of eye-straining, small-print transcription from debates, the *Daily Mail* reader would rarely see more than a column of parliamentary reporting, and even that was seldom verbatim reports of speeches. The difference meant that while *The Times* supported the government, *The Times* reader would also have learned what the opposition had to say. Not so the reader of the *Daily Mail*. Because the paper did not transcribe the debates, it had more freedom to summarize, to indicate which side it felt had won, or to ignore the debates entirely. So the *Daily Mail*'s style of journalism meant that it could come out in favor of the war and against the British anti-war movement much more strongly than *The Times* could, simply by virtue of what it left off its news pages.

An example of this pattern comes from the 19 February 1901 parliamentary coverage of both newspapers. *The Times*'s coverage of that day noted David Lloyd George's complaint about the fact that, in the Boer concentration camps, the families of burghers still on commando were receiving reduced rations until the fighters surrendered. Lloyd George said that "the remnant of the Boer army who were sacrificing everything for their idea of independence were to be tortured by the spectacle of their starving children into betraying their cause" if the reduced-rations policy were continued. Secretary of State for War St. John Brodrick denied the accusation (in fact, reduced rations were standard policy in the camps at the time [Pakenham *Boer War* 505]), blasting Lloyd George for "trying to establish a charge for which he has not a particle of evidence." Lloyd George defended himself, citing his source: "a telegram from Pretoria," the Reuter news agency report on the subject, which had appeared in *The Times* and the *Daily Mail* a month before.[12] "No telegram could come from Pretoria that was objected to by the military censor there," noted Lloyd George. "Did the right honourable gentleman mean to say that the telegram with the stamp of the military censor on it was not a particle of evidence?" he asked Brodrick.[13]

The *Daily Mail* reported nothing at all about Lloyd George's complaint. The sole mention it gave the exchange was: "After Mr. Brodrick denied that there was necessarily any truth in a telegram because it passed the censor ... Mr. Lloyd George ... continu[ed] his tirade."[14] No mention of the subject of the tirade. The *Daily Mail* reader never learned from that newspaper about the reduced-rations debate. The question of reduced rations was a touchy one, and a jingo newspaper bent on portraying as just the war and all its tactics could not risk the inconsistency of appearing to sympathize with Boer women and children. Like all other British newsapers of the turn of the century, the *Daily Mail* strove for consistency in its editorial stances on major issues, especially the war. Where the Harmsworth paper was innovative was in extending that editorial consistency beyond the leader and into the news pages. If a piece of news such as the reduced-rations debate might supply ammunition to the anti-war side, then that news did not appear in the *Daily Mail*.

PRO-BOER

Until January 1901 no major London daily challenged *The Times*, the *Daily Mail*, and the other pro-government or pro-war newspapers. Although the halfpenny radical *Morning Leader* maintained an anti-war stance throughout the conflict, it was not of sufficient stature in the London press to worry anyone. The *Manchester Guardian* was influential but was nevertheless primarily a provincial paper. London Liberals and radicals against the war grew increasingly frustrated at having their say limited to the pages of J. A. Spender's weekly *Speaker*, and in late 1900 a group of "pro-Boers," headed by David Lloyd George, decided that the capital city needed a strong Liberal voice against the war. Starting a new daily proved too expensive, so the coalition, funded largely by chocolate manufacturer George Cadbury, reclaimed the *Daily News* from Liberal imperialism. They bought the paper in January 1901, telling pro-war editor E. T. Cook on a Tuesday "that he would go on the following Thursday," according to Herbert Gladstone.[15]

The *Daily News*, its masthead boasting the "largest circulation of any Liberal newspaper in the world," had been solid behind Gladstonian principles before the 1896 hiring of Cook (Koss *Rise and Fall* 366), who rallied the paper behind imperialism. With his replacement by the Radical journalist A. G. Gardiner and the addition of H. W. Massingham and Herbert Lehmann as parliamentary correspondent and leader-writer, respectively, the pro-Boers had built a paper that looked a good bet to achieve what Massingham explained to C. P. Scott was their goal: "to put Liberalism here on the basis which the *Guardian* has so firmly established in Manchester" (quoted in Koss *Rise and Fall* 398). In the spirit of Cadbury's Quakerism, the paper became the major London opponent of the concentration camps. The pro-Boer stance did not pay off for the investors. Harold Spender of the *Manchester Guardian* told the story of George Cadbury revealing after the war that the early months of his chairmanship of the board of directors of the *Daily News* cost him £10,000. When Spender reminded Cadbury that the paper had probably "saved ten thousand lives" by reporting on the conditions in the concentration camps, "his face brightened with a beautiful smile. 'Ah! in that case,' he said, 'I will willingly bear the loss'" (quoted in Koss *Rise and Fall* 400).

But despite Massingham's assertions that the *Daily News* would aim to serve the function of the *Manchester Guardian*, the two papers varied in their approaches to the concentration camps, the most important humanitarian issue of the war. The *Daily News*, considered a bit hysterical by most other dailies, publicized the camps from the earliest days of Emily Hobhouse's visits to them in 1901, with many letters to the editor from prominent pro-Boers condemning the camps. The *Manchester Guardian*, however, while including special wire service reports on the deportation of women and children earlier than any other paper – in the fall of 1900 – was later than the *Daily News* with protests against the camp system.

Even before the pro-Boer takeover, the *Daily News* had editorialized in support of the efforts of the South African Women and Children's Distress Fund when it announced the fund's formation in the letters columns of 8 December.[16] The paper constantly carried news agency reports of British troops bringing in women and children to the camps, the same telegrams that appeared in *The Times*. But as soon as the new management took over, the *Daily News* published a letter from the South Africa Conciliation Committee (19 January), drawing attention to the Reuter's telegram that had appeared in *The Times* on 17 January and that would come to cause the first big flap over the camps in the House of Commons – the half-rations telegram that had revealed the policy of reduced food for families of men on commando.[17] In addition, the *Daily News* published long letters from the South African Women and Children's Distress Fund, reporting on Emily Hobhouse's progress through the camps.[18]

News reporting from South Africa also varied among these four newspapers. The first news of the camps in *The Times* was its report at the end of December of Kitchener's 20 December proclamation that surrendered burghers would now "be allowed to live with their families in Government laagers [camps] until such time as the guerrilla war now being carried on will admit of their returning safely to their homes."[19] Although the camps were already being loaded with women and children whose farms had been burned, and not only with the families of surrendered burghers, the proclamation did not go any further (Warwick *Black People* 147–48). Three days later *The Times* featured the first mention that anyone was finding fault with the camps, in an article on "The Alleged Ill-Treatment of Boer Women." The article quoted a letter from a Dutch clergyman, T. J. Ferreira, rebutting charges against the British military regarding "the bad treatment exiles are receiving from the military." Ferreira said he visited the camp at Port Elizabeth "determined to find out the truth." So he stayed to dinner. "The food was excellent," he declared, describing the meal from the roast beef to the coffee. "The women and children are happy, have no complaint, and are quite content to stay where they are until they can return to their homes."[20] *Times* articles would continue to deny bad conditions in the camps even when the government reports about the death rates were released, often, as with the Ferreira story, refuting specific charges that had never appeared in the paper: "As for the statement that women go ragged and barefooted and had to bathe within sight of the military, it is a shameful falsehood."[21] *The Times* maintained a defensive posture throughout the controversy about the camps; charges against the British never appeared in the paper – only refutations of them.

No one could have accused the *Daily Mail* of being defensive. Its early news coverage of the camps from South Africa was scanty; it, too, reported on Kitchener's proclamation about the surrendered burghers and their families, but it did not feature the refutations of charges against the British that *The Times* ran. Its first leader-page notice of the camps called for "Stern Methods of War" such as those employed by the North in devastating parts of the South during the American Civil War – "reduction to poverty," as practiced by Generals Sherman and Sheridan. The *Daily Mail* advocated burning Boer farms and removing civilians from the countryside. The American Civil War theme recurred throughout the paper's leaders about the war.[22]

Daily Mail leader-writers in April 1901 called for the abolition of the concentration camps as part of a British effort at "War in Earnest." The camps were not too harsh, but too humane and too expensive. "The policy of feeding the wives and children of the burghers now in the field against us has been tried and proved a failure," said the leader. "It has been misunderstood and regarded as one more sign that England is to be played with. There is every objection to it on the score of economy and common sense."[23] So it was not out of humanitarianism that the *Daily Mail* opposed the camps, but out of financial concern. The leader pointed out that Uitlander, "loyalist" refugees from the republics, who fled their jobs at the gold mines at the outbreak of war, were "starving in every South African port, while the Boer women are rioting in comparative plenty." Comparisons between the situations of the English refugees and the Boers in camp were plentiful in both newspapers. It was a theme especially popular with letter-writers.[24]

The *Manchester Guardian* reported from early December about the British army's treatment of non-combatants, especially women in South Africa. Throughout December its Cape Colony correspondent reported on the situation of a group of Boer women and children from "Fauresmith, Jagersfontein, and other southern portions of the Orange River Colony," who had been marched through the streets "under an escort of soldiers with fixed bayonets" and who were being kept "in a location practically prisoners," "in the most Jingo town in South Africa."[25] These women were housed in wood and corrugated iron sheds and guarded by British soldiers, in what was already referred to as a "refugee camp," although the military admitted that it had forcibly deported the women for helping Boer fighters.[26]

THE DEATH RATES

Death rates in the camps rose steadily, largely due to disease brought in with the wagonloads of women and children. The people arrived in poor condition after traveling for days in open wagons and introduced pneumonia, measles, and other ailments to the overcrowded and often underfed populations of the camps (Hobhouse *Brunt* 38). In the white camps the death rates peaked at a rate of 344 per 1000 per annum in October 1901, while in the black camps the worst rate was 372 per 1000 per annum, reached in December 1901 (Warwick *Black People* 145). The subject of health conditions in the camps first appeared in *The Times* in February 1901, when a Reuter's story said that at the Kroonstadt camp in the Orange River Colony, "The medical officer's report for January shows that a normal state of health prevails here. The authorities are doing their best to make the lot of the refugees as comfortable as possible. Schools will shortly be established in the camps under qualified teachers."[27] Schools were indeed established in the camps for whites, and the camp administrators came to regard the schools as their greatest success, largely because they were able to teach English to thousands of Afrikaans-speaking children.[28] But as the camps grew, the camp education news was quickly overshadowed by reports of poor health conditions. The deaths in the camps made their way into *The Times* initially by way of a wire service transmission of a Boer military proclamation that was found on a surrendered burgher. "Many women's deaths have been occasioned because the so-called Christian enemy has no consideration for women on a sick bed or for those whose state of health should have protected them from rough treatment," the proclamation said.[29] The *Daily Mail* did not run the report.

The *Daily News* obtained, "from a thoroughly accurate and trust-worthy source," the first set of mortality statistics from the camps, complete with names of the dead. The information appeared in the paper on 12 June 1901, just before the publication of Hobhouse's report. The *Manchester Guardian* cited the *Daily News* statistics, but the jingo papers pulled out all the stops to refute them, calling on doctors and demographers to prove that the camp death statistics were either exaggerated or were no worse than the figures in the average English town. The battle over the numbers persisted between the newspapers almost until the end of the war.[30] The *Guardian* challenged the government statistics at the release of every new Blue-book, relying for medical interpretations on Dr. F. S. Arnold, brother of the *Guardian*'s W. T. Arnold (and nephew of Thomas, cousin of Matthew).[31]

By mid-June even the *Daily Mail* could not ignore parliament's discussion of the concentration camps, as the House of Commons exploded over the publication of Emily Hobhouse's report to the South African Women and Children's Distress Fund. Hobhouse was the first civilian to examine all the camps for whites, and she was shocked at what she found. When her report was released to parliament and the newspapers, the *Daily Mail* fumed about the "anti-national press" that had reported on Hobhouse's findings, and how the press had "concocted preposterous statistics to convict the horrible Mr. Chamberlain and the odious Lord Milner of atrocities to women and children."[32] The 17 June parliamentary debates on the Hobhouse report took up more than a page of *The Times* and more than a column of the *Daily Mail*, a considerable amount for both papers.[33] Both devoted leaders to the debate, supporting Brodrick in his defense of the conditions in the camps, and summarizing the debate on the leader page.[34]

During the debate opposition leader Sir Henry Campbell-Bannerman called for Hobhouse's report "to be published, so that the British people may know the state of things."[35] In his famous "methods of barbarism" speech about the camps and farm-burning, Campbell-Bannerman leapt off the fence and into the pro-Boer camp, to the fury of much of his party. Neither *The Times* nor the *Daily Mail* published any extracts from the Hobhouse report, although both criticized it, *The Times* as "blood-curdling descriptions and ... false or inaccurate stories,"[36] the *Daily Mail* as "hysterical assertion."[37] All the papers assumed a knowledge of the report, whether or not they had published any of it. They assumed a cross-fertilization of news – people did not get their news from just a single source. *The Times* assumed a knowledge of information from the *Daily Mail*, and readers of other papers were also influenced by the news coverage of the halfpennies.

The *Manchester Guardian* did not excerpt the Hobhouse report either, but the *Daily News* release of the mortality rates, coincident with the report, prompted the *Guardian*'s first leader devoted to the subject of the camps, on 13 June.[38] And the *Guardian* took particular exception to *The Times*'s critiques of the Hobhouse report, devoting a leader to defending the "general moderation" of the report.[39] Such cross-referencing is what makes it so difficult to identify the influence of either "the press" or a single newspaper on public opinion.

The Times's concentration camp reports take on an even more defensive tone after the June debates. On 19 June 1901, the day after the newspaper reports of the camp debates, *The Times*'s "special correspondent" in Bloemfontein telegraphed that "there is nothing in Bloemfontein which does not point to progress – progress, that is, as far as possible under the present difficulties. In no department is this more marked than in the burgher refugee camps under the administration of the Orange River Colony." The death rate, the reporter said, "may seem high, but many reasons have conduced to this high rate, which is rapidly decreasing."[40] By now *The Times* and the *Daily Mail* acknowledged that the death rates in the camps were abnormally high. The *Daily Mail* blamed the British pro-Boers: "they, and they alone, are responsible for the fact that the war was not over nearly a year ago, and, in consequence, all the mortality in the concentration camps, and the devastation tactics which they, in their hypocritical humanitarianism, so loudly denounce, lies at their door."[41] (The pro-Boers prolonged the war by giving the Boers hope that Britain might give in, according to the *Daily Mail* argument.)

The Times began to blame Boer women for the deaths in the camps. The 19 June article from Bloemfontein explained that the women in the camps "are absolutely without appreciation of the necessity of careful sanitary cleanliness. The women take but small care of their children."[42] (Emily Hobhouse's report noted that soap was not included in the rations for the Bloemfontein camp [*Report to the Committee* 4–5.]) Blaming the victims, in this case the Boer mothers, became very popular, starting with the publication of the first Colonial Office Blue-book on the camps in November, described in *The Times* on 18 November. The newspaper said that the Blue-book, "after tracing the high death-rate from measles to the extremely cold nights, goes on to say that the Boer mother is greatly to blame."[43] The paper then cited instance after instance from the book of Boer mothers treating their sick children with useless or dangerous remedies. Readers sent in letters for months to come, focusing on how the British officials were working against great odds in trying to lower the death rates in the camps. The death rates, many of these readers held, were due to the "callousness to all hygiene of many of the women and their tendency to have recourse to remedies of a most detrimental and dangerous character."[44]

The *Manchester Guardian* came out with guns blazing after the publication of the November Blue-book. It attacked the haphazard way the report was put together, charging that the lack of structure was meant to obfuscate:

Almost the only passages in a volume of 379 pages which it is possible to read consecutively are those in which the inmates of the camps are attacked for the backward state of their medical and sanitary knowledge. This, indeed, may be said to be the one "theme" in the Blue-book; all other aspects of the question are presented in scattered sentences, hidden away in separate reports which are bundled together at random, without any discoverable system of arrangement and without even an index or a summary.[45]

The emphasis on bad habits among the Boers, the paper charged, was inappropriate and "monstrous," and had "no bearing on the moral question raised by the mortality in the camps." But the emphasis had its effect in *The Times*, the *Morning Post*, the *Daily Telegraph*, and other pro-government newspapers that were to stress the "filthy habits" of Boer mothers in their leaders on the mortality rates. The *Guardian* was proud of its "careful reading and re-reading" of the Blue-book, that "enables one to discover underneath the surface of official optimism the real causes of the mortality which has shocked the country."[46] The *Guardian* noted that while some of the "Ministerialist press" still maintained that the camps had been formed for the protection of helpless Boer women and children, the more accurate picture of the families having been deported from their homes at a moment's notice against their will was attested to in the Blue-book: "There is evidence even in this Report, prepared as it is by British officials and exclusively from the official point of view."[47] The paper delighted in turning the government's own statistics and reports on the camps back against the government.

The *Daily Mail* did not report on the Blue-book at all and carried no articles or letters blaming Boer mothers for camp deaths. Even when its war correspondent Edgar Wallace scooped the rest of the London papers with his advance report of the findings of the Ladies Commission sent out by Chamberlain to inspect the camps, Wallace avoided sensationalism. He gave a straightforward account of the findings and recommendations of the group and did not cite any of the mother-blame stories that would later appear in the commission's Blue-book. Wallace, however, could not resist, or his editor in London couldn't, commenting that the commission was unnecessary in the first place and "need never have been appointed."[48] *The Times* encouraged the Ladies Commission investigation into the camps, convinced that investigation would vindicate the government of any fault in the operation of the camps.[49]

A major difference between *The Times'* and the *Daily Mail's* coverage of the camps was *The Times's* regular inclusion of reports of European and American opinion about the camps. Foreign correspondents of London dailies enjoyed more freedom in their reporting than local reporters (Brown *Victorian News* 105). It was up to the foreign correspondent to determine what was news in international capitals, and their reports were often more pro-British than those of reporters in London. *The Times* Vienna correspondent reported in late 1901, for example, that "the combined efforts of Sir Henry Campbell-Bannerman and Miss Hobhouse have now enlightened foreigners in the remotest corners of Europe as to the 'barbarous methods' practiced by the British army in South Africa."[50] *The Times* emphasis on "foreign calumnies" was consistent with its image as an influential paper for the middle classes and above, while the *Daily Mail's* lack of interest in foreign opinion of the camps also fits that paper's image of parochialism.

The *Daily News* and the *Manchester Guardian* relied on translations of reports in foreign newspapers for their news on foreign opinion about the camps. Since the foreign news was all anti-British, it was the same in the conservative papers as it was in anti-government papers. The *Guardian,* however, stressed the loss of reputation and honor involved in foreign disapproval of the camps, while *The Times* thumbed its nose at the continent.

None of the controversy around the conditions or the death rates in the camps for Boers spilled over into public concern in Britain for the inhabitants of the camps for Africans. When Africans appeared in news stories in either *The Times* or the *Daily Mail,* it was in articles about whether or not African men should be allowed to carry guns if they were working for the British army or in articles about Boer troops committing atrocities on blacks.[51] The former stories were exemplary of the British effort to see the war as a "white man's war,"[52] and the latter played an important role in keeping before the British public the notion that the war was being fought at least partially to secure better treatment for Africans in the republics.[53] *The Times* did mention the black camps occasionally, but never to cite conditions in them; the articles focused on how the men in the camps were being employed by the British and how the inhabitants were growing their own crops for food.[54]

The only direct mention of African women in any of the newspapers during the course of the war was the *Daily News*'s Arthur Hales's attempt at a literary sketch, "In a Boer Town," which appeared on 10 May 1900:

The girls are rather pleasing in appearance though far from being pretty... The Kaffir girl is very dark, almost black. The bushman's daughter is dirty yellow, like river water in flood time... But whether they are black, brown, or coffee-coloured, they are all alike in one respect – every daughter of them has a mouth that is as boundless as a mother's blessing, and as limitless as the imagination of a spring poet in love... It is amusing to watch them flirting with the soldier niggers. They try to look coy, but soon fall victims to the skilful blandishments of the vainglorious warriors, and after a little manoeuvering they put out their lips to be kissed, a sight which might well make a Scottish Covenanter grin. (3)

Hales's description of the African woman's mouth is couched in mock-praise, but the point is that the mouth is "boundless" and "limitless," a mouth that could swallow up a poor unsuspecting man.[55] Hales follows up his description of the African women with the white man's anxiety about his abilities in comparison to the black man; apparently, the "soldier niggers" "do enough love-making in twenty-four hours to last an ordinary everyday sort of white man four months, even if he puts in a little overtime." Generally, however, Africans appeared in the papers only in their capacities of helping or hindering the British war effort. The extent of the *Manchester Guardian*'s interest was to lament the lack of mortality statistics for the "native camps." Africans in the war were not of sufficient concern to war correspondents and editors to warrant frequent stories, and the operative assumption was that they were not of concern to the British reader.

PUBLIC OPINION AND THE CAMPS

To sum up, in its coverage of the concentration camps, *The Times* was much more responsive to parliament than was the *Daily Mail*. The *Manchester Guardian* took a great deal of initiative in its camp coverage, commissioning articles from Emily Hobhouse and spending hours sifting through the government's statistics to try to get a larger picture of the situation in the camps, and losing a great deal of readership along the way. The *Daily News* also contributed painstaking analysis of the camp statistics and lost a great deal of money over its opposition to the war and the camps. From the first parliamentary debate on the concentration camps until the end of the war, *The Times* followed up the controversy about the camps with more wire service items, more foreign news, more interest from its own correspondents in South Africa, more leaders, and, consequently, more letters to the editor about the camps than appeared in the *Daily Mail*. *The Times* coverage and editorial attitudes came from long-established traditions of parliamentary reporting and a certain amount of loyalty to the Conservative government. As George Boyce explains, "It seemed to be representative of a certain kind of public opinion – that is, of the enlightened, educated middle classes; and it set out to give its readers a constant stream of information and free comment necessary for the public to form a considered judgement" ("Fourth Estate" 22, 23). The *Daily Mail*, on the other hand, was starting a new tradition – presenting what readers want to read, so as to sell newspapers. Neither *The Times* nor the *Daily Mail* presented the "pro-Boer" side to the question of the camps, and neither addressed the issue of the African camps. But both saw themselves as influencing British public opinion in favor of British imperial interests and in favor of the policy of pursuing the Boer War.

Pioneering New Journalist Kennedy Jones said that the *Daily Mail*'s service to imperialism could be compared with Kipling's (quoted in Palmer "British Press" 217). The comparison between journalism and literature effectively indicates these media's similar roles in the creation and sustenance of the ideology of imperialism. But where literature, such as Kipling's fund-raising poem "The Absent-Minded Beggar," can be seen in its role as supporting such ideological notions as nationalism or imperialism or home-front patriotism, newspapers are more associated with influence on "public opinion," which was concerned with policies that required demonstrable public support in order to function well. The newspapers believed that they could influence public opinion, and the provision of such information as camp death rates does seem to have created a level of public concern that transcended party affiliation. But the camps debate highlights changes that were coming with the new century. Some ideologies remained firmly in place – all the newspapers seemed to share the same attitudes toward Africans in the war, for example. But while the New Journalism was giving voice to the new jingoism, it was also allowing the expression of attitudes that had been impermissible. The newspaper that most represented things to come, the *Daily Mail*, never expressed concern about the women and children in the camps; the ideology of man as protector of woman was fast giving way. The popular press could advocate half-starving Boer women and children at the same time as the more old-fashioned newspapers were invoking the more old-fashioned spirit of chivalry in defense of the camps. The ideological shifts represented by the new tabloid journalism were helping to insure that the South African War would be "the last of the gentlemen's wars."

CHAPTER 3

Gender ideology as military policy – the camps, continued

With the concentration camps controversy, stories about women appeared in the war reports for the first time in the South African conflict. The war had boasted no Florence Nightingale and, because the Boer republics had no communities of British women and children (all had fled to the British Cape Colony at the start of trouble), chivalric patriotism could not be invoked in defense of helpless memsahibs as in the Sepoy Rebellion of 1857 (Sharpe *Allegories of Empire*, Brantlinger, *Rule of Darkness*). The Boer War, coming as it did at the cusp of Victorianism and Edwardianism, featured new anxieties and uncertainties about men's role in relation to women. The "last of the gentlemen's wars" marked a transition in Britain for both imperialism and Victorian conceptions of men's duties towards women. In the concentration camps controversy, the press and other public discourse frequently invoked shared ideology about gender and race – that is, much writing about the camps, on both sides of the issue, assumed certain shared notions in its readers about men's obligations to women and the position of Africans in relation to Europeans. These shared ideas were called upon in support of notions about Empire and about the Boer War in particular that were *not* shared ideology – that is, questions about Britain's role in South Africa and about its methods of prosecuting the war were matters of opinion rather than of ideology, to be openly debated in the public sphere, especially the newspapers. The changes made by the popular press at the turn of the century – the expanded readership, the shift toward sensationalism and personality and away from parliamentary reporting and exclusive attention to political figures – made it possible for the camps controversy to become news and to then force political action. The changing status of women in the late-Victorian period coincided with the emergence of the popular press, and this chapter will explore the emergence of the camps as a new category of political danger: the "women's issue."

In the South African camps and back in Britain, women influenced the course of the Boer War and South African history through a curious set of circumstances whereby they were simultaneously victims, symbols, and political actors, sometimes all in the same person. In looking at the ways women were portrayed and portrayed themselves in the controversy over the concentration camps, we see the simultaneous operation of competing discourses about women's duties, obligations, and place. After examining what the average Briton would have been reading about the Boer women in the camps, this chapter discusses the careful ideological work done by the two women at the heart of the camps controversy, Emily Hobhouse and Millicent Fawcett.

Recent critics have addressed the roles of gender and sexuality in the literature of imperialism and of Empire in the literature of women. Anne McClintock's broad study of imperialism in nineteenth- and twentieth-century culture examines H. Rider Haggard, Olive Schreiner, Empire-oriented advertising, and much more. Sandra M. Gilbert and Susan Gubar explore the "heart of darkness" in the literature of Haggard and Joseph Conrad, as well as the connections between imperialism and women's desire for "home rule" in the fiction of such writers as Schreiner and Charlotte Perkins Gilman. Susan Meyer explores Victorian women novelists' complicated relationship to questions of race and empire. Jenny Sharpe's work on both literary texts and other public and private discourse – such as newspapers, narratives of the Sepoy Rebellion, and diaries – makes clear the extent of imperial ideology's reliance on the figure of the white woman, especially the sexually threatened white woman. Deirdre David also addresses both literary and "cultural documents" in her study of women in the construction of Empire, and this chapter can be said to begin with her assertion that "in the late-nineteenth-century questioning of British engagement abroad, worries about empire and race are inseparable from patriarchal worries about female cultural assertion" (*Rule Britannia* 9).

Joan Wallach Scott advocates the study "of processes, not of origins, of multiple rather than single causes" (*Gender* 4), and this chapter explores the multiple processes involved in the sustenance of the idea of imperialism in late-Victorian Britain. Imperialism cannot be said to originate solely in economics; even J. A. Hobson's analysis of the capitalist roots of the phenomenon, examined in chapter one, acknowledged the importance of cultural and social supports for an imperial policy. Language is the terrain in which the contradictions involved in the creation of hegemony are worked out, and British writing about the

concentration camps reveals the process of this working out, the reconciling of contradictions, the co-opting of ideas. During the Boer War,
the contradictions often overrode the hegemonic power of the discourse
of public officials. British journalism, government Blue-books, and War
Office and Colonial Office correspondence reveal the fragility of certain
ideas that had been strong ideological supports for imperialism.

Rather than aiming to recreate the consciousness of the Boers and
Africans in the concentration camps, this chapter focuses on the discursive relationship between these groups and political figures and journalists in Britain. The presence of these subordinate groups within the
discourse of elites in Britain is essential to the constitution of those elites,
who operate only as "part of an immense discontinuous network ('text'
in the general sense) of strands that may be termed politics, ideology,
economics, history, sexuality, language, and so on" (Spivak *In Other
Worlds* 203). Imperialism in Britain, in its many manifestations, cannot
be seen separately from the colonial or, in this consideration, the
colonial woman. British imperialism depended on particular discursive
relationships of British policy-makers to British women, Boers, and
Africans in South Africa.

New contradictions that arose within imperial ideology during the
Boer War were approached differently by the different sides on the
concentration camps issue. While all the Britons whose writings I
examine had a stake in maintaining British hegemony in some way,
some were willing to challenge aspects of it and some worked hard to
strengthen its hold. Emily Hobhouse and her sympathizers tried to take
advantage of the split in public opinion caused by the camps, while
Brodrick and Millicent Fawcett tried to heal the break and reclaim
British imperial hegemony.

THE DISCURSIVE POSITION OF WOMEN IN THE WAR

Fewer British women made the trek to the Transvaal than went to India
in the nineteenth century, because the British presence in the Witwatersrand was not an administrative or military one. Most British in Johannesburg had come for one reason – gold. These "Uitlanders," with little
stake in the politics and social life of the region save what affected the
money they could take home, brought no community of women from
England to keep domestic and social order for them. There was no need
for the memsahib in the South African republic of the Transvaal. The
British colonies of Natal and Cape Colony were different from the

Transvaal in this regard, maintaining a social structure closer to the usual patterns of colonial settlement.

The British government and British mine-owners and workers in the Transvaal expressed little interest in those British women who had come to the region before war broke out in 1899, except during the Jameson Raid of 1895. The raid was the trigger to the Afrikaner disaffection with the British that culminated in the Boer War. When in the autumn of 1895 Cecil Rhodes and Leander Starr Jameson hatched their plot to take over the Transvaal for Britain, they decided that a plausible premise for such an invasion would be the need to liberate the oppressed Uitlanders. But it was first necessary to prove that the Uitlanders wanted liberating. So Rhodes and mine-owner Alfred Beit organized a committee of mine-owners to write a letter of appeal from the Transvaal British that would be left undated for future use: "Thousands of unarmed men, women and children of our race will be at the mercy of well-armed Boers, while property of enormous value will be in the greatest peril ... All feel that we are justified in taking any steps to prevent the shedding of blood, and to insure the protection of our rights" (quoted in Woods and Bishop *Story of the Times* 168). Thomas Pakenham points out that "it was stirring stuff about the women and children, but not the precise truth, they knew," especially since the letter was written a month before it was used as an invitation to invade (*Boer War* 2–3). The only danger in Johannesburg to Uitlanders was the danger of losing a substantial part of their income to Boer taxes. The fact that the letter came to be known as the "women and children letter" indicates a certain amount of self-awareness on the part of the players involved as to how such images were used. Nevertheless, the British were to return to the powerful picture of helpless women and children in South Africa a few years later when they were called upon to justify the concentration camps.

THE CONCENTRATION CAMPS

The decision to clear the Boer republics and deport Boer women and children and African men, women, and children into what had previously been "refugee camps" for surrendered Boers was not well considered. Pakenham points out that the initiative was Lord Kitchener's and "had all the hallmarks of one of Kitchener's famous short cuts. It was big, ambitious, simple, and (what always endeared Kitchener to Whitehall) extremely cheap" (*Boer War* 494). The camps had been started, Kitchener said in a 20 December 1900 cable to War Secretary

Brodrick, because: "Every farm is to [the Boers] an intelligence agency and a supply depot so that it is almost impossible to surround or catch them." The inhabitants of these farms were largely women and children, most men being out on commando. Kitchener therefore decided, in order "to meet some of the difficulties," "to bring in the women from the more disturbed districts to laagers near the railway and offer the burghers to join them there."[1] So Kitchener saw himself as solving a military problem by deporting women from their farms and establishing the concentration camps. He was not concerned about how the camps would be received by the British public or the Boers in the field, let alone by newspapers on the European continent. Those public relations problems fell to Brodrick.

According to Kitchener, the first lot of white women were brought into concentration camps for spying.[2] After the early stages of the war, however, white and black families appear to have been brought in because the British had confiscated or burned their homes and food. Even with burned crops and homes, however, many Boer women begged British officers to be allowed to stay on the veldt and await the return of their men rather than enter the camps.

In March, after questions in parliament forced Brodrick to cable Kitchener for information about the camps, Kitchener was reassuring about the need for the camps: "The refugee camps for women and surrendered boers are I am sure doing good work[;] it enables a man to surrender and not lose his stock and movable property... The women left in farms give complete intelligence to the boers of all our movements and feed the commandos in their neighbourhood."[3] Just over a week before, when asked by John Ellis whether "the persons in those camps [were] held to be prisoners of war" and by Irish M.P. John Dillon "Are they guarded by sentries with bayonets?" Brodrick had told the House of Commons, "[T]hese camps are voluntary camps formed for protection. Those who come may go."[4]

Why didn't the War Office from the first admit that the camps were established to keep the Boer women from passing intelligence along to the commandos? In admitting that, they would have been admitting that the women were imprisoned because of their military activities, and were in fact, as the Liberals and the Irish M.P.s were saying, prisoners of war. Part of the reason for their reticence was that Brodrick had been virtually in the dark about the camps himself from the formation of the earliest ones in September 1900. Information was extremely slow in coming from the closed-mouthed Kitchener, and Brodrick does not appear to have known whether or not women could leave the camps. But if the War Office was going to make any assumptions in parliament about the status of the camp inhabitants, it was going to err on the side of making the women out to be grateful guests, not prisoners. Although Brodrick insisted that "those who come may go," the women were not free to leave the camps.

But even Brodrick had not settled, this early in the controversy, the way in which the camps should be portrayed. When, in the exchange cited above, Brodrick was asked by John Ellis for details he could not supply, the Secretary betrayed his confusion. He admitted that "a certain number of women had been deported to the laager." Dillon, to loud Irish cheers, asked, "What civilized Government ever deported women? Had it come to this, that this Empire was afraid of women?" Brodrick stepped deeper into it when he responded that "Women and children who have been deported are those who have either been found giving information to the enemy or are suspected of giving information to the enemy." An outraged Dillon returned: "I ask the honourable gentleman if any civilized nation in Europe ever declared war against women... A pretty pass has the British Empire come to now!"[5] The government soon stopped referring to the deportation of women and children and to the camps' function in keeping potential spies off the farms.

The opposition, in parliament and in the press, continued to harp on the women's status as prisoners until, at Emily Hobhouse's recommendation in June, Brodrick agreed to allow camp inhabitants to leave if they had relatives or friends to go to. He wrote to Kitchener on 21 June that "Our line has been that they are not *penal* but a necessary provision for clearing the country of people not wanted there and who cannot be fed separately. In consequence if you can allow any who can support themselves to go to towns so much the better."[6] Hobhouse noted, however, that this policy declaration took quite a while to filter down into actual practice in the camps. As of September, Alice Greene wrote to Hobhouse from South Africa that "At the meeting last Friday at the Ladies' Central Committee in Cape Town no one seemed to know any instance of any one released in answer to Mr. Brodrick's concessions" (van Reenen *Hobhouse Letters* 468). And as late as 9 April 1902 Hobhouse was pleading in the *Guardian*: "Pressure of public opinion has brought about reforms in the material conditions of the camps; can no similar pressure be brought to bear such as shall remind Mr. Brodrick of his promise that women able to leave the camps should be allowed to do so? That promise has proved itself worthless and worse than worthless, for hopes were raised by it in vain."[7]

Farm-burning was a point of contention in the British press, with the sides breaking down into pro-Boer versus pro-war over the issue. Few people who supported the war were prepared to quarrel with the methods by which Roberts and Kitchener were fighting it. Letters in newspapers revealed that it was primarily opponents of the war, the "pro-Boers," who were speaking out strongly against the farm-burning. But the camps were another matter. The Great British Public could get upset about the death rates and the conditions in the camps without criticizing the generals, the soldiers, or the government's war policy. While farm-burning was military strategy, the camps could be seen as a humanitarian issue. "Non-political" churches passed resolutions deploring the conditions in the camps. Imperialist groups such as the Victoria League formed committees to help the camp inhabitants. The *Manchester Guardian* complained that the camps had become a party issue, but in fact people broke party rank much more often on the question of the concentration camps than on the farm-burning issue.[8]

Brodrick noted as early as April 1901 in a letter to Kitchener that "some of our own people are hot on the humanitarian tack"[9] on the subject of the camps. In May, Brodrick noted that he was preparing papers for the House on farm-burning and the camps. For farm-burning, he had "arranged so as simply to show the farms-dates-cause," while he was a bit more worried about the camps because "we have a demand from responsible people headed by some MPs to allow (1) Extra comforts to be sent in (2) some access by responsible and accredited people who can assist in measures for improving the life in the camps (3) some latitude as to visitors – friends of the refugees." Brodrick was prepared to go along with points 1 and 2, especially because "they have also shown considerable discretion as they have had and communicated to Govt some harrowing accounts of the condition of the earlier camps (Janr. & Febr.) and have not used them publicly."[10] Kitchener's reply was: "I do not think people from England would be any use or help to the families in camp as they already have a number of people looking after them but fund might help them if properly administered. I wish I could get rid of these camps but it is the only way to settle the country and enable the men to leave their commandos and come in to their families without being caught and tried for desertion."[11] Kitchener,

then, saw the camps almost exclusively in terms of the men in them – a
tiny percentage of the inmates. He described the camps in terms of their
military function in getting Boers to surrender. On the other hand, the
camps, as Brodrick indicated, were being seen in Britain strictly in terms
of their women and children inhabitants.

Brodrick was forced to press the point with Kitchener for the sake of
public opinion in Britain and in the future colonies in South Africa: "If
we can get supplies and interest in these unlucky people we shall not
only still public feeling here, but smooth the path for the future. I
imagine the returns from St. Helena &c will be much affected in temper
by the care taken of their women kind."[12] The opinions of the camp
inhabitants did not worry Brodrick; public opinion in South Africa
meant the opinions of white men, although in England public opinion
appeared also to include women of the upper classes – "responsible
people" such as Mary Ward. Brodrick was prophetic about Boer public
opinion on the camps; the Boer fighters who returned from prisoner of
war camps in Ceylon and St. Helena to the new colonies after the war
were "much affected in temper by the care taken of their women kind,"
but it was by the huge number of deaths in the camps that they were
affected. Relations between Britain and South Africa were soured by
memories of the camps for decades to come. Kitchener continually
brushed off attempts from the War Office to address the camps in the
terms in which they were being discussed in London, as an issue about
women and children.

Except for a few pro-Boer holdouts, the people of Britain had proved
willing to believe the best about the necessity for the war in the first
place. But would the public stand for its military locking up white
women wholesale to keep them from spying? The War Office had its
doubts, and Brodrick realized that he should play down the idea that the
women's imprisonment might be related to their own potential for
military activities. If the British were going to imprison the Boer women
and their children, they were going to have to do it within a discourse
that fit nineteenth-century male-female relations. The government
framed its policy in terms of the need of white women to be protected by
white men.

NATIVE OUTRAGES

By establishing the camps, the argument ran, British men were adopting
the duties shirked by the unmanly Boers on commando who had

"deserted" their families, leaving them to starve.[13] In *The Times*, Britons read Brodrick's parliamentary reply to Lloyd George in June 1901 that if the Boer fighters had been willing "to provide for their women and children, many of those difficulties which are now complained of would never have occurred."[14] Boers were not behaving as men should toward "their" women and children. In addition, *The Times* leader-writers reminded readers that, "To release most of these women now would be to send them to starve and to expose them to outrages from the natives which would set all South Africa in a flame."[15]

Thus the discourse of the government and the government-supporting press brought together two central ideologies of Victorian Britain – the weakness of woman and the sexual savagery of the black man towards the white woman.[16] Black women figured hardly at all in these writings about the camps – no category existed for them, since "women" were white and "natives" were men.[17] This discourse of protection of white women had of course been employed earlier in British imperialism, starting, as Jenny Sharpe argues, with the Sepoy Rebellion of 1857. As Patrick Brantlinger (*Rule of Darkness* 209) and Sharpe (*Allegories of Empire* 64) show, sexual atrocities against British women were commonly attributed to the Indian mutineers, even after investigations had disproved such allegations. The significance of this rhetoric lies in the way it uses racism to produce a particular chivalric reaction in the British male, a reaction that serves a particular political or economic purpose.

Jenny Sharpe's analysis of the emergence of the trope of the native rapist in British accounts of the Mutiny emphasizes "the slippage between the violation of English women as the object of rape and the violation of colonialism as the object of rebellion" (*Allegories of Empire* 68), and this slippage would seem to be in operation as well in the spread of lynching throughout the southern United States after the Civil War. As Hazel V. Carby explains, the charge of raping white women stood in for a charge of rebellion against white superiority. In 1892, Ida B. Wells's *Southern Horrors* analyzed the rhetoric about lynching to reveal the political and economic repression that was the real cause of the horror, despite white propagandists' attempts to invoke the image of the black rapist. As Carby explains:

Wells recognized that the Southerners' appeal to Northerners for sympathy on the "necessity" of lynching was very successful. It worked, she thought, through the claim that any condemnation of lynching constituted a public display of indifference to the "plight" of white womanhood... Black disenfranchisement and Jim Crow segregation had been achieved; now, the annihilation of a black political presence was shielded behind a "screen of defending the honor of [white] women." ("On the Threshold of Woman's Era" 269)

The image of endangered white womanhood was invoked during the Boer War for political and economic reasons as well, but the absence of British potential rape victims meant that the deployment of the black rapist stereotype was less straightforward. Chivalry was indeed used as a justification for aspects of Boer War imperialism. But where the Mutiny victims had been portrayed as proper upper-class ladies who needed to be protected or revenged, in the South African case, the potential rape victims were not only not British or upper class, they were actually the property of the enemy.

It is a testimony to the enduring power of the image of the black rapist to see that image used to justify "defending" the wives of the enemy in the Boer War and, indeed, to see it used by both sides in the concentration camps debates. One of the central themes of Emily Hobhouse's *The Brunt of the War and Where It Fell* is the cruelty of the British military for subjecting Boer women to humiliation at the hands of "Kaffirs." Hobhouse quoted a petition from Boer women in the Klerksdorp camp citing the circumstances of their being brought in:

On this occasion Kaffirs were used, and they equalled the English soldiers in cruelty and barbarity. The women knelt before these Kaffirs and begged for mercy, but they were roughly shaken off, and had to endure even more impudent language and rude behavior... When the mothers were driven like cattle through the streets of Potchefstroom by the Kaffirs, the cries and lamentations of the children filled the air. The Kaffirs jeered and cried, "Move on; till now you were our masters, but now we will make your women our wives." (*Brunt* 219)

The "you" who is addressed by the jeers is not the Boer woman who is portrayed as the victim – it is the male Boer, and male Boers appear nowhere in the narrative. Hobhouse creates an image of Boer women and children, unaccompanied by "their" men, under threat from hostile, predatory Africans. But the words the Boer women themselves attribute to the Africans in their petition seem to contradict the picture, for they assume a male auditor. Indeed, the Boer women's petition is the closest Boer War narratives get to the Mutiny writings Sharpe describes – jeering, threatening black men assert their new power over their old masters by claiming sexual privileges over white women.[18] In the Mutiny stories, the image for the rebellion itself became the image of Sepoys humiliating British men by sexually violating their wives and daughters.

In the Boer War, the threatened violations by black men were not of English women at all but of the enemy of the English. It would appear from the petition that that enemy considered carefully what notes to strike to inspire sympathy in their British captors. Surely the British would not approve of white women, even white women who had aided and abetted the enemy, being driven through the streets by black men and sexually taunted. Nevertheless, the deportations continued. The protection of white womanhood was invoked by the British only when it suited, such as in justifying the camps and the deportations. White womanhood, it seems, was not as strong a signifier as *English* womanhood.

And black womanhood could hardly be said to exist at all. "Kaffirs," for Hobhouse and the Boer women she quoted, were always men. Only occasionally do black women feature in any of Hobhouse's narratives, and never are they dangerous to white women. One of Hobhouse's correspondents, a Mrs. G, told of how her "two old Kaffir servant-girls, who had been with her for years and years," had suffered at the hands of the same soldiers who had burnt Mrs. G's house. As Hobhouse told the story,

Back at Norval's Pont the little party was separated. The Kaffirs had to go into one camp and the white people into another. There was a strict rule against keeping any servants in the white camp, but they ventured to keep the two little orphan girls, as they had been brought up in the house and were like their own ... Mrs. G thereupon stated her case to the Commandant, saying, "They are orphans; I have had them ever since they were babies, and I am bringing them up as my own." He was very kind, and said he would give her a permit ... The only stipulation he made was that they should go back to the Kaffir camp at night. (*Brunt* 262)

Mrs. G and Hobhouse here present the two versions of white-black relations in South Africa at the time. In the first, blacks are hostile to whites, always waiting their chance to turn the tables on their "masters," especially sexually. Hobhouse's reports included many instances of African men gloating over Boer women in their captivity, often accompanied with sexual jokes. Black male sexuality would have been a powerful threat to the white man, whether Boer or Briton, and Hobhouse knew to exploit it.

In the second version of Boer-African relations presented by anti-war discourse, Hobhouse cleverly uses standard British ideas about Africans. One justification for the war given by the government had been Boer mistreatment of Africans. British High Commissioner Sir (later Lord)

Alfred Milner had claimed publicly that he aimed to "secure for the Natives ... protection against oppression and wrong," and in Joseph Chamberlain's ultimatum that started the war, the Colonial Secretary had declared that Britain would offer "most favoured nation treatment" to Africans in British colonies in South Africa (quoted in Pakenham *Boer War* 120, 112). By painting a sentimental picture of Boer and African mutual attachment, Hobhouse was countering common horror stories about Africans being mistreated by Boers, such as the *Daily Mail*'s tales of "Boer barbarity towards loyal coloured subjects."[19]

Hobhouse also exploited another popular British idea of what white-black relations should be: her version of events placed Boer women in the position in which the British saw themselves – the benevolent protector watching over the childlike blacks. To demonstrate a good, loving relationship between the Boer and the black African, Hobhouse chose what seemed the least problematic kind of relationship: the bond between a white woman and two female black servants. Other combinations would involve sexual complications: a Boer woman wanting to stay with her African male servant while her husband was away on commando would have been improper, and an Afrikaner man showing affection for an African woman servant would certainly not have been seen as benign by Hobhouse's readers. It was the imaginative impossibility of lesbian desire between a Boer woman and an African woman that made it possible for Hobhouse to use the story of Mrs. G.

BRITISH NEWSPAPERS AND BOER WOMEN

When Hobhouse published her report on the camps, the War Secretary's immediate appointment of a committee to investigate was a tacit acknowledgment that there might be reason to be concerned about the camps. But the jingo newspapers were not about to give in to sentiment about the Boer women. The *Daily Mail*, fierce in its support for the war, stressed the bitterness of the Boer women and their anti-British activities. War correspondent Edgar Wallace (later to become famous for his mystery and adventure novels and plays) had no fear of offending women or those who wished to accord them special status:

There have been many occasions since the war started when I have wished most earnestly that the friends of emancipated womanhood had had their way, and that the exact status of woman had been made equal to that of man. I have often wished her all the rights and privileges of her opposite fellow ... to be honoured for her gallantry – and shot for her treachery. Especially to be shot for her treachery.

Women have played a great part in this war, not so much the part of heroine as of spy... We have decided that we do not make war upon women and children, and if through ill-nature women and children make war on us, we loftily refuse to acknowledge they are making war.[20]

As Lord Ripon wrote to J. A. Spender in the heat of the June debates, "Verily, the age of chivalry has passed."[21]

Wallace and the new *Daily Mail* saw themselves as representing the future of British journalism as well as of British social attitudes. If women were going to demand emancipation, Wallace noted, they were going to have to take the good with the bad. The woman who made war was, perhaps, "ill-nature[d]," was going against the nature of womanhood. But since she was doing so, men no longer had an obligation to chivalry. Although in parliament British politicians would not paint a picture of a cold-blooded fierce Boer woman spying for the enemies of Britain, Alfred Harmsworth's *Daily Mail* felt able to. Perhaps the newspaper felt fewer constraints than the War Office because of its readership, so different from that of *The Times*, where parliamentary speeches were so thoroughly covered. Perhaps the *Daily Mail*, which prided itself on being in touch with the opinion of the "masses," saw that although "quality" newspaper readers were not prepared to see women as combatants in war and patted themselves on the back for Britain's manly support of "deserted" women and children, the rest of the nation had no difficulty hating Boer women. The *Daily Mail* and other jingo newspapers editorialized against the money spent on the camps as money spent aiding the enemy. The new member for Oldham, a certain Winston Churchill, in his maiden speech in parliament on 18 February 1901, argued in favor of reduced rations in the concentration camps for wives and children of Boers who had not surrendered:

No consideration of humanity prevented the German army from throwing its shells into dwelling houses in Paris and starving the inhabitants of that great city in order to compel the garrison to surrender. He [Churchill] ventured to think his Majesty's Government would not have been justified in restricting their commanders in the field from any methods of warfare which were justified by precedent set by European and American generals during the last 50 or 60 years.[22]

For Churchill, anything good enough for British generals ought to be good enough for the British public. But even Brodrick had trouble swallowing the idea of starvation rations for women and children, and he changed the policy as soon as it was exposed by Lloyd George. Clearly, there was disagreement about what was acceptable policy toward women and children.

While the jingo journals called Boer women spies and complained about the "comforts" of the concentration camps, campaigners for the elimination of the camps consistently tried to point out the ideological discrepancy of the government refusing to name the women as "prisoners of war" while it was nevertheless keeping them confined to the camps. The *Manchester Guardian* and the *Daily News*, two newspapers that opposed the war, often referred to the camps as "prison camps." Once the mortality figures from the camps began to come to light in Britain, the *Daily News* escalated the terminological battle by labeling the camps "death camps." Emily Hobhouse criticized the military and the jingo papers: "Their line generally is to speak of 'refugee' camps and make out the people are glad of their protection. It is absolutely false. They are compelled to come and are wholly prisoners."[23]

Newspapers writing about farm-burning and the concentration camps often compared the South African situation to the American Civil War, in which Generals Sherman and Sheridan aimed to destroy the morale of the Southerners by destroying the South itself. But while papers on both sides of the controversy cited the Civil War analogy, neither mentioned another Civil War parallel: the Boer women and the women of the Confederacy. Jean Bethke Elshtain's discussion of the Confederate women's inheritance from the mothers of Spartan soldiers easily fits the Boers (*Women and War*). Olive Schreiner described the Boer woman's role in the first Anglo-Boer War, of 1881:

The Transvaal War of 1881 was largely a woman's war; it was from the armchair beside the coffee-table that the voice went out for conflict and no surrender. Even in the Colony at that time, and at the distance of many hundreds of miles, Boer women urged sons and husbands to go to the aid of their northern kindred, while a martial ardour often far exceeding that of the males seemed to fill them. (*Thoughts on South Africa* 201)

Although the image of the Spartan mother has always had a place in the history of military nations, nevertheless these women, whether Spartan, Confederate, or Boer, had never been treated by military men as combatants. The concentration camps were a new departure both for Britain and for Western ideas about women in war.

As the women in the war zone became factors to be taken into consideration by the military, so did the women at home in Britain.

Newspapers reflected this change; after the concentration camps became news, letters to the editor appearing in *The Times*, the *Daily Mail*, the *Daily News*, and the *Manchester Guardian* increasingly came from women who were writing as women, invoking traditional associations. The women who wrote to the *Daily Mail* were furious about the "pandering" to Boer women and children: "Blencathra" noted, "It is time for the women of England to speak. Why should the Government be at the expense of sending out ladies to the concentration camps? . . . Let the ladies of this commission stay at home and visit the fatherless and the widow."[24] British women's duties were at home, cried the patriotic letter-writers. Compassion is an appropriate quality in a woman, but an Englishwoman's compassion should be directed toward the widows and orphans of British soldiers, not toward the enemy. Not so, argued the letter-writers in the "pro-Boer" press. "An Englishwoman" proclaimed her "heartache" and "shame" in the *Manchester Guardian* after the release of Hobhouse's report,[25] and another noted that the British should "have pity on *all* children, not just those in England."[26] Compassion was a female trait and duty, both sides agreed. The significant difference came in the way each side explained the appropriate uses of feminine compassion in this national debate. Such arguments in the press among women about women's role in the camp controversy reveal the ways traditional associations with women's duties could be turned to the advantage of either side in such a national question as the concentration camps.

HOBHOUSE AND FAWCETT

The women most involved in the public debates about the concentration camps were Emily Hobhouse and Millicent Fawcett. Hobhouse was active against the war but sought to portray her work in the camps as non-political. Fawcett saw herself as a patriot and supported Britain's war effort but maintained that she, too, was non-political in her writings about the camps. Although the women held opposite positions on the issues of the war and the concentration camps, the reports they published about the camps came to virtually identical conclusions about the conditions in the camps. The language and examples they used upheld their own positions in the debate, but the reforms they called for were strikingly similar. Fawcett's Blue-book was accepted as legitimate by pro-government newspapers and its recommendations were acted upon, although it was called a "whitewash" by some of those against the war. Hobhouse's earlier report was not acknowledged publicly by the government or its supporters in the press, although the War Office took it seriously enough to appoint the Fawcett Commission in response to it. Hobhouse often pointed to the thousands of camp deaths that occurred between the publication of her report and the appearance of Fawcett's and noted that had her report not been undermined by the government and the jingo press when it was first released, immediate change would have resulted. She wrote in her memoir that as soon as the report appeared, "Instantly, the sentiment of the country was aroused and had it been allowed its true expression, not only would the camps then and there have been adequately reformed, but very possibly the war would also have dwindled in popularity and been ended" (van Reenen *Hobhouse Letters* 122–23). As we saw in the previous chapter, Secretary of State for War St. John Brodrick and Secretary of State for the Colonies Joseph Chamberlain were also quite concerned about the effect of a "wobble" in public opinion on the issue of the camps.

Concern over the concentration camps became the main focus of anti-war activism for the period from June 1901 through the end of the war in May 1902. The government itself directed a large amount of public attention to the camps from September 1901 until January 1902. During the publicity campaigns of the pro-Boers and the government about the camps, the central focus was not government policy in maintaining the camps but the fate of women and children within them. The image of these women and children became a rallying point in Britain – either Hobhouse's image of the starving, noble mothers with their doomed children, or Fawcett's image of ignorant, selfish mothers with their neglected children. In both cases, women were seen in Britain as representing the Boer nation.

Public calls for changes in the camps were calls for action from the key male players, notably Brodrick and Chamberlain. The eventual drop in the death rates was attributed by most anti-war factions to Emily Hobhouse and by the government to the Fawcett Commission. Men had been blamed for the conditions in the camps, and women were credited for the reforms, even though the women themselves had no power to order reforms but could only recommend them to male officials. What purpose did it serve each side to credit women with the reforms?

From the time they became a major public controversy, the camps were a women's issue. Initially, they were formed to house surrendered Boers and their families and were administered much as the male prisoner-of-war camps were. But when these towns of bell-tents came to be overwhelmingly populated by women and children, women in Britain began to take a special interest in them. The South Africa Conciliation Committee, formed before the outbreak of hostilities as the Stop the War Committee, propagandized against the war and on behalf of the Boers' "fight for freedom." When in the autumn of 1900 women in the SACC read about the camps, they took the traditionally feminine step of collecting clothing, blankets, and money for the women and children in the camps and organized themselves into the separate South African Women and Children's Distress Fund. Emily Hobhouse sailed out to the Cape with the goods and money, to distribute clothing and food among camp inhabitants and to investigate on behalf of the Fund the conditions in the camps.

Hobhouse, who had no parents and no husband, was a natural choice. She had traveled to Minnesota a few years before to engage in temperance and social work with what she had thought was a Cornish mining community in the city of Virginia. Both the Minnesota and the South Africa missions were somewhat larger-than-life versions of the kind of philanthropy normally associated with upper-class women such as Hobhouse.

Only when Hobhouse went to South Africa and released her report on the camps did the camps become a women's issue in the eyes of the public. In the months leading up to the publication of her report, scattered news about the camps had appeared in the newspapers in Britain, and the camps had been, as we have seen, a topic of correspondence between Kitchener and the War Office, but it was not solely in terms of women and children that they were discussed. Rather, they had been portrayed as a military strategy, as had farm-burning. But with Hobhouse's report, the terms of the debate changed. The issue was now one of gender – of gallant men protecting helpless women and children or of unmanly men allowing helpless women and children to starve. Hobhouse helped to set these terms, referring in her report to the "women's camps," the "camps of women and children." Her focus on the women and children in the camps was natural, given their overwhelming majority compared to men. But this focus also must be seen as a political strategy, countering the government's emphasis on the inhabitants as "refugees" of war rather than as victims of a British policy of interference with non-combatants. Hobhouse saw clearly the public relations maneuvering about questions of gender.

Joshua Rowntree had reported on his visits to the concentration camps in the *Daily News*, owned by fellow Quaker George Cadbury.

Rowntree's judiciously worded reports contrasted with Emily Hobhouse's letters home, printed in the *Daily News* and in the *Manchester Guardian*. While both visitors were careful not to blame individual officers for conditions in the camps,[27] Hobhouse told of directly intervening to try to improve squalid conditions. And the Distress Fund was careful to point out that "the military authorities have shown themselves willing to adopt some of the various suggestions which her woman's wit has enabled her to put forward on behalf of her suffering sisters."[28] Thus Hobhouse's publicity from the very start emphasized her gender.

For Hobhouse, the camp system was a gendered one. The problems were due largely to "crass male ignorance, stupidity, helplessness and muddling," she declared to her aunt, Lady Hobhouse, in her first month of visiting the camps. But she seems in those early days to have been willing to excuse the "male" ignorance as that of sorry little boys: "I rub as much salt into the sore places of their minds as I possibly can, because it is good for them; but I can't help melting a little when they are very humble and confess that the whole thing is a grievous and gigantic blunder and presents an almost insoluble problem, and they don't know *how* to face it."[29] Hobhouse's cheerily sadistic image of what is "good for" the blundering army officials indicates that she saw herself as having the power to solve the "insoluble problem" for the "very humble" men. And although she had no policy-making power, Hobhouse was able to effect changes in the camps. But, as the previous chapter showed, it was only through rubbing salt into their sore places, through negative publicity back in Britain and abroad, that Hobhouse was at last able to shame the officials into action.

Once Hobhouse's report entered the public sphere through newspaper stories about House of Commons proceedings, hers became the terms of the public debate. The government countered her approach head on by appointing its own Ladies' Commission to investigate conditions in what it now acknowledged were women and children's camps.[30] So the public discourse about the camps had gone from one of military necessity, in which women had no voice, to a new form in which women had the central place, the main voice. The men in charge of public representations of the war – the War Office, the Colonial Office, the newspaper editors and M.P.s on both sides of the issue of the war itself – had been forced to change their strategies and the language they used in relation to the camps.

Just as Hobhouse criticized men in charge of the camps in gendered terms, so too she attacked the Ladies' Commission: "great and shining lights in the feminine world, they make one rather despair of the 'new womanhood' – so utterly wanting are they in common sense, sympathy and equilibrium" (van Reenen *Hobhouse Letters* 462). The problem with Fawcett and her commission, according to Hobhouse, was their inability to sympathize with the Boer women in the camps. Fawcett's advocacy of women's rights in Britain did not, as Hobhouse noted, lead her to sympathize with women in South Africa. In fact, the only link Fawcett made between South Africa and the status of women in Britain was to equate Boer oppression of Africans with British men's oppression of British women.[31] So, for this suffragist, Boer and African women's positions were not comparable to British women's.

THE FAWCETT COMMISSION

Millicent Fawcett had made up her mind about the necessity for the camps before she set off for South Africa. In early July she wrote an article for the *Westminster Gazette*, critiquing Hobhouse's report and asserting that the creation of the camps was "necessary from a military point of view." Fawcett said nothing in her article about the camps being protection for Boer women and children. She was firm in her assertion that Boer farms had been centers for supplying "correct information to the enemy about the movements of the British. No one blames the Boer women on the farms for this; they have taken an active part on behalf of their own people in the war, and they glory in the fact. But no one can take part in war without sharing in its risks, and the formation of the concentration camps is part of the fortune of war."[32] After her meeting with St. John Brodrick for orientation before her voyage to South Africa, Fawcett recorded in her diary that Brodrick had said "it was the first time in the history of war that anything of the sort had been attempted – that one belligerent should make himself responsible for the maintenance of the women and children of the other."[33] But Fawcett never adopted the War Office's line on the function of the camps as protection for the Afrikaner families. She maintained only that they were a military necessity, while Brodrick alternately asserted that forming the camps was a humanitarian gesture and that it was a military necessity, never admitting, as Fawcett did, that the women were compelled to remain in the camps as part of the "fortunes of war" because of their role in the combat.

Fawcett set out on her camps investigation suspicious of anyone who might be "pro-Boer"; she accepted no help from people in South Africa who had been associated with Hobhouse on her visit. When she met members of the Ladies Central Committee for Relief of Sufferers by the War, she recorded in her diary:

> I led off by asking if they were non political but I quickly found they were intensely pro Boer. They recited various tales of horror ... I said our commission was non political ... Mrs. Purcell said how could our commission be considered non political if Miss Waterston [a fierce anti-Boer] were on it. I replied of course we all knew that Miss W had strong political views but she was capable of seeing and advising in matters relating to sanitation, diet, etc without bringing in political considerations.[34]

For Fawcett, then, sanitation and diet, both female domestic concerns, were apolitical. Apparently, Fawcett saw those with "strong political views" on the other side of the issue, such as Hobhouse, as incapable of advising in such matters.

Fawcett's report included numerous accounts of Boer mothers using folk remedies for their ailing children, remedies that appeared ludicrous and dangerous to the commission and its supporters. One oft-cited passage reports a Boer mother covering her child with green paint. Hobhouse liked to refute that example in her speeches, pointing out that the "green paint" was only an herbal medicine mixture. In addition, the report blamed Boer mothers when they refused to let their children be taken into camp hospitals. Fawcett ranked the causes of camp mortality: "1. The unsanitary condition of the country caused by the war. 2. Causes within control of the camp inhabitants. 3. Causes within the control of the administrations" (*Report on the Concentration Camps* 14). It was to cause number two that the Commission gave the most graphic evidence, and the jingo press naturally seized upon it.[35] One particular passage cropped up again and again in speeches, letters, and newspaper articles aimed at vindicating the British government for the death rates:

> Even at the best of times, and especially if anyone is sick in the tent, the Boer woman has a horror of ventilation; any cranny through which fresh air could enter is carefully stuffed up, and the tent becomes a hot-bed for the breeding of disease germs.
>
>   It is not easy to describe the pestilential atmosphere of these tents, carefully closed against the entrance of all fresh air. The Saxon word "stinking" is the only one which is appropriate ... It is, therefore, no wonder that measles, once introduced, had raged through the camps and caused many deaths; because the children are enervated by the foul air their mothers compel them to breathe and fall more easy victims to disease than would be the case if the tents were fairly ventilated. (Fawcett *Report on the Concentration Camps* 16)

The Blue-book mixed this kind of mother-blame with pronouncements about the Boer "race." Fawcett cited many "unsanitary habits" of the Boers, including "the fouling of the ground," a particular bugbear of hers. "The inability to see that what may be comparatively harmless on their farms becomes criminally dangerous in camps is part of the inadaptability to circumstances which constitutes so marked a characteristic of the people as a race," Fawcett opined (*Report on the Concentration Camps* 16).

Her report reveals a woman appalled at the people she's reporting on, yet struggling to appear even-handed. When she complains of the Boers giving inappropriate foods and strange home-made medicines to sick people, she notes:

This is a difficulty with which every doctor in England is familiar, and, with regard to the character of the Boer domestic pharmacopoeia, no doubt parallel horrors could be found in old-fashioned English family receipt books of 150 or 100 years ago. But whatever parallels can be found, or excuses made, for these practices, we are bound to take them into account. A large number of deaths in the concentration camps have been directly or obviously caused by the noxious compounds given by Boer women to their children. (*Report on the Concentration Camps* 17)

Fawcett acknowledged that "parallels can be found" and "excuses made" for the habits of the Afrikaner women, but she could not bring herself to accept any of them. The Boers, to Fawcett, were comparable with "old-fashioned" English families of "150 or 200 years ago." She has to double-remove these women from the English: Boers are even more old-fashioned than the average British seventeenth-century family. No wonder they are not fit to govern Britons. But in fact, because it was frank about the unsatisfactory conditions in the camps at the same time as it supported the war effort, the Fawcett Commission report, wrote Mrs. Arthur Lyttleton to Millicent Fawcett, "has apparently done the impossible and pleased everyone."[36]

Jingo newspapers gleefully seized on the Blue-book's anecdotal evidence of Boer ignorance as justifying the concentration camp policy, despite the overall tone of the report, which was highly critical of camp operations. The horror stories of Boer mothers took root throughout Britain, playing into the British stereotype of the Boers as a nation of ignorant peasants. Newspapers talked of the war being fought to "civilise the Boer," thus linking the Afrikaner and the African in the minds of British readers as uncivilized peoples to be raised out of ignorance by the British.[37] An article in *The Nineteenth Century* focusing on

British women's emigration to South Africa noted the unsuitability of marriage between British men and Boer women: "As a rule the Boer women of South Africa are devoid of many of the qualities which are essential to make a British man's home happy and comfortable. Cleanliness is a virtue too often foreign to the Boer character, and it is not unfrequently replaced by an ignorance of the laws of hygiene which produces habits of slovenliness both injurious to health and distasteful to British ideas (Cecil "Female Emigration" 683). The article cited the Fawcett report as evidence for its claims about Boer women.

The Ladies Commission criticism of the Boers, focusing on the backwardness of the Boer women and their "filthy habits," had much in common with the reports of British women sanitary inspectors when they recounted visits to working-class and poor homes.[38] Fawcett, like Hobhouse, was an upper-class woman. At least part of her inability to sympathize with the Boer women was class-related. Hobhouse, on the other hand, sympathized with Boer women based on a class affinity she constructed herself. She tried to present the Boers as a society with their own class structure, comparable to Britain's. In the *Manchester Guardian* Hobhouse wrote of a Mrs. Pienaar and her family, evicted from their farm. The British "took everything away from her – amongst other things, 4,500 sheep and goats, 150 horses, and about 100 head of cattle." This cataloging of wealth ended with the sad pronouncement that "Once rich, they now have to live on charity."[39]

Hobhouse's sympathy with upper-class Boer women led her to sympathize with Boer racial hierarchy as well. On her return to South Africa after the war, Hobhouse's class pride was outraged, and she wrote to her aunt, Lady Hobhouse, about the "poor white" problem in the former republics. She related the story of a particular Boer woman and her children, who "sit there face to face with starvation, that terrible kind which is combined with perfect respectability... It is so awful to people of this good class to say they are in want, or even seem to beg."[40] Their new poverty sat even harder with the Boers, Hobhouse explained, because of their contrast with the Africans. "Recollect these blacks have recently been armed against them, the Boers have been at their mercy, and the Kaffirs are now living in luxury with flocks and herds, while the Boers are in penury around them."[41]

For all the justification in England of the necessity for the camps as protection for white women and children, the War and Colonial Offices felt no need to similarly justify the imprisonment of thousands of Africans. While white women were in the camps ostensibly for protection from African men, African men, women, and children were in camps simply because it was a military necessity for the British to put them there. Districts had to be cleared, so Africans had to be cleared from them. No further justification was needed and none was ever called for, not in Britain or in Europe, despite all the fuss about the camps for the whites. The writing about the African camps, in government reports and in newspapers, merely related information about farm work and recorded death rates, usually inaccurately. The *Guardian* did refer to the camps for Africans in one leader, however: "There are some who think the war a glorious thing because the Boer was so cruel to the Kaffir," the leader noted, pointing out that "the Kaffir is suffering pretty heavily in these camps, but his friends make no objection."[42] Hobhouse never visited an African camp. Millicent Fawcett recorded in her diary no narrative about any of the black camps – only captions on photos of African camp inmates, such as "Natives at work. Singing."[43]

Questions of gender and writing about the Boer War arise not from the positioning of the nations involved as masculine and feminine, as colonizer and colonized or subject and other. Oppositions, indeed, are problematic in the case of a two-sided war for the land of a third party. Instead, the study of gender in discourse about the Boer War brings up a more complex set of relationships among male and female Britons, Boers, and Africans. These relationships are revealed in public and governmental writings during the war – newspapers, Blue-books, military despatches, and ministry telegrams – as well as in private correspondence among public figures involved in the war. The writings about the concentration camps reveal a public controversy that encapsulates the profound difficulties over imperialism with which turn-of-the-century Britons were wrestling.

It was necessary for men to protect women and children and for the British to guard the interests of Africans and upgrade the backward white civilization of South Africa if the imperial relationship of mother country to colony was to be maintained. But during the Boer War, especially with the controversy over the concentration camps, these assumptions were under negotiation by both sides of British public opinion about the war. Millicent Fawcett, advocate of women's right to the same careers as men, saw Boer women as soldiers in their country's war just as their men were. But this ostensibly pro-woman interpretation of Boer women's lives led Fawcett and those who subscribed to her version of the war to believe that the deaths in the camps were the fault of the Boer mothers. Fawcett's nationalism and the class privilege that allowed her to see the Boer mothers in camps as ignorant, lower-class women who, like slum-dwelling English, needed housekeeping lessons from the middle class, prevented her from letting her feminism challenge British imperialism. Emily Hobhouse sympathized with Boer women as women but was unable, as Fawcett was unable, to look at the conditions of African women in their camps. She exploited the image of the black man as a sexual threat to white women and so contributed in her own way to the maintenance of one of the key ideologies working in support of British imperialism.

The appointment of the Fawcett Commission to investigate the camps was truly a remarkable move on the part of the War Secretary. Never before had there been a government commission, official or unofficial, made up entirely of women, let alone a commission led by a suffragist. The appointment of the commission, and the action taken in response to its (and, uncredited, Emily Hobhouse's) recommendations, testifies not only to the changing status of women in public life but also to the increasing priority of women's issues in public discourse, especially the press. The new position of women within the "public" whose opinion counted with people like Milner was reflected as well in the new priority of women's concerns in the new popular press, from fashion coverage, to Lady Sarah Wilson's Mafeking articles, to the coverage of the concentration camps. No longer was the English woman's discursive position in imperialism the one described by Jenny Sharpe – one of victim or potential victim of rape. But neither had the Englishwoman achieved agency, either in defense of her Empire or in opposition to it. The women players in this debate were dependent on Brodrick, Milner, and Chamberlain to put into action the reforms they recommended, having no powers actually to initiate change themselves. The women in the camps were the women heard from least during the war, of course. As during the Mutiny the stories of women were less important than the stories about them, so the concentration camp inhabitants were most significant in the versions of them as starving and noble or crude and foolish. British women are able to take control of some of the public discussion of this imperial war with the emergence of the concentration camps issue, but they are able to do it only by seizing control of the public information about both Afrikaner and African women, thus effectively silencing those women themselves. The image of the noble Boer mother with her dying children in the camps came to be an important one in Afrikaner nationalism later in the twentieth century, and narratives by Boer women were published, some even in English translations. But no narratives have emerged about the African camps, not from Hobhouse or Fawcett, and not from the inmates themselves, who were unlikely to have the literacy skills to produce diaries. The concentration camp issue demonstrated the growing place of women's issues in public discourse about imperialism, but the women whose discourse mattered were a very limited group still.

CHAPTER 4

Cannibals or knights – sexual honor in the propaganda of Arthur Conan Doyle and W. T. Stead

Images of women were manipulated by both sides in the debate over the Boer War concentration camps, with neither side giving much attention to the lives of actual women in the camps. The army and the Colonial Office eventually had to recognize the importance of the women and children in the camps because the camps' death rates were reflecting badly on men whose duty was to protect women and children. The public debate surrounding the camps became a debate about gender. This chapter examines another public debate that involved women but was controlled by men. The exchange of war propaganda between Arthur Conan Doyle and W. T. Stead focuses on the sexual honor and conduct of the British soldier, but women are rarely given voice. The terms of the debate arise from the phenomenon of Victorian medievalism – Victorians went so far as to stage jousting matches and tournaments in their nostalgia for a medieval past, filtered through Victorian sensibilities.[1] The core nostalgic notion of Victorian medievalism, its central metaphor, was the notion of chivalry as the right conduct of men toward women. The chivalrous man needed a woman to inspire him, but codes of chivalry were written for men; chivalry, for the Victorians, was a male-oriented set of ideas about how to be a good man. Although the Doyle-Stead debate about masculine sexual honor is couched in the terms of medievalism, it nevertheless marks the South African War as the beginning of a twentieth-century sensibility about what could be expected of men as men. Public opinion about war, and especially about such matters as the concentration camps, depends on shared ideas about proper wartime conduct, but ideas about proper wartime conduct relied on ideals about masculinity – about proper *male* conduct.

This chapter examines Doyle's and Stead's uses of the Victorian idea of chivalry, exploring the importance of chivalry as part of a functioning ideology of the proper conduct of war. A military policy that uses chivalry as a justification can have very practical implications for women's lives in wartime. Although it regulates male conduct, chivalry as a working ideology depends on assumptions about relations between men and women. Even in the homosocial system of war, women or the idea of women must have an important place. In public discourse about the concentration camps, white women were described as being vulnerable to rape by African men, and so chivalry was called into action to justify the Boer women's deportation and confinement in the camps. Similarly, in Doyle's and Stead's propaganda discussing the conduct of the war and especially of the soldiers in the war, women appear primarily as victims or potential victims of rape – but rape by British soldiers. The Doyle-Stead debate about the sexual honor of the British soldier was a public, wartime expression of the contested nature of gender roles in Britain at the turn of the century. The newspaper and pamphlet battles over the war reveal the ways that assumptions about gender and social obligations get worked out in relation to imperial and military concerns.

The texts on which this study relies are the productions of an anti-war propagandist, radical journalist W. T. Stead, and a pro-war propagandist, popular fiction writer Arthur Conan Doyle. Stead and Doyle use the notion of chivalry as a key trope for the discussion of the ethics of the conduct of the war itself, but both men eventually focus specifically on one particular type of misconduct in war – rape by soldiers. Doyle and Stead's debate about soldierly sexual honor reflects, among other things, British concerns about a military force that was no longer a professional one but that was, by mid-war, composed largely of under-trained and unfit volunteers. What were the moral standards of such volunteers, far from home and far from the force of British public opinion? Was a British man in khaki a noble representative of his nation, carrying British ideals abroad? Or was he simply "a single man in barracks," as Kipling wrote? Soldiers had always been seen as sexual threats. But volunteer soldiers, with less of the discipline of military training, might be an even bigger problem. Kipling's returning volunteer wondered how he could ever fit in again: "me, that 'ave been what I've been?"[2] The soldiers were an unknown quantity, but Doyle and Stead were participating in an effort to construct the new soldier of the Empire within a framework that could contain and manage him, for the people of Britain and for the returning soldiers themselves. Chivalry was a useful way of teaching the soldier how to behave and teaching the British public how to think about the soldier during a war that saw the recruitment of an entirely different kind of soldier. Before the Boer

War, officers were gentlemen and footsoldiers were rough-and-ready types who took the Queen's shilling for lack of a job, to escape troubles at home, or for adventure. With the large-scale recruiting necessary during the Boer War, the middle and lower middle class Volunteer corps meant that much of the fighting would now be done by non-career soldiers who had left decent jobs at home. Public ideas about soldiers needed revising.

Public discourse about the Boer War did not feature a strong rhetorical focus on the home front. The women of Britain were in no danger and were not especially called upon to encourage their men to join up. To be sure, Kipling's "The Absent-Minded Beggar" raised money for the troops and their families by calling up an image of wives and children left behind, but there was no overwhelming sense of "Women of Britain Say, Go!" and no posters of bestial, ravaging Boers. Chivalry's place as one of the central ideologies in support of the war, and the proper conduct of it, had to depend on women, but with the lack of British women in the war's rhetoric, the female place in the chivalric ideology had to be filled by the women on the battle front – Boer women. For the anti-war propagandist Stead, Boer women were rape victims and potential rape victims. For Doyle, who supported the war, Boer women were, significantly, *not* victims of rape; this testified to the chivalry and purity of the British soldier. For Stead and for Doyle, women's place in the chivalric world of war marked either the uncontrollable lust of the British soldier in wartime or the self-controlled lust of the British soldier in wartime.

In one of the last of the great British penny pamphlet controversies, W. T. Stead's propaganda pamphlet *Methods of Barbarism* and Arthur Conan Doyle's reply, *The War in South Africa, Its Cause and Conduct*, battled for the hearts and minds of the British in the latter stages of the Boer War. While Stead's anti-war propaganda, in *Methods of Barbarism* as well as in *Shall I Slay My Brother Boer?* (One response was called *Shall I Kick My Brother Stead?*), and many other publications, tackles many different themes, including the concentration camps, farm-burning, and capitalist inspiration for the war, Doyle's rebuttal to Stead takes issue especially with a single aspect of Stead's charges – the assertion that British soldiers raped Boer women. Doyle's pamphlet purports to discuss the "cause and conduct" of the war, but he focuses on the conduct, on questions not of military policy but of individual behavior. Doyle links military honor to sexual honor, just as Stead connects military misconduct with sexual misconduct.

This propaganda debate, with all its class- as well as gender-based assumptions, reveals the impact on turn-of-the-century imperialism of ideologies honed in domestic settings. Both Stead and Doyle preached the virtues of sexual restraint, but for Doyle restraint came from within, from the British soldier's sense of honor and chivalry, while for Stead restraint had to be imposed on the soldier. For both Stead and Doyle, sexual honor was an English issue at the same time as it was an imperial one, and concerns about male sexual behavior in the Empire reflected concerns about male sexual behavior at home.[3] Stead's anti-war position is almost as influenced by ideas of chivalry drawn from Victorian medievalism as Doyle's pro-war position, and Stead and Doyle's fight about the nature of the Victorian soldier appears to have less to do with their positions on the Boer War than with their relations to turn-of-the-century notions of masculinity, Darwinism, and social progress.

STEAD AS A PUBLIC FIGURE

W. T. Stead supported women's rights. He campaigned against the Contagious Diseases Acts and in favor of women's suffrage. His 1885 *Pall Mall Gazette* series on child prostitution in London, "The Maiden Tribute of Modern Babylon," included vivid descriptions of the sexual debaucheries of a class of aristocratic men who preyed on the "daughters of the people." These men, styled "minotaurs" by Stead, had so indulged in sexual excess that for them stimulation could come only from the rape of young virgins. Judith Walkowitz and others have discussed the Maiden Tribute's attitudes toward male sex drives and Stead's own satisfactions from playing the part of a sexual predator in the drama he staged to "purchase" a thirteen-year-old girl. Upper-class sexuality is unnatural sexuality, for Stead, because it has been corrupted by excess. Stead's assessments of male sexuality take a different form in his Boer-War propaganda, however, as the sexuality of the working-class Tommy Atkins becomes the issue, and predatory sexuality becomes equated not with aristocratic men but with men in a kind of primitive, natural state.

Stead was the loudest voice in the pro-Boer movement even if the work of Leonard Courtney and Frederic Harrison was, in the long run, more influential (Davey *The British Pro-Boers* 87). Because of Stead's public stature as a journalist, he was sure to be read, if not believed. The Liberal leader Sir Henry Campbell-Bannerman thanked Stead for his "sound rating" early in the war, before Campbell-Bannerman declared himself a "pro-Boer."[4] South African High Commissioner Alfred Milner worried when Stead came out strongly against war in South Africa in August 1899. Milner wrote to English South African journalist (and former Stead protégé) Edmund Garrett, "It is rather a serious matter that Stead has taken the line he has. Of course he is not the power he once was – still he touches a large public" (quoted in Davey *The British Pro-Boers* 84). That public shrank considerably during the Boer War, as Stead irritated Britons by openly encouraging the Boer forces and by castigating the British government for prosecuting the war. While other pro-Boers more quietly lobbied for an end to the war, Stead met publicly with Boer representatives and cheered them on to victory (Davey *The British Pro-Boers* 86). The first issue of his weekly publication, *War Against War in South Africa*, printed a translation of the "War Hymn of the Boers," "sung by the Boers in their camps during the Majuba campaign" (Majuba was the scene of the infamous Boer defeat of the British in the first Boer War of 1881).[5] This kind of slap in the face was pushing the British public a little too far, and sales of Stead's mainstream organ, the *Review of Reviews*, began to drop dramatically as a result of his pro-Boer activities.

Stead's anti-war work was a huge undertaking. *War Against War*, sixteen pages of newsprint, came out weekly from 20 October 1899 until 26 January 1900 and included regular articles from Stead as well as transcripts of speeches about war issues, news summaries, articles reprinted from the dailies, poetry, and much material from foreign newspapers. Stead wrote many pamphlets and published many more, selling and distributing them through the Stop the War Committee and the *Review of Reviews* office and offering bulk discounts for mass distribution.

War Against War is definitively Stead's production – he uses the first person in its leaders and in many unsigned articles, and it was he personally who was both attacked and credited for the views the journal contained. On the cover of the 24 November issue, Stead prints a private letter to him from Olive Schreiner ("Though it is a private letter, I am sure our correspondent will forgive me for bringing it before my readers"). Readers of *War Against War* were, for Stead, "my readers." Stead was seen, by himself and by observers on both sides of the war question, as the patron saint of the anti-war movement. So the strategies Stead would use in his propaganda to characterize the British soldier were strategies that had to be met head-on by propagandists on the other side of the issue.

DOYLE AND THE WAR

One of the most important propagandists opposed to Stead was Arthur Conan Doyle. The creator of Sherlock Holmes is not the first Victorian writer we associate with the promotion of the aims of Empire. Rudyard Kipling and Rider Haggard come to mind more readily, with their tales of adventure in India and Africa. Although Doyle's most popular and most lasting works, the Holmes stories, often contain imperial details, the stories are not set in the outposts of British civilization. Holmes is a Londoner, rooted firmly in the metropolis, making occasional excursions to the surrounding countryside. Nor is Doyle's other fiction imperial, unless we count the delightfully comic Brigadier Etienne Gerard, who served a different Empire. Doyle's fiction is, however, often about war, and it is because he is concerned about war that Doyle becomes an important public figure in support of British imperialism at the turn of the century. Empire per se did not interest Doyle, but war was important, with its opportunities to show British mettle, to demonstrate the manly spirit at its best. So while Doyle penned as important a contribution to imperial propaganda as Kipling, he did so out of support for his country in wartime rather than out of a strong commitment to the project of empire. No British literary figure was as engaged with the fate of his country at the turn of the century as Doyle, who spent months fighting an enteric epidemic in a field hospital on the battle front and who would be credited with turning much foreign public opinion around on the question of British conduct in the war. But rather than support for the policy of imperialism, it was Doyle's conception of the link between the concepts of personal honor and national honor that pushed him into the role of public spokesperson for Britain.

On the occasion of the centenary of Doyle's birth, Adrian Conan Doyle, the author's son, noted the senior Doyle's frustration at being known chiefly as the creator of Sherlock Holmes. For Adrian, "his creation of Holmes is far overshadowed by that long list of lesser known yet nobler accomplishments by which he served his country," especially his writings on military matters and legal and ethical concerns such as divorce reform and the Congo atrocities (*Doyle Centenary* 7). For serving his country through propagandizing on its behalf during the Boer War, Doyle earned a knighthood. But personal glory was not his object when he undertook the task. Early in the war Doyle had tried to enlist, at the age of forty. He explained to his horrified mother that, as he had written

to *The Times* to suggest the use of mounted infantry, when the government called for such a force, "I was honor-bound, as I had suggested it,
to volunteer. What I feel is that I have perhaps the strongest influence
over young men, especially young sporting men, of anyone in England
bar Kipling. That being so, it is really important that I should give them
a lead" (quoted in Carr *Life of Doyle* 155). He was not accepted into the
military, but he was able to reach the fighting by another route. Resur-
recting his dormant qualifications as a physician – he had abandoned
his practice when he became a literary success in the early 1890s – he
went out to South Africa as senior surgeon of a hospital for British
soldiers funded by a friend, John Langman.

DOYLE THE PUBLIC FIGURE

From his first fame as a writer until his death, Doyle lived in the public
eye, speaking out on many issues of public controversy of the times. He
felt it was his obligation as a public figure to help defend the honor of his
country as well as to make recommendations to its leaders as to what the
best and most honorable courses of action would be. It was during the
Boer War that this newly bestselling author made his first foray into
public debate. His sense of himself as an important example for young
British men led him to volunteer for active military service during the
conflict, and his sense of his talents as a writer led him to produce a
propaganda pamphlet in defense of Britain's conduct during the war.
He suggested, in letters to the War Office and to the newspapers,
innovations in military strategy and equipment – rifle fire that would be
able to drop into trenches rather than shooting straight over them, metal
helmets and lightweight body armor, and militia drill at home in
England to train an ever-ready defense force. (His suggestions, however,
were not enthusiastically welcomed by the War Office.) He even ran for
parliament in the Khaki Election of 1900.

War had always interested Doyle, and he had had a brief encounter
with it in 1896, when he happened to be in Cairo when war was
declared. "Egypt had suddenly become the storm centre of the world,
and chance had placed me there at that moment," he wrote later in the
autobiographical *Memories and Adventures*. "Clearly I could not remain in
Cairo, but must get up by hook or by crook to the frontier" (134–35). He
was unable to reach the fighting in Egypt, but things were different a few
years later, when he met up again with many of his military acquaintan-
ces from Egypt, in the thick of the war in South Africa. Even before he

set off for South Africa to work in the Langman Hospital, Doyle was planning to write a book about the war, and he started collecting information from his fellow passengers on the voyage to Cape Town. He published *The Great Boer War* while the conflict was still going on, basing the book on notes from his experiences in South Africa, government documents, and voluminous correspondence from soldiers, officers, and newspaper correspondents. He collected material from eyewitnesses he met at the Langman Hospital and on his travels, and he used his time in South Africa to gather information as efficiently as he could, and as quickly, for he wanted his history to be the first to appear. The book, first published in 1901, was well received, and sixteen editions of it were published during the war itself, each with fresh additions and revisions. His research was extensive, much like the painstaking research he had done for his historical novels. And, indeed, *The Great Boer War* is reminiscent of the historical novels, with its stirring descriptions of battles and individual acts of heroism.

As Sir Nigel Loring, in Doyle's *The White Company* and the post-Boer-War *Sir Nigel*, was always seeking a worthy opponent, so Doyle continuously constructed the Boers in his military history as competitors worthy of the noble British. Doyle opens *The Great Boer War* with a recipe:

Take a community of Dutchmen of the type of those who defended themselves for fifty years against all the power of Spain at a time when Spain was the greatest power in the world. Intermix with them a strain of those inflexible French Huguenots who gave up home and fortune and left their country forever at the time of the revocation of the Edict of Nantes. The product must obviously be one of the most rugged, virile, unconquerable races ever seen upon earth. Take this formidable people and train them for seven generations in constant warfare against savage men and ferocious beasts, in circumstances under which no weakling could survive, place them so that they acquire exceptional skill with weapons and in horsemanship, give them a country which is suited to the tactics of the huntsman, the marksman, and the rider. Then, finally, put a finer temper upon their military qualities by a dour fatalistic Old Testament religion and an ardent and consuming patriotism. Combine all these qualities and all these impulses in one individual, and you have the modern Boer – the most formidable antagonist who ever crossed the path of Imperial Britain. (11)

This enemy bore little relation to the stupid, backward farmer many Britons had thought they would find in the South African republics. Of course, a rude peasant enemy would not have allowed the British a chance to shine – they needed a worthy opponent. In addition, however, Doyle had to account for why the war had not proceeded as expected. The general feeling in Britain had been in accord with the lieutenant of the Irish Fusiliers who wrote to his parents in early October 1899: "I don't think the Boers will have a chance, although I expect there will be one or two stiff little shows here and there . . . I think they are awful idiots to fight although we are of course very keen that they should" (quoted in Pakenham *Boer War* 125). The war was *not* over by Christmas 1899, as General Lord Roberts had predicted it would be.

Doyle's Sir Nigel himself, with his eternal hopes for "some opportunity for honorable advancement" through contest with any "worthy gentleman," would have been proud to do battle with *The Great Boer War*'s version of Boer leader Piet Joubert. Joubert, Doyle wrote, "came from that French Huguenot blood which has strengthened and refined every race which it has touched, and from it he derived a chivalry and generosity which made him respected and liked even by his opponents" (70). The enemy were generally "brave" (85), "gallant Boers" (227, 263), "clever and audacious" (283). Doyle resisted the tack taken by many war commentators who dwelt on reported Boer abuses of the white flag and shooting of wounded. For almost every report of a Boer violation, Doyle described a British one, excusing neither. He wanted an honorable battle, and he found many occasions to report chivalrous or honorable behavior by Briton and Boer. In describing the battles at Elandslaagte and Rietfontein, Doyle reported of Sir George White that "[i]t is typical of White's chivalrous spirit that within ten days he refused to identify himself with a victory when it was within his right to do so, and he took the whole responsibility for a disaster at which he was not present" (82–83). Such selflessness was the mark of an honorable British *officer*; the honorable British *soldier* was perhaps best represented in the following description of an act of heroism:

The idea of an ambush could not suggest itself. Only one thing could avert an absolute catastrophe, and that was the appearance of a hero who would accept certain death in order to warn his comrades. Such a man rode by the wagons – though, unhappily, in the stress and rush of the moment there is no certainty as to his name or rank. We only know that one was found brave enough to fire his revolver in the face of certain death. The outburst of firing which answered his shot was the sequel which saved the column. Not often is it given a man to die so choice a death as that of this nameless soldier. (*Great Boer War* 285)

The death of the nameless soldier was the death of the average Briton doing his duty for his country. Such a soldier had no name in *The Great Boer War* but was simply a necessary component of a narrative of honorable combat. Tommy Atkins had an essential nobility of spirit that revealed itself in moments such as these. Honor was available to all soldiers, regardless of class, but the Tommy and the upper-class officer earned very different sorts of honor.

After Doyle's return to London, he remained deeply concerned about the war. He continued to revise *The Great Boer War*, interviewing as many key participants as he could and keeping up with all the details of the war's progress. But what disturbed him the most about the war was the increasingly anti-British tone of the newspapers on the Continent. The European press was printing more and more accounts of the misconduct of British troops. Doyle recounted in the *Cornhill* after the war that:

> To anyone who knew the easy going British soldier or the character of his leaders the thing was unspeakably absurd; and yet, as I laid down the paper and thought the matter over, I could not but admit that these Continental people were acting under a generous and unselfish motive which was much to their credit... How *could* they know our case?... Nowhere could be found a statement which covered the whole ground in a simple fashion. Why didn't some Briton draw it up? And then, like a bullet through my head, came the thought, "Why don't you draw it up yourself?" ("Incursion into Diplomacy" 745)

Thus began what Doyle called his "incursion into amateur diplomacy" (744). Having already written *The Great Boer War*, Doyle was in a good position to draw up a defense of Britain's part in the war. His defense was *The War in South Africa: Its Cause and Conduct*, a book-length pamphlet which Doyle raised funds to have translated into twenty languages and distributed for free throughout Europe, the Americas, and north Africa. The recipients Doyle designated – the press, ministers, and professors – were the ones J. A. Hobson would list that very year in *Imperialism* as the public figures who wielded the largest influence on public opinion on imperialism.

CHIVALRY

Chivalry came back into fashion in Victorian Britain on a wave of revived interest in things medieval. While this Victorian medievalism might seem to be an essentially conservative ideology, a harkening back to less troublesome (because less democratic) times, in fact medievalism had an appeal for social critics across the political spectrum. The socialism of Ruskin and Morris was no less nostalgic about the days of chivalry than the backward-looking vision that in 1839 prompted the Earl of Eglinton to produce the rain-soaked Eglinton Tournament,

featuring jousting and other knightly displays, at a cost upwards of
£30,000. By the time of the Boer War, chivalry had its satirizers, but it
was still an operative ideology, and the pro-feminist W. T. Stead was
able to make as effective use of the notion of chivalry as did the
anti-suffragist Arthur Conan Doyle.

As Mark Girouard's lavish *The Return to Camelot* illustrates, the revival
of "the code of medieval chivalry, and the knights, castles, armour,
heraldry, art and literature that it produced" (131) started in Britain in
the late eighteenth century and held until World War I. Medieval castles
went up on country estates, rich men collected armor and held tournaments, and, of course, the Pre-Raphaelite Brotherhood painted
Galahad, Lancelot, and Guinevere. But artists, aristocracy, and country
gentry were not alone in the craze for the courtly. Victorians were
searching for something deeper than a facade of the heroic. They
wanted an alternative to the materialist values that were accompanying
industrialization (Girouard *Return* 131). Carlyle, in his opposition to
Mammon-worship, called for a "Chivalry of Work," which would make
the aristocracy into a real governing class, would build the character of
manufacturers until they were worthy "Captains of Industry." John
Stuart Mill, too, wanted heroes – but not Carlyle's kind. In 1838 Mill
wrote of his resentment of the popular novels of the time, which "teach
nothing but (what is already too soon learnt from actual life) lessons of
worldliness, with at most the huckstering virtues which conduce to
getting on in the world." Instead, Mill longed for the "old romances,
whether of chivalry or of faery," which had "filled the youthful imagination with pictures of heroic men, and of what are at least as wanted,
heroic women" (quoted in Houghton *Victorian Frame of Mind* 316–17).
The chivalrous gentleman who was the hallmark of Victorian and
Edwardian Britain had been, Girouard explains, "deliberately created"
(*Return* 260). In a century that saw the class struggle of Chartism, calls for
extension of voting rights and universal education, it seemed necessary
to many to recreate a medieval, aristocratic ruling class. No longer
would England be ruled on the middle-class basis of capitalism and
private property. "The aim of the chivalric tradition was to produce a
ruling class which deserved to rule because it possessed the moral
qualities necessary to rulers," Girouard notes (*Return* 261).

Although much of the revival of chivalry and its values was for-
mulated by the upper classes for the greater glory of the upper classes,
the ideology had its implications for the workers, too. A new chivalric
Britain would contain a working class bound by affection and loyalty to

its betters, rather than banded together to fight for its own interests. This class relation appears in uniform in Doyle's Boer War writings – Doyle was concerned with the relationship between the gentlemanly British officer and Tommy Atkins, who was distinctly not a gentleman. Doyle's defense of British honor was not simply a defense of the English gentleman, the officer who was responsible for whether his troops followed the rules of war, but was also a defense of the honor of the soldier in camp. As chivalric codes would come to apply to working class boys through such groups as Baden-Powell's Boy Scouts, Doyle declared the British Tommy chivalrous, the upholder of the honor of his country.

To understand Doyle's outrage at aspersions on the sexual honor of the British soldier it is useful to understand Doyle's personal relationship to the concept of chivalry. Doyle himself had been brought up to value the ancient ideals of chivalry and family honor, thanks to his mother, the formidable Mary Doyle, who had trained him as a child to be keenly conscious of his noble heritage – she traced the family back as far as the Plantagenets.

Doyle is often eulogized for not divorcing his tubercular wife, Mary Louise ("Touie"), in favor of the younger woman, Jean Leckie, with whom he had fallen passionately in love. His maintenance of a "Platonic" relationship with Leckie for ten years until his wife's death was thought by friends to be tremendously admirable. Adrian Conan Doyle and subsequent biographers cite J. M. Barrie's tribute as representative: "There can never have been a more honorable man than Arthur Conan Doyle" (quoted in Jaffe *Arthur Conan Doyle* 14). The honor in question was clearly sexual honor – self-restraint. Doyle and Leckie, who married a year after Touie's death, wrote to each other every day for the last ten years of Doyle's first marriage and saw each other whenever they could. During all that time, we are told, neither Touie nor the Doyle children, Mary and Kingsley, were aware of the relationship. For Doyle's sister Connie and brother-in-law E. W. Hornung, the relationship with Leckie was wrong, despite the fact that Doyle, as Jacqueline Jaffe puts it, "conducted this affair in a manner he felt was consistent with his position as a married man" (*Arthur Conan Doyle* 12). According to John Dickson Carr, Hornung told Doyle, "It seems to me you attach too much importance to whether these relations are Platonic or not. I can't see that it makes much difference. What *is* the difference?" to which Doyle replied, "Only the difference between innocence and guilt" (*Life of Sir Arthur Conan Doyle* 130). An honorable man would not sleep with one woman when he was married to another. An honorable man had desires, certainly, but he did not allow them to overcome his morals.

Doyle's clinging to the notion of sexual purity as part of a chivalric code is a holdover from earlier Victorians' reinterpretation of the Middle Ages to fit an image the Victorians were creating of themselves. Girouard notes that sexual purity was grafted onto chivalry only with Tennyson's *Idylls of the King* and the "Muscular Christianity" of Charles Kingsley and Thomas Hughes (*Tom Brown's Schooldays*) (*Return* 198). Medieval chivalry, while it included the concept of "courtly love," an unconsummated love between a knight and an unattainable lady, did not stress chastity as much as did the Renaissance and Victorian versions of the Middle Ages.

By the mid-nineteenth century, women had become increasingly important to the ideals of Victorian chivalry. In 1865 Ruskin declared, in "Of Queen's Gardens," "The first and necessary impulse of every true knight and knightly heart is this of blind service to its lady"[6] (104). And this "impulse," for Doyle and for other proponents of chivalric ideals, was extended beyond one's lady to all women. It did not matter if the woman was physically unattractive (Doyle once struck his son for referring to a woman as "ugly") or of a lower class. We may look at Sir Nigel Loring's instructions to his squires in Doyle's historical novel *The White Company* for an only slightly tongue-in-cheek version of the code:

> "But what have we here? A very fair and courtly maiden, or I mistake."
> It was indeed a tall and buxom country lass, with a basket of spinach leaves upon her head, and a great slab of bacon tucked under one arm . . .
> "Fear not, fair damsel," said Sir Nigel, "but tell me if perchance a poor and most unworthy knight can in any wise be of service to you . . ."
> "Lawk no, kind sir," she answered, clutching her bacon the tighter, as though some design upon it might be hid under this knightly offer. "I be the milking wench o' fairmer Arnold, and he be as kind a maister as heart could wish."
> "It is well," said he . . . "I would have you bear in mind," he continued to his squires, "that gentle courtesy is not, as is the base use of so many false knights, to be shown only to maidens of high degree, for there is no woman so humble that a true knight may not listen to her tale of wrong." (173)

For Doyle, reverence for women was a crucial part of the honor of the British gentleman and of the British soldier, whether gentleman by rank or not. But by the turn of the century women were agitating for the right to higher education, to be admitted into the professions, and to vote. The desire to be revered was not at the top of the New Woman's agenda. And women's rights activists did stretch Doyle's reverence beyond its limits. Although gentle courtesy was due to women of every class, once she had stepped outside the behavior required in the gentleman's code of honor, a woman might no longer expect respect from a gentleman. Doyle had no qualms about maligning the militant suffragettes. John Dickson Carr explains that "it was not a matter of political principle. What he disliked was their behaviour. He considered it grotesque, a reversal of roles" (*Life* 276). Revering women was part of being a Victorian gentleman, but women had an obligation to be worthy of reverence. Doyle suggested to the press on his 1914 American tour that the suffragettes were likely to be lynched, calling them "wild women" (Carr *Life* 285). His ferocity against the suffragettes became legend, and he argued against the vote for women: "When a man comes home from his day's work, I don't think he wants a politician sitting opposite him at the fireside" (Carr *Life* 210).

But Doyle's attitudes towards women were not that simple – not if we take into account his fiction. Who could forget Irene Adler, the woman who defeated Sherlock Holmes and so became, to him, simply "the woman"? Doyle's fiction includes another female character who becomes "the woman" for the story's hero: in "The Doctors of Hoyland," from Doyle's collection of medical stories called *Round the Red Lamp*, Dr. Verrinder Smith, the new physician who has moved into Dr. James Ripley's town, turns out to be a woman. Ripley is hostile: "Not that he feared competition, but he objected to this lowering of his ideal of womanhood" (304). After all, he had noted in the medical directory that Dr. Smith had been trained at Edinburgh, Paris, Berlin, and Vienna, and "[a] man, of course, could come through such an ordeal with all his purity, but it was nothing short of shameless in a woman" (304). Ripley is proved wrong, for Smith has not been, as he predicts, "unsexed" by her education and achievements. After the humiliation of having his own medical article corrected by her, and after losing all his patients to her, he comes eventually to renounce his bad attitudes and behavior when Smith attends him in an emergency and sees him through his convalescence. He proposes marriage, but Dr. Smith gently refuses him, for she intends to devote her life entirely to science. After all, as she tells Ripley, "There are many women with a capacity for marriage, but few with a taste for biology" ("Doctors" 314). Ripley remains sad and single for the rest of his life, and Smith goes off to a research career at the Paris Physiological Laboratory, as, it turns out, she had always intended.

Doyle does not stint in creating his woman doctor – she is a better researcher and a better physician than her male counterpart. And, while

Ripley is certainly prejudiced, he never doubts that women are *capable* of being doctors. The prejudice he must overcome is slightly different: Ripley learns that a true woman is capable of maintaining her purity and her femininity in the face of a medical education. But neither the narrator nor Ripley quarrels with Smith's assertion that, for a talented woman, marriage is incompatible with a career. The story features a professional woman, but she is no New Woman: she is gentle, kind, and feminine. Nevertheless, she emasculates; men can offer her nothing she needs, and she must remain unattainable. How can you be chivalrous to a woman who has won more research awards than you? Dr. Verrinder Smith cannot represent the future for women; she is very productive, but she cannot, or will not, reproduce.

STEAD AND CHIVALRY

Chivalry has a different place in the life and writings of Stead than it does in Doyle. The author of "The Maiden Tribute of Modern Babylon" was certainly motivated by a desire to protect women from the foul conduct of men. But chivalry extended beyond British borders for Stead. He was a driving force in organizing the 1899 Hague Convention, at which the major European powers agreed to rules of warfare. His anti-Boer War publications emphasize the importance of following the Hague Convention and other, unspecified, rules of civilized combat. His journalism valorizes the Boers for their generous conduct in battle and with their British prisoners, holding them up as superior in chivalry to the British despite being backward, dirty farmers.

In *War Against War in South Africa*, Stead declares, "We can make war like cannibals or make war like Knights" (114). Fighting a war on chivalrous principles, he believed, brought greater honor to the countries at odds. The alternative to chivalry for Stead is not simply dishonorable fighting but "cannibal" fighting – primitive, unrestrained warfare. War releases the primitive in man's nature, and "[t]he progress of civilisation is attested by the extent to which mankind is able to restrain the aboriginal savage who is let loose by a declaration of war within that continually narrowing limit" (*WAW* 114). The primitive man is concealed inside the civilized man, unleashed when man is given permission to kill. The argument is based on a Darwinian notion of progress toward civilization, moving away from the savage primitive.

The issue of chivalry in Stead relies on notions of class difference. J. A. Hobson saw the masses as misled by the press and the music halls, as prey to passions whipped up for political ends. The primitive was on the surface in the working classes, who were, for all their franchise and new literacy, not yet to be trusted, not yet civilized. For Stead as for Hobson, the problem was that public-opinion-shapers in middle-class Britain were not doing their duty. When one newspaper reported uncritically an anecdote about a British Lancer refusing mercy to a surrendering Boer because "You didn't show us any mercy at Majuba," Stead is furious. How can it be, he asks, that:

because we were fairly beaten by brave men in a stand-up fight we now deem it right to slay a disarmed enemy who goes down on his knees and begs for mercy! This is not civilized War. It is sheer butchery . . . Yet our Press and our parsons have not a word to say . . . It is perhaps as well that they should be silent. For they have been the cause of this recrudescence of aboriginal savagery. The newspapers have fanned the flames of race hatred, they have fed the fire of revenge.[7]

In this sentiment Stead resembles Hobson and other crowd-theorists, blaming middle-class figures of influence for not doing their job in guiding in the right direction the easily-influenced, in this case the soldier rather than the jingo crowd at home. Like Hobson, Stead blames the newspapers for stirring up nationalism. Stead castigates the press and clergy for permitting, or even encouraging, the British soldier's degeneration into "aboriginal savagery." The soldier is at risk of a slide into the savage from the moment he is permitted to kill, and it is only the force of middle-class public opinion that can restrain him.

Although both Stead and Doyle are concerned with national honor, for Stead, the nation and the soldier are two different entities. A British public that would not object to the prosecution of an unjust war was a disgrace: "The degradation of the national character follows naturally from the national apostasy," he asserted, when the British public failed to respond to charges of atrocities among British soldiers.[8] For Stead, the Boer War was an unjust war that brought out the worst in the British troops and the British public.

Stead asserts that public opinion in Britain should be a strong enough force to rein in the excesses of the military in South Africa, who under royal commission perform unspeakable acts: "When we read of similar deeds to those which are now being perpetrated in our name in the South African Republics, as having occurred centuries since, we marvel that the contemporaries of such events, men humane, enlightened, and Christian, were not able to exercise any effective restraint upon the savagery of their soldiery" (*WAW* 3), he writes. Soldiers who act in barbaric ways are not necessarily representative of their contemporaries at home, who might be "humane, enlightened, and Christian," but not strong enough to speak out. But while the army need not represent the national character, its savagery arises from the natural man. So is the true Englishman a more disciplined, restrained version of the English soldier? The horror of the atrocities of the British soldiers, according to Stead, is that they are carried out with the sanction of the British public:

For to-day the nation at home witnesses every morning and evening, in the camera obscura of its daily press, the whole hellish panorama that is unrolled in South Africa. The work of devastation is carried on before our eyes. We see the smoke of the burning farmstead; we hear the cries of the terrified children, and sometimes in the darkness we hear the sobbing of the outraged woman in the midst of her orphaned children, and we know that before another sunset British troops carrying the King's commission, armed and equipped with supplies voted by our representatives, will be steadily adding more items of horror to the ghastly total which stands to our debit in South Africa. (*War* 3)

The goal of such bombast can only be to shame readers into action, as patriotic Englishmen or women, to stop such evils being carried out in their name. Thus Stead, who entertained and encouraged his country's enemies during the war, was nevertheless truly English-identified and public-spirited as an Englishman. It was because he expected so much of his country, he would argue, that he held it to such high standards and refused to sanction what he saw as its betrayals of true British values.

If progress demanded moving from the primitive to the civilized, for Stead that progress is best exemplified by the state of man, in the gendered sense of the word. Man is naturally, at his most basic, "primitive" level, a killer. And it is up to the laws of civilization to curb, tame, and repress that instinct to kill. But civilization and its forces, such as legislation and public opinion, cannot, or dare not, completely eradicate men's capacity or inclination to kill. That capacity is necessary for warfare. So the more civilized a nation becomes, the more necessary are laws and customs for civilized warfare: these regulations are the "continually narrowing limit" on the natural brutality of men.

In *The Truth about the War*, a pamphlet published in 1900, Stead notes, "Not even the worst enemies of the Boers allege that any Outlander women have suffered outrage at their hands" (12). Stead charges neither Boer nor British with rape at this stage in the war. But he does associate the British with rape:

Within the last few years the Turks and their Kurdish allies have massacred more Armenians than all the Outlanders who are claiming the franchise in the

Transvaal. In the same period, Armenian women more than twice or thrice the number of the whole female population in the Transvaal have been subjected to the last extremity of bestial outrage at the hands of savages whose lust was whetted by fanaticism. These wretches were our proteges in a far more real sense than is the Outlander who wanders to the Rand to make his fortune. (*Truth* 12–13)

British soldiers are rapists by proxy – their protégés do the dirty work for them in Armenia, including wholesale rape. Turks and Kurds are savages who live by their urges, without the restraints that are necessary on men released to kill. Here Stead makes the connection between killing and rape – when men are released from the restraints of civilization and told that they may kill, the natural outcome (at least in the case of "fanaticism") also includes rape.

In his December 1900 pamphlet *How Not to Make Peace*, Stead is happy to recount Lord Roberts' assessment of the conduct of his troops: "exemplary." Stead cites Roberts' accounts of women and children who had been warned to fear the British troops – they soon came to see that "they had nothing to fear from the 'man in khaki.'" The pamphlet quotes a letter from an anonymous British officer who goes into great detail about the British soldier's lapse into "moral degeneracy" during the war, but rape is not one of the charges laid against Tommy Atkins. Instead the letter says that "[g]eneral conventions, customs of civilized war, respect for women, tenderness to children, which were the common phrases in England, are treated as foolish cant" (42). The "Officer in the Field" asserts that "one of the causes which has lent to this recklessness is the isolation of the theatre of war, and the entire absence of any public opinion" (42). The officer charges that the second-most evil of the British army in South Africa (after the destruction of property!) is the "deliberate exposure of women and children to horrors worse than those of the battle-field," that is, "the passions and lusts of the natives" (50). Stead's pamphlet also quotes General Buller's declaration that there had been no cases of rape involving British soldiers (71). In criticizing the troops' conduct in South Africa, Stead notes that he is not concerned to vilify individual soldiers: "What I attacked was not the individual soldier, but the policy which he was compelled to carry out" (85). "I also admit," he says,

and am very glad to do so, on first-hand evidence of officers in command of General Buller's army, that there has been a gratifying and unprecedented absence of outrage of women on the part of British soldiers. But that crime I never laid to their charge. What I complained of was that the policy of denudation and devastation led naturally, not to the forcible violation of women, but to their degradation by famine. (88)

This was a charge to which Arthur Conan Doyle would respond quite strongly when Stead reiterated it in *Methods of Barbarism*. In his response, Doyle conflated the charge of rape with that of reducing women to degradation (prostitution) by robbing and starving them. For a man with the chivalric values professed by Doyle, the charges might indeed seem equal. But Stead had been careful to distinguish between the two charges, disavowing any desire to call the British soldier a rapist but noting that "surely it is not necessary at this time of day to ask what the result must be if you deprive a woman of all means of subsistence and place her penniless and friendless in the midst of a military camp. It is not outrage by force, but degradation by famine" (88–89). Rape as a violent crime, a "recrudescence of aboriginal savagery," perhaps, was different than a man asking a woman for sex in return for money, food, or shelter, Stead asserts. But it would be hard to say that he was declaring men's behavior in either situation "unnatural."

In *How Not to Make Peace*, Stead reminds his readers of Josephine Butler's struggles to repeal the Contagious Diseases Acts, asking if, after that long struggle,

it is too much to ask us to believe that the whole of the British troops in the Transvaal have been converted into an army of St. Josephs? For making the suggestion that it was possible for British soldiers to lead a celibate life of chastity, Mrs. Butler was ridiculed in every military club in London, and yet, when we have a hundred thousand men liberated from all the restraints of public opinion, let loose to burn and destroy in an enemy's country, is it rational to believe that the Dutch women can escape untouched from such proximity? (89)

But then he retreats to racism to save himself from having to make such charges against British soldiers, resorting, again, to rape by proxy as a charge against Britain:

But, for the sake of argument, I am willing to admit that every British soldier in the Republics leads a life of virginal purity. The crowning horror and worst outrage of all was not the violation of Dutch women by English soldiers, but the exposure of these unfortunate white women to the loathly horror of compulsory intercourse with the Kaffirs. That this has taken place repeatedly is proved by the executions of Kaffirs, which have been ordered in punishment of this crime; but, although we may shoot the Kaffir for outraging a white woman, the inexpiable outrage remains. (89)

By charging the African man with rape, Stead again avoids discussing British male sexuality as potentially violent. Charges of rape against

Africans allow rape a status as a violent crime. Stead replaces the rape charge against British soldiers with, as we saw above, a charge of the creation of poverty-induced prostitution – British soldiers force women to *choose* to have sex with them.

Neither Stead nor Doyle allows any place for reciprocated desire in South Africa – that a British soldier and a Boer woman (let alone an African woman) might have consensual sex. Arthur Hales, war correspondent for the *Daily News* before its purchase by pro-Boers mid-war, sketched a picture of a young Boer woman who was unlike either the monster usually seen in the British daily press or the victim portrayed in anti-war propaganda. Hales, much respected for his detailed, evocative reporting from South Africa, constructs himself as a man's man, perhaps not unlike a soldier. He is captivated by the youngest daughter of a Boer family:

[T]he fourth had a face like a young preacher's first public prayer. A face that many a man would risk his life for. So much of my whole career has been passed amidst the rougher and more rugged scenes of life that a description of dainty womanhood comes awkwardly from me. But I have read so much about the ugliness and clumsiness of the Boer women in British journals that I should like to try and describe this daughter of the veldt, although only a farmer's daughter. I do not know if she was short or tall, but her cheek could have nestled comfortably on the shoulder of a fairly tall man.[9]

Her hands were the kind of hands that could "help a husband back to paths of rectitude when all the world had damned him past redemption." This is not a woman who appears in either Stead or Doyle's writing on the war – it is a Victorian woman with whom an English man would fall in love. So little of the British writing about Boer women allows them as potential objects of desire that Hales' portrait stands out starkly. Although such a picture of a Boer woman could appear in a pro-government newspaper during the war, the Boer woman as desired or desiring could not exist in propaganda, in publications that were aimed at constructing the British soldier as either a rapist or as entirely self-controlled. Neither Doyle nor Stead could allow a British soldier to form a romantic attachment to a Boer woman.

Rape by British soldiers does make it into Stead's propaganda in one important place. *Methods of Barbarism* includes actual testimony of Boer women rape victims, excerpted from the transcript of the Spoelstra censorship trial of 1901, in which a Dutch journalist defended a letter he had written to a Dutch newspaper and had tried to have smuggled past the British censors. The letter had charged British troops with "shameful treatment of women and children" (69), including farm-burning, the herding of women and children into concentration camps, and British rudeness to anyone Dutch. The Spoelstra letter had not mentioned rape, but when he called as witnesses the sources he had used for the letter, some of the women told detailed tales of rape and attempted rape by British soldiers. One witness described the manner in which a soldier raped her and reported that her husband had not filed a complaint in the matter, because, she asserted, "We were all frightened." The President of the Court is then reported to have said, "If such a most awful thing happened to a woman as being raped, would it not be the first things for a man to do to rush out and bring the guilty man to justice? He ought to risk his life for that. There was no reason for him to be frightened. We English are not a barbarous nation" (89–90). Stead was unable to resist making the last sentence of the judge's statement into a headline.

DOYLE'S RESPONSE

Doyle's defense of the British soldier in *The War in South Africa: Its Cause and Conduct* had been prompted initially by Continental "calumnies," but it responded even more directly to *Methods of Barbarism*. Doyle indignantly quotes huge passages of the Stead pamphlet in *The War in South Africa*. He particularly objects to Stead's assertion that the British soldier would take advantage of sexual opportunities whenever possible. Doyle quotes Stead's assertion of how far one could trust the sexual honor of the British soldier:

We all know him at home. There is not one father of a family in the House or on the London Press who would allow his servant girl to remain out all night on a public common in England in time of profound peace in the company of a score of soldiers. If he did, he would feel that he had exposed the girl to the loss of her character. This is not merely admitted, but acted upon by all decent people who live in garrison towns or in the neighborhood of barracks. Why, then, should they suppose that when the same men are released from all the restraints of civilisation, and sent forth to burn, destroy, and loot at their own sweet will and pleasure, they will suddenly undergo so complete a transform-ation as to scrupulously respect the wives and daughters of the enemy.(sic) It is very unpopular to say this, and I already hear in advance the shrieks of execration of those who will declare that I am calumniating the gallant soldiers who are spending their lives in the defence of the interests of the Empire. But I do not say a word against our soldiers. I only say that they are men. (quoted in Doyle *War* 119)

Doyle takes issue with Stead's charge that it is natural for men to rape, especially in wartime. Stead has constructed the British soldier as a natural man with primitive, violent instincts to which he gives in when freed from the constraints of civilization. In describing the British soldier thus, Stead normalizes behavior of which Doyle can never believe Tommy Atkins guilty. According to Stead's description, in wartime, when women are available, they will be taken advantage of:

No war can be conducted – and this war has not been conducted – without exposing multitudes of women, married and single, to the worst extremities of outrage. It is an inevitable incident of war. It is one of the normal phenomena of the military Inferno. It is absolutely impossible to attempt any comparative or quantitative estimate of the number of women who have suffered wrong at the hands of our troops. (quoted in Doyle *War* 119)

"When stripped of its rhetoric it amounts to this," writes Doyle, "'250,000 men have committed outrages'" (119). Doyle mocks Stead's voice, "'How do I prove it? Because they are 250,000 men, and therefore *must* commit outrages'" (*War* 119–20). Doyle could not muster a rebuttal to such a charge – he could only expect that in repeating Stead's claims he would reveal their ridiculousness. What Doyle reveals instead is his own lack of language with which to rebut an assertion that masculinity includes the potential to rape. Such a charge was unfathomable to one who put forward the chivalric ideal as a model in his fiction and in his personal life, and who saw the conduct of war through such a lens as well.

DOYLE'S SOLDIERS

Doyle's military men, in his history and his fiction, are chivalrous to the core. Their bravery and fierce sense of honor make them masculine, not their sexuality. Micah Clarke defends the weak and even prevents his friend from killing an enemy soldier when he is down. Brigadier Gerard is a stickler for honor in fighting, and our view of his masculinity comes from his military exploits – he breaks many women's hearts, but only offstage. Most other adventure writers of the turn of the century had nonsexual heroes, of course, especially Rider Haggard. These stories are, after all, aimed at least partially at pre-pubescent boys.[10] But the Kipling who is so often invoked in discussions of the British soldier during the Boer War had never hidden the sexuality of the soldiers he drew; they were, after all, only "single men in barracks." Honor and masculinity went hand-in-hand in Kipling. But masculine honor is not sexual restraint in Kipling, as any of "The Ladies" of the poem of that title could have testified.

In Doyle's writings on South Africa, women have as small a place as they do in his fiction about war. Boer women occasionally crop up, where they can fit Doyle's defense of British male honor. But even in his discussions of the concentration camps, Doyle did not give much attention to Boer women. Instead, he focused on male visitors to the camps and their praises of the camp conditions.

War was men's business. The focus on sexual honor in Doyle was a question of conduct toward women, but it was an issue for discussion among men, and it was a question that arose only in single-sex circumstances. Only when men were away from the company of women did they get a chance to shine in battle, for Doyle, and did they succumb to their primitive instincts to rape, for Stead. The homosociality of war was either an inspirer to greatness or a spur to immorality, depending on whose version you believed. Doyle's was the traditional version of war and its single-sex glories. Stead's perhaps represents twentieth-century, post-Oscar Wilde, fears that a single-sex environment might be a dangerous one. Once homosexuality had sprung up as possibility, it was difficult to make innocent an environment contaminated by now-spoken possibility. Stead does not have to articulate a fear of homosexuality in his description of the life of the soldier – he simply locates disorder in the soldier's sexuality. "Normal" sexuality is not possible in the abnormal condition of war. Doyle solves the problem by ignoring the possibility of sexual expression by soldiers – their sexuality is submerged into their chivalry.

Doyle's *The Great Boer War*, like *The War in South Africa*, did not devote much space to women. When Boer women did appear in *The Great Boer War*, they were cruel or devious. During the siege of Ladysmith, for example, "the [British] garrison could see the gay frocks and parasols of the Boer ladies who had come down by train to see the torture of the doomed town" (*Great* 164–65). And when the British were "clearing" the southeast, "Troops were fired at from farm-houses which flew the white flag, and the good housewife remained behind to charge the 'rooinek' extortionate prices for milk and fodder while her husband shot at him from the hills" (*Great* 303). Doyle never got more personal, nor more general, than these casual mentions of Boer women. When he wrote in *The Great Boer War* about the concentration camps, he never referred to Boer women directly, never characterized them as a group or individually. In the single paragraph devoted to the camps in all the book's 500 pages, Doyle said that the camps had been formed for surrendered Boers. He then added his only use of the word "women": "As to the women and children, they could not be left upon the farms in a denuded country" (*Great* 468). He summed up the controversy about the camps by noting that "Some consternation was caused in England by a report of Miss Hobhouse, which called public attention to the very high rate of mortality in some of these camps; but examination showed that this was not due to anything insanitary in their situation or arrangement, but to a severe epidemic of measles which had swept away a large number of the children" (*Great* 468). While Doyle's summary of the concentration camps controversy certainly left out key elements of the camps story, it was remarkably free of that emphasis so prevalent in most writing about the camps – Boer-blame. Doyle did not malign the Boers as a nation in the way other pro-Britain writers had. He could not. For Doyle's version of the South African drama to work, the Boers could not be a backward, slovenly nation. The Boers had to have a nobility that made them a fitting enemy for the noble Britons. Nevertheless, sticking too closely to that formulation would have landed Doyle in some trouble as well: the noble mother dying with her child in the British-run camp was a potent propaganda image for the other side, the pro-Boers. So Doyle was left with no choice but to pass as quickly as possible over the camps controversy in *The Great Boer War*, blaming a non-partisan measles epidemic rather than his British soldiers or ignoble Boer women.

THE CAMPS AND HONOR

But in *The War in South Africa*, Doyle devoted much more attention to the camps – they were an important part of his defense of the sexual honor of the British soldier. First Doyle gave his version of the origin of the camps: "Considerable districts of the country [had been] cleared of food in order to hamper the movements of the commandos," therefore "it was the duty of the British, as a civilized people, to form camps of refuge for the women and children" (*War* 81). In this he conflated two approaches to the camps – the pro-camps definition of them as "refugee" camps for women and children in danger on the veldt and the anti-camps assertion that the camps were formed not because women and children felt the need for refuge but because the British had cleared their country and deported them from the farms. Were the camps simply an unavoidable part of the fortunes of war or were they places of refuge for needy women and children? Doyle waffled – it could never simply be unavoidable for women to suffer, yet he had seen too much of the war to assert that the camps were a purely chivalrous gesture.

Stead had attacked the chivalry of the British government in its policies towards women and children in South Africa, and Doyle would have a tough job defending the policies that were resulting in hundreds of deaths a week in the camps. Stead asserted that the British were "waging war upon women and children. Under the plea of military necessity, we have destroyed the homes and sustenance of 60,000 women and children; we have denuded their farms of all the live stock and grain upon which they were able and willing to sustain themselves without asking for help; we have burnt the roofs of their houses over their heads" (*WAW* 7). According to Stead, the army had dug itself into a hole by burning the Boer farms and was left with only three possible courses with regard to the women and children: first, and "most merciful," would have been "to have followed the precedent of Elizabethan times, to have put the women and children to the sword" (*WAW* 7), next, "to leave them, homeless and foodless, to cower round the ashes of their ruined homes, at the mercy of all the Kaffirs and Cape bastards who form a kind of diabolic fringe to every British column" (*WAW* 8). The third option was the course actually adopted, "that of carrying off as prisoners of war the women and children whose homes we had destroyed, and to supply them with the necessaries of life" (*WAW* 8). Stead again employs an image of rapists who are British protégés. In Stead's reading of the possibilities, the Africans who threaten the Boer women accompany every British troop and so would not be a threat were it not for the actions of the British. This is another image of rape by proxy. It must be noted that the Africans Stead blames for rape are those affiliated with the British – he takes pains to point out that the Boer women "did not seek to be protected from the Kaffirs, with whom they appear to have lived on very good terms" (*WAW* 50). So he does not subscribe to the War Office's and even Emily Hobhouse's rhetoric that Boer women on the farms needed protection from the African men of the warring districts, although he does quote State Attorney Smuts' language about the "Cape boy and the Kaffir" who "infest" the British troops and threaten the Boer women (*WAW* 52).

In Stead's subsequent discussion of the conditions in the concentration camps, his focus is not so much on the women and children in the camps as the inhumanity of "journalists, university graduates, and orthodox Christians" who expressed their dismay at the waste of British money that the camps represented. Stead lambasted the government for "mak[ing] babies prisoners of war" (*WAW* 8) and then feeding them with bully beef. The policy whereby the wives and children of men on commando were kept on half-rations (a policy abandoned after the press got wind of it) came in for the full Stead treatment:

> It was then deliberately determined ... to subject the women and children whose husbands and fathers were still obeying the orders of their Government, in defending their country against the invader, to a policy of systematic starvation. To a woman whose husband was on commando, to the helpless child of a man who had not yet laid down his arms, the decree went forth that they should be deprived of one half of the rations necessary for their proper sustenance. (*WAW* 9)

To an image of the Boer soldier as defender of his country from invasion Stead weds the language of the Slaughter of the Innocents (a "decree went forth").

In attacking Stead and the other critics of the camps, Doyle noted that "the British nation would have indeed remained under an ineffaceable stain had they left women and children without shelter upon the veldt in the presence of a large Kaffir population" (*War* 81). According to Doyle, "It was not merely that burned-out families must be given a shelter, but it was that no woman on a lonely farm was safe amid a black population, even if she had the means of procuring food" (*War* 81–82). This, of course, was an extension of the arguments used by the British government to make racism work to its benefit. The government had pointed out that it needed to bring in white women and children from farms if they had no sustenance, because of the threat from blacks. But Doyle declared further that it was unsafe to leave women on the farms, even if they had food. All Boer women without men at home were in danger from black men. So Doyle's earlier assertion that the camps were formed for families without food is supplemented by this new assertion that white women who could support themselves were nevertheless brought into camps because they were in danger from black men. At the same time that he offered this blanket indictment of black men, Doyle was working to vindicate white British men from the very thing of which he was accusing African men.

When rumor in Britain had it that women and children without food were to be left on the veldt, Stead had vehemently criticized the British army. Doyle complained about what he termed Stead's "harrowing pictures of the moral and physical degeneration of the Boer women in the vicinity of British camps" (*War* 81). Stead, Doyle declared, was assuming that Boer women would give themselves to lascivious British soldiers in return for food and other necessities. But when Doyle proposed a corrective to that image, it was not the character of the women that he sought to redeem – it was that of the British soldier. "It is impossible without indignation to know that a Briton has written ... of his own fellow-countrymen that they have 'used famine as a pander to lust'" (*War* 81). Male honor was the guarantee of female chastity in the chivalric code. Virtuous British soldiers would keep the Boer women from moral degeneration.

The concept of degeneration that Doyle invoked implied a moral responsibility on the part of the woman. A Boer woman who would sleep with a British soldier would be choosing that course of action herself, Doyle implied, even if famine had been her motivation. It was fortunate that the British soldier was pure and controlled enough to resist such an opportunity. The Boer woman, then, had the potential to act in a sexual way toward a British soldier, as Stead allowed as well, in his escape clause from his charges of sexual violence against British soldiers. But there is no ambiguity in either Doyle's or Stead's descriptions of the Boer woman's potential for agency in sexual contact with a "Kaffir." No Boer woman would submit to a black man voluntarily; such a connection could only be rape. For Doyle, as for Stead in his earlier propaganda, black men became the locus of animal sexuality to be counterposed against the white man's controlled, civilized sexuality. African men had to be rapists of white women if Doyle were to vindicate British soldiers of the charge.

Making use of such assumptions, Doyle shifted the focus of the arguments against the concentration camps. Rather than arguing over the morality of leaving women and children vulnerable to starvation once the British had burnt down their farms, Doyle could emphasize the sexual vulnerability of white women. He could make Stead a villain for suggesting that the British soldier was a sexual predator, confident that his readers in Britain would assume that to call the average Tommy a rapist was going too far. At the same time, he could call the average African man a rapist. To justify the formation of the concentration camps, Doyle chose to focus on the sexual vulnerability of white women and the necessity for the British government to protect those women. He could then ignore the economic vulnerability of the same women – a vulnerability created by the British when they burned farms and crops.

The aspect of medievalism that survived from Scott through to Ruskin and then to Doyle was the notion of chivalry as primarily a sense of the protection of the weak by the strong. We see this sentiment in the way Doyle discusses the concentration camps. The final appendix he added to *The War in South Africa* was a testimony from an Austrian visitor to South Africa during the war. "What struck me most," Count Huebner reports, "was the elaborate and generous system devoted to the amelioration of the condition of the old men, women, and children in the Concentration Camps" (Huebner "Appendix" 270). The protection of the weak by the strong is late Victorian medievalism's strongest value, and if Doyle is the inheritor of Scott and Ruskin's medievalism, then his horror at the charges of sexual misconduct against the British soldier is wholly logical. His fictional Micah Clarke even declares that a man's duty toward a woman in distress supersedes his duty to a superior officer, "For the duty which we owe to the weak overrides all other duties and is superior to all circumstances, and I for one cannot see why the coat of the soldier should harden the heart of the man" (Doyle *Micah Clarke* 423). In such a system, what more blatant violation of the code of chivalry could there be than rape?

If chivalry is a guiding ideology for Doyle's soldiers past and present, then he cannot portray the kind of soldier Kipling can portray, complete with moral compromises. So Doyle never depicts his Boer War soldier in the kind of detail he provides for the soldiers in his historical fiction. His fictional soldiers are all set safely centuries in the past, while his real-life soldiers are all stick figures in histories of events rather than stories about men. The soldier is the ultimate figure of masculinity, combining bravery with honor and strength. But he is also the ultimate figure of the nation: Micah Clarke is the better instincts of Dissenting Britain ready to throw off the corrupt King James; Sir Nigel, comic as he can be, is nevertheless the pure and brave Englishman who is the ancestor of the British soldier of the twentieth century.

Doyle was at a distinct disadvantage in trying to defend British honor in the South African War, fought for control of land and goldfields. The conflict was not the stuff of noble quests. But Doyle had rehabilitated a war before – *Micah Clarke*'s portrait of the Monmouth Rebellion made that conflict a noble and valorous one, even if it could not rewrite history to make it a successful one. Doyle's efforts for the Boer War were not unlike those in *Micah Clarke*, and he did his best to draw noble lessons from what was essentially an ignoble event. Doyle was one of the last great defenders of British chivalry, and his knighthood, conferred in 1902 for his propaganda efforts, rewarded him for his chivalric defense of what would, in a few decades time, seem to have been essentially indefensible.

The Doyle-Stead debate reveals the extent to which public discourse about imperialism relied not only on assumptions about gender and race but also assumptions about class. Sexual honor was, of course, a gendered notion. But class status, whether of the soldier or of the woman, played an important role in the defining of proper honorable conduct in general. The Boers, often cast in British writing as an entire country of the lower class, took on a nobility in both Doyle and Stead that made them either worthy opponents or worthy pastoralists to be left alone on their land. In either case, the Boers are not the uneducated, unlovely peasants seen often in Boer War writing. Race certainly came into play in public debate about the war, and in the Doyle-Stead debate both sides maligned Africans in much the same way as the writers about the concentration camps had. Sexual honor during the Boer War was a white notion, and, for the most part, a white British male notion, while always dependent on shared attitudes about both white women and black men. In the end, sexual honor was an important construct for both soldiers and officers, but it remained important to maintain in public the distinctions between those two categories, distinctions of class that reveal the difficulty of looking at gender and race as independent of class in public debate during this imperial war.

CHAPTER 5

Interpreting South Africa to Britain – Olive Schreiner, Boers, and Africans

Just as British imperial policy depended on colonial as well as domestic factors, so did public discourse on imperialism. This chapter examines the writings of a South African literary figure, perhaps the South African most well-known in Britain during the Boer War, apart from Boer president Paul Kruger. Olive Schreiner's nonfiction about South Africa, addressed to British audiences, was a different kind of journalism from the press coverage of the Boer War, a different kind of propaganda from the kind practiced by Doyle and Stead. Schreiner's efforts in periodicals and pamphlets are the most important pro-Boer writings by a literary figure in a public debate that was notable for the presence of literary figures. Schreiner's pro-Boer writings were published before the war and were aimed at promoting British fellow-feeling toward the Boers. The Boers would, Schreiner argued, be mixing with Britons to produce the future, blended white race of the united British colony of South Africa.

British relations with South Africa were affected by questions of race, but it is important to note that the questions of race that were of most immediate concern to the British in the years just before as well as during the war were questions of the compatibility of the two white "races" in South Africa. The prosperous South African colony that the British hoped would result from the Boer War was a colony not unlike Australia or Canada – a colony in which the indigenous population was seen as hardly significant. South Africa, of course, was complicated by two major differences from those colonies of longer standing: the indigenous population formed a much larger percentage of the population, and the British were preceded by another settler population, the Afrikaners. Public discussion of British-South African relations focused much more extensively on the latter point than the former. So while no discussion of British Boer War writing can ignore the presence of African races in the discourse about South Africa, it is the presence of

Afrikaners *as a race* that was more significant for a future English South
Africa.

Schreiner's presentation of the Boer to the British public contextual-
izes the sense of the Boer character we see in the press coverage and
propaganda of the Boer War and complicates our understanding of the
significance of "race" in the British view of South Africa during the war.
Schreiner, an English-speaking South African, proposed in the British
periodical press that the central question for British-South African
relations was a racial question: how do problems of race, especially
racial definition among white peoples, prevent the consolidation of an
English-speaking union between South Africa and Britain?

Critical work on Schreiner has focused primarily on her fiction – *The
Story of an African Farm* (1883) was a bestseller in Britain, and it and the
unfinished *From Man to Man* (1923) mark Schreiner as an important early
feminist novelist.[1] Schreiner's participation in the intellectual discussion
group called the Men and Women's Club in London in the 1880s, with
Karl Pearson, Eleanor Marx, and others, has also been spotlighted.[2] But
Schreiner's writings on her black fellow South Africans have recently
come in for a good deal of attention as well. When critics have examined
Schreiner's writings about Africans, they have either praised her for her
progressivism in not being as bad as everybody else, as Joyce Avrech
Berkman does, or chastised her, as does Nadine Gordimer, for letting
her feminism distract her from the *real* struggles of South Africa. This
chapter argues, however, that Schreiner's writings on Africans are not
her most important writings on race. Race, for Schreiner, means the
differences between Briton and Boer as much as between black and
white, and Schreiner's articles and pamphlets that discuss the Boer are
her most significant attempts to define the racial future of the South
African nation.

Schreiner's writing about her homeland attempts to shape British
perceptions of South Africa and so to shape British-South African
relations. She tries to envision a political future for South Africa within a
British imperial culture that is already in decline by the turn of the
century. She attempts to define a South Africa of the future by fixing a
cultural identity called "South African" out of a region of disparate and
sometimes hostile communities. Shaping that South African identity
means defining a national identity that is South African rather than
English-South African or Afrikaner, and that takes account of Africans
without actually incorporating them into the concept of the nation. To
create such a national identity, Schreiner defines a South African "race"

in the definition of which we see the complexities of the notions of race and nation in turn-of-the-century Britain and South Africa. South (or, perhaps more properly, southern) Africa in the period leading up to the Anglo-Boer War of 1899–1902 consisted of British colonies and protectorates in uneasy alliance with Boer republics; in Schreiner's writing of the Boer War period we see how languages of race are invoked to create a nation out of two peoples – a nation of one white race in a land of many African races.

In the lead-up to the Boer War, Schreiner wrote a series of essays and pamphlets about her homeland for British readers, hoping to create sympathy and understanding of the Boer position and so to avert war. In these essays, Schreiner finds her own position as an intellectual and a South African, a position that demands that she interpret Boer to Briton. Schreiner interprets a culture that is not her own, though it is from her own country, to a culture that *is* her own, but not of her own country. The 1890s essays, which Schreiner considered "personal" writing ("simply what one South African at the end of the nineteenth century thought, and felt, with regard to his [sic] native land" [*Thoughts on South Africa* 14]), combine with her more overtly political tracts of the same period (*The Political Situation* [1896] and *An English-South African's View of the Situation* [1899]) to reveal the importance of race to considerations of national identity at the turn of the century. Schreiner employs definitions of race that rely on both socialism and evolution, in what Saul Dubow has called "a curious mix of political radicalism and biological determinism" (*Scientific Racism* 72). But the discourses of evolution and socialism prove incompatible in Schreiner's analysis of late-Victorian imperialism, with the result that even this most progressive of Victorians is incapable of envisioning a truly multi-racial or non-racial future for South Africa.[3]

In turn-of-the-century Britain and South Africa, many definitions of race were in circulation at once, with race-as-ethnicity, race-as-nationality, and race-as-color each tied to a particular discourse and political purpose. Then, as now, the concept of race was politically charged yet virtually indefinable. During the Boer War, definitions of race that distinguished between English South Africans and Boers took on more significance than definitions of the African races of South Africa, and Schreiner's contributions to the debates point up the significance of the racializing of white populations – defining the characteristics of separate groups as racial characteristics – at the turn of the century.[4] Schreiner asks, "How, of our divided peoples, can a great, healthy, harmonious and desirable nation be formed?" (*Thoughts on South Africa* 63). To answer that question, she has to create a national identity that can eliminate the "racial" issues that divide the two groups. She must racialize South Africa – define the characteristics of its separate groups – in order to construct a future, "blended" South African who inherits the characteristics of both groups. The British public Schreiner addresses has a stake in South Africa; Schreiner assumes that her readers understand the advantages of a South Africa formed of "our divided peoples."

Schreiner is able to look ahead to a day when the Afrikaners and British would not hold all the cards in South Africa. In *An English-South African's View of the Situation*, she notes that no "white race" had ever "dealt gently and generously with the native folks" (26) in South Africa, and that "[t]here is undoubtedly a score laid against us on this matter, Dutch and English South Africans alike; for the moment it is in abeyance; in fifty or a hundred years it will probably be presented for payment as other bills are, and the white man of Africa will have to settle it ... when our sons stand up to settle it, it will be Dutchmen and Englishmen together who have to pay for the sins of their fathers" (27). This forecast betrays a lack of faith in a natural evolution of South African society to the control of white peoples. Evolution will take care of the differences between Briton and Boer, but it cannot take care of the other kind of racial difference in South Africa – the one between white and black. For Schreiner, the erasure of the Boer in the evolution of South African society is not paralleled by an erasure of Africans.

SCHREINER AS SOUTH AFRICAN

As a figure located both within and outside the social structures of late Victorian Britain, Olive Schreiner was uniquely placed to influence British ideas about race and South Africa. Born in South Africa of an English mother and a German missionary father, Schreiner came to London just before the 1883 publication of *The Story of an African Farm*, and she soon became active in progressive intellectual circles, living in London through much of the 1880s. Throughout her life, like many other English South Africans, she referred to Britain as "home." Yet she spent, off and on, only about twelve years in Britain. After her return to South Africa in 1889, she wrote a series of articles about her homeland, focusing on the character of the Boer, for British periodicals including the *Fortnightly Review* and the *Contemporary Review*, and for the American magazine *Cosmopolitan*.[5] These essays were collected after her death as

Thoughts on South Africa (1923). Schreiner's other 1890s writings include *Trooper Peter Halket of Mashonaland* (1897), an extended allegory aimed at stirring public opinion against Cecil Rhodes' Chartered Company in Rhodesia and *An English-South African's View of the Situation* (1899), which, on the eve of the Boer War, calls for British understanding of the Boer position. Once the Boer War broke out, Schreiner helped to organize anti-war congresses; she spoke out against the war and against the concentration camps and was much in demand for her fiery oratory.

Schreiner had faith that her writing could help make political change. When she published *Trooper Peter* in 1897, it was in hopes of staving off war between Britain and the Boers: "If [the British] public lifts its thumb there is war, if it turns it down, there is peace; if, as in the present case they are indifferent and just letting things drift, there is no knowing what they may be surprised into at the last moment. It is for them . . . that the book is written. They must know where the injustices and oppression really lies, and turn down their thumbs at the right moment."[6] Schreiner's sense of the power of the "public" goes along with her sense of the power of writing addressed to that public. She believed in the power of writing to make political change and said that her criticisms of Cecil Rhodes' Chartered Company's policies toward Africans in Rhodesia in *Trooper Peter* were her most important work.[7] Although Schreiner's pro-Boer views were unpopular in Britain, her political pamphlets and journalism sold well in Britain as well as in her native South Africa. In July 1899 she heard from her publisher that *An English-South African's View of the Situation*, her pamphlet aimed at preventing the Boer War, had sold 3,500 copies at a shilling apiece in its first five days. Her pamphlets were reviewed widely – she had received thirty-two notices of *An English-South African* in the same post with the letter from her publisher.[8] The major South African newspapers ran leaders about her political writings, commenting on her speeches and articles as well as her books and pamphlets. As "the one woman of genius South Africa has produced" (Garrett "The Inevitable in South Africa" 479), Schreiner was noticed, though not always taken seriously as a political commentator. Edmund Garrett, the English journalist who edited the *Cape Times* and was a member of the Cape parliament, charged in the *Contemporary Review* in July 1899 that *An English-South African* "supports the logic of a schoolgirl with the statistics of a romanticist, and wraps both in the lambent fire of a Hebrew prophetess" ("The Inevitable in South Africa" 480).

Although much contemporary anthropological and ethnographic discussion centered on categorizing the many African groups who made up late-Victorian South Africa,[9] Schreiner does not draw on such literature in her writing on race in South Africa. Despite her interest in social Darwinism, Schreiner does not join the debates on ranking African "tribes," as such discussion was irrelevant to her political goal for South Africa – reconciling Briton and Boer. Nevertheless, Schreiner as a South African is incapable of discussing the future of South Africa without considering Africans. She sees the possibility of a non-British, non-Boer white South Africa because she thinks of the British and Boer "races" in social Darwinist terms. Africans cannot be part of the South African of the future; Schreiner's writings on South Africa describe Africans less in terms of social Darwinism than in terms of the other major discourse available to her as an English South African progressive – political economy. Schreiner sees Africans as the working class of the new South Africa. The irony of her use of social Darwinism is that the language of evolution was most commonly used to discuss African inferiority to Europeans in late Victorian Britain; Schreiner, however, uses evolution to account for Boers and turns instead to political economy to account for Africans. Strategically, her choices were subtle. If she had argued for a South Africa in which all races interbred, she would have lost political credibility in both South Africa and Britain. Neither white South Africans nor white Britons were likely to look forward to a future in which white and black intermarried. But a future in which Briton and Boer eventually melted into each other to form a strong white breed of vaguely British-flavored South Africans was an evolutionary result that was palatable – South Africa could become an America that remained loyal to the mother country. Schreiner could not argue for a future in which the Boers were a political entity because Boer political strength was the South African threat about which Britain was most worried in the late 1890s. Instead, the Boers became a racial entity, to be absorbed in an evolutionary progression. The threatening political category becomes the non-threatening racial category.

By the same token, Africans moved from racial category to political category. One of the most common ways to discuss Africans in this period of high imperialism was, of course, through the language of evolution. Colonialism was justified by the language of social Darwinism: Africans were lower on the evolutionary scale than Europeans and in need of guidance, direction, and encouragement so that they could eventually reach the Europeans' level. In her essays on the Boers and South Africa, Schreiner refuses the prevailing discourse of evolution for discussing Africans; instead, she discusses Africans as a political and economic category, as a class. This reversal enables her to avoid the fraught area of miscegenation while taking Africans seriously as a political group. Schreiner's strategic construction of categories means that she can posit a future in which Africans remain important *for* South Africa but not *as* South Africans. They will do the manual labor for the future South African, who is white. And they will then be entitled to the rights of working classes worldwide. By eliminating Africans from her vision of the ideal South African, Schreiner can argue for Africans' political and economic rights. By giving in to fear of miscegenation, Schreiner wins herself a position from which to construct an argument based on political rights.

SCHREINER AND THE BOER

Schreiner understood her own inability to sympathize fully with the majority of the population in her country, and she knew how racism and other ethnocentrisms were reproduced. She knew, for example, that she had to explain to her British readers how it was that she (and they) could sympathize with the Boer. In the introduction to the essays that were eventually collected as *Thoughts on South Africa* she writes: "Neither do I owe it to early training that I value my fellow South Africans of Dutch descent. I started in life with as much insular prejudice and racial pride as it is given to any citizen who has never left the little Northern Island to possess... I cannot remember a time when I was not profoundly convinced of the superiority of the English, their government and their manners, over all other peoples" (*Thoughts* 15). Schreiner explains her bias against Boers as "racial pride" and goes on to illustrate her "insular prejudice" with this example:

One of my earliest memories is of ... making believe that I was Queen Victoria and that all the world belonged to me. That being the case, I ordered all the black people in South Africa to be collected and put into the desert of Sahara, and a wall built across Africa shutting it off; I then ordained that any black person returning south of that line should have his head cut off. I did not wish to make slaves of them, but I wished to put them where I need never see them, because I considered them ugly. I do not remember planning that Dutch South Africans should be put across the wall, but my objection to them was only a little less. (*Thoughts* 15–16)

This story is about *Africans* transgressing what Carolyn Burdett has called Schreiner's "apartheid wall." Why would Schreiner think she was using it to illustrate her prejudice against Boers? She recounts her childhood reluctance to eat sweets given to her by a Boer child and her refusal to sleep in a bed that had been slept in by a man she mistakenly believed to be "a Dutchman" (*Thoughts* 15). Boers were "dirty." Schreiner explains that "[l]ater on, my feeling for the Boer changed, as did, later yet, my feeling towards the native races; but this was not the result of any training, but simply of an increased knowledge" (*Thoughts* 17). Throughout Schreiner's writing on South Africa, the pattern of these childhood reminiscences recurs – relations with Afrikaners are concrete, described in the detail of personal acquaintance, sometimes of fondness, while relations with Africans are rarely described, and when they are, it is in abstract, not personal terms. When Africans appear in Schreiner's writing, it seems almost accidental – a description of her aversion to Boers turns into a description of her aversion to Africans. In 1901 Schreiner wrote that she wished she had had the health to write, "above all," "what I think and feel with regard to ... our Natives and their problems and difficulties" (*Thoughts* 14), but she never did so. Africans remain fantasy figures or metaphors in most of her writing. Although she never systematically explores the condition of black Africans, they inhabit her discourse about South Africa probably much as they inhabited her everyday life in South Africa: always present but only within the terms established by white communities.

In her essays about the Boers, Schreiner was working against British anti-Boer feeling that had originated early in the nineteenth century, when Britain took possession of the Dutch-occupied Cape of Good Hope. Boer rebellions against British rule, especially its regulations about the treatment of African servants, had cropped up periodically through the first part of the nineteenth century, culminating in the Boers' 1837 Great Trek into the "unoccupied" lands beyond the Orange and Vaal Rivers, where they set up independent Boer states after bloody battles with Dingaan's Zulus in Natal. The first significant British skirmish with the Boers came in 1881, when the Boers, with a humiliating defeat of the British at the Battle of Majuba Hill, won back the sovereignty of the Transvaal, which had been annexed by Britain four years before. British public opinion maintained that the Boers were stubborn, cruel to their African servants, and trapped in the seventeenth century. By the time of the South African War, British anti-Boer sentiment had taken on increasingly anthropological tones. "A Situation in South Africa: A Voice from the Cape Colony," by the Reverend C. Usher Wilson, which appeared in the *Nineteenth Century* just after war was declared in 1899, rebutted the defenses of the Afrikaner that came from Schreiner and other "pro-Boers": "The Boers are supposed to be a simple, pastoral and puritanical people, who plough their fields and tend their cattle during the day, and read their Bibles at night... Truly, distance lends enchantment. Instead of this the Boers are nothing more nor less than a low type of the *genus homo* ... In self-sought isolation they have tried to escape the tide of civilisation" (522–23). The description has a tint of science, but it also employs another discourse – that of the necessity for "civilising" Africa. Various British entrepreneurs and explorers had throughout the century justified incursions into Africa by citing Africans' need for civilization, which was billed as Christianity but more often meant commerce (with Britain). The Boers, however, were a special case. Descended from Dutch and Huguenot settlers, they were already Christian, but they were still agricultural and decidedly not modern.

Schreiner's characterization of the differences between Boer and Briton was both scientific and sentimental. Perhaps the most controversial of her descriptions of the Afrikaner for a British audience was her essay called "The Boer," which appeared in the *Daily News* and the *Fortnightly Review* in 1896, although it had been written in 1892. Its appearance followed directly on the Jameson Raid, the ill-fated attempt by Cecil Rhodes to stir up the English in Johannesburg to armed rebellion against the Boer government of the South African Republic. Schreiner's essay presents the Boer, the descendent of early Dutch and French Huguenot settlers, as a survival of the seventeenth century. She describes the Boers as completely cut off from the intellectual life of the rest of the world for two hundred years.

Victorian and especially Boer War stereotypes of Boers presented illiterate and crude peasants who never washed or changed their clothes; South African Republic President Paul Kruger was described as blowing his nose through his fingers. Metaphors alternated between social class and evolutionary status – the Boers were a nation of peasants, paralleled in the British working classes and poor, but they were also holdovers from an earlier stage of European civilization, either in a state of arrested development or culturally degenerate. Although Schreiner chooses the terms of evolution rather than those of social class to describe the Boers, she refuses the evolution-inflected discourse of degeneration. Degeneration theorists declared that the Boers had, through their isolation and their too-close contact with Africans, backslid as a European race.[10] Schreiner's purpose, however, is to create a sympathetic British perception of the Boers as a pastoral race whose uncomplicated love of the land would mix well with British intellect and progressive spirit to make the South African of the future.

South African critics of "The Boer" charged that Schreiner had focused too much on the up-country Boer, the descendent of the early Dutch voortrekkers, rather than the better educated Capetown shop-keeper, who spoke both English and Afrikaans. But Schreiner had chosen the farming Boers because she saw them as uniquely South African. "[T]he Boer, like our plumbagos, our silver-trees, and our kudoos, is peculiar to South Africa," she explains (*Thoughts* 65). The real South Africa, in Schreiner's estimation, was to be found in the species of human, like the species of plant and wildlife, that had developed in response to the conditions of the country.

Schreiner emphasizes the impact of the relatively small number of Huguenot ancestors on the national character of the Boer. She cites the Huguenots as the primary cause for the development of the Boer identity as South African, as distinct from Europe. The Boer, Schreiner argues, "is as much severed from the lands of his ancestors and from Europe, as though three thousand instead of two hundred years had elapsed since he left it" (*Thoughts* 69). This distinct separation resulted from the religious exile of the Huguenots. Unlike the Pilgrims, who left England because of their disagreements with the political party in power, the Huguenot, Schreiner argues, "left a country in which not only the Government, but the body of his fellows were at deadly variance with him; in which his religion was an exotic and his mental attitude alien from that of the main body of the people. To these men, when they shook off the dust of their feet against her, France became the visible embodiment of the powers of evil" (*Thoughts* 82). This attitude, combined with a sense of religious entitlement to the land that became the Boer view of South Africa as the Promised Land, produced the separation from Europe that made the Boers unlike settler populations anywhere else.

Schreiner's religious freethinking produced her profound admiration for the Huguenot history of the Boers: "They were not an ordinary body of emigrants, but represented almost to a man and woman that golden minority which is so remorselessly winnowed from the dross of the conforming majority by all forms of persecution directed against intel-lectual and spiritual independence" (*Thoughts* 75). Ironically, Schreiner's own religious dissent meant that she could praise the Boer for the very aspect of that civilization that others saw as representing its backward-ness: its seventeenth-century, Calvinistic, bible-based thinking. But

Schreiner does recognize Boer biblical literalism as a problem: she cites the Transvaal parliament's majority view that the insurance of public buildings was an insult to Jehovah, who should be allowed to burn down a building if it was his will (*Thoughts* 99). For all her affection for the Boer, Schreiner nevertheless sees Boer culture as lagging far behind that of England and the rest of Europe. But for that fault she sees a clear cause, and one that would, she thought, soon be remedied.

Much of "The Boer" is devoted to explaining how the language of the Afrikaner, the Taal, had stifled intellectual development in the Boer: "[S]o sparse is the vocabulary and so broken are its forms, that it is impossible in the Taal to express a subtle intellectual emotion, or abstract conception, or a wide generalization; and a man seeking to render a scientific, philosophic, or poetical work in the Taal, would find his task impossible" (*Thoughts* 87). She cites a story of two South African students evicted from their Edinburgh rooms for repeatedly disturbing the house with peals of laughter – it seems they were engaged in translating the Book of Job into the Taal (*Thoughts* 88).

Schreiner's focus on the shortcomings of the Boers' language has a familiar ring for students of Victorian writings on the Celts. Celtic languages had been discussed in similar terms – they were corruptions of earlier languages, and they isolated and restricted the people who spoke them. An 1866 leader in *The Times* attacking Matthew Arnold's championing of Welsh cultural heritage used the same arguments with which Schreiner would criticize the Taal thirty years later:

The Welsh language is the curse of Wales. Its prevalence and the ignorance of English have excluded, and even now exclude, the Welsh people from the civilization, the improvement, and the material prosperity of their English neighbours... [T]he Welsh have remained in Wales, unable to mix with their fellow-subjects, shut out from all literature except what is translated into their own language and incapable of progress... Their antiquated and semibarbarous language, in short, shrouds them in darkness. If Wales and the Welsh are ever thoroughly to share in the material prosperity, and, in spite of Mr. Arnold, we will add the culture and morality, of England, they must forget their isolated language, and learn to speak English, and nothing else. (Dawson and Pfordresher *Matthew Arnold* 161–62)

In her discussion of the Taal in "The Boer," Schreiner never makes this final move – she never calls for the abolition of the Taal and its replacement with English. But we can see it coming. Boers still believe in witchcraft and biblical literalism because they missed out on the European Enlightenment. According to Schreiner, "If it be asked whether the Taal, in making possible this survival of the seventeenth century in the Boer, has been beneficial or otherwise to South Africa, it must be replied that the question is too complex to admit of a dogmatic answer" (*Thoughts* 105). The Boers are the equivalent of a medieval village preserved into the nineteenth century:

[We] might find in it much to condemn; its streets narrow; its houses overhanging, shutting out light and air, its drains non-existent; but over the doors of the houses we should find hand-made carving, each line of which was a work of love; we should see in the fretwork of a lamp-post quaint shapings such as no workman of to-day sends out; before the glass-stained window of the church we should stand with awe; and we might be touched to the heart by the quaint little picture above the church-altar; on every side we should see the material conditions of a life narrower and slower than our own, but more peaceful, more at one with itself. Through such a spot the discerning man would walk, not recklessly, but holding the attitude habitual to the wise man – that of the learner, not the scoffer. (*Thoughts* 105)

Schreiner's is a distinctly ambivalent sentimentality: the Boers are noble, but they are medieval.

PERSONAL AND POLITICAL WRITING

The differences between the "personal" essays, written in the early 1890s, and *An English-South African's View of the Situation* (1899), the Boer War pamphlet, are striking. Schreiner in *An English-South African* describes "cultured and polished Dutch-descended South Africans, using English as their daily form of speech, and in no way distinguishable from the rest of the nineteenth-century Europeans," (28) as being more representative of the late-nineteenth-century Dutch South African than the up-country Boer.[11] Schreiner is consistent with nineteenth-century language theorists such as Ernest Renan in her argument that if the Boers were to learn to speak English as well as the Taal, the "natural" result would be that "in another generation the fusion will be complete. There will be no Dutchmen then and no Englishmen in South Africa, but only the great blended South African people of the future, speaking the English tongue and holding in reverend memory its founders of the past, whether Dutch or English" (*Thoughts* 30). The amalgam of Englishman and Boer that will make up the future South African sounds much like the blend of Teuton and Celt that Arnold saw as the Englishman. It was natural, for the Victorians, for a more advanced culture to displace an outdated one. And just as the Teuton dominated the softer, more primitive Celtic elements of the English character, so the Englishman would dominate the primitive Boer elements in the South African of the future. In *An English-South African*, Schreiner asserts that the Taal must be supplanted by English in the end. Schreiner's prediction of a "blended" South Africa, "speaking the English tongue," would have seemed a sad, if inevitable, vision to the author of "The Boer."[12] But the author of *An English-South African* is pragmatic and knows that the way to appeal to the better instincts of the English people is not to parade the seventeenth-century Calvinism of the Boers but their kinship with the nineteenth-century Briton and, indeed, their eventual cultural subordination to Britain.

Schreiner constructs the Boer-Briton union as positive, despite her professed fondness for the Boer, because she sees the melding of the two in terms of nationalism and evolution, not imperialism. Eric Hobsbawm points out that in the late nineteenth century:

the only historically justifiable nationalism was that which fitted in with progress, i.e. which enlarged rather than restricted the scale on which human economies, societies and culture operated, what could the defence of small peoples, small languages, small traditions be, in the overwhelming majority of cases, but an expression of conservative resistance to the inevitable advance of history. The small people, language or culture fitted into progress only insofar as it accepted subordinate status to some larger unit or retired from battle to become a repository of nostalgia and other sentiments. (*Nations and Nationalism* 41)

This is the position, derived in significant part from her reading of Herbert Spencer, to which Schreiner assigns the Boer within the new nation of South Africa in the twentieth century.[13] Her formulation allowed the idea of an English South Africa, with close ties and loyalties to Britain, while disallowing actual imperial acquisition of the region.

That Schreiner could be anti-imperialist and yet see the Anglicizing of South Africa as natural and good is consistent with evolution-influenced political progressivism at the turn of the century such as that of J. A. Hobson, who saw the "civilising" of the "lower races" as a good thing, but only if it was not imposed by capitalism. According to Hobson, if, as a result of contact with white people, "many of the old political, social, and religious institutions [of "lower races"] decay, that decay will be a natural wholesome process, and will be attended by the growth of new forms, not forced upon them, but growing out of the old forms and conforming to laws of natural growth" (*Imperialism* 280). The natural growth model applied by imperialist and anti-imperialist alike to African races is applied by Schreiner to the Boers as well, marking the Boers as one of the "lower races" by analogy. Schreiner constructs the Boers as a race, defining what makes them unique, in order to hold on to those characteristics for her future South African citizen. She can skirt the political issue of Boer treatment of Africans because the language she uses to describe the Boer race is the language of social Darwinism, not "politics." So the Boer she creates is a sentimentalized portrait of a people through whom one, as a future South African, might want to trace one's heritage but among whom, in the twentieth century, one would not want to live.

IMAGES OF AFRICANS

The picture of African peoples that was in circulation in British periodicals during this period also relied on the discourse of evolution. The Canon of Grahamstown Cathedral, A. Theodore Wirgman, asserts in an article on "The Boers and the Native Question," published in the *Nineteenth Century* during the early stages of the war, that the South African republics could no longer coexist with British colonies in the region because of the two peoples' incompatible notions of justice. "It is a question of survival of the fittest," declared Wirgman, "and, quite apart from national feeling and patriotic fervour, there is no doubt in the mind of any right-minded man, who knows the facts, that peace, order, and justice to the natives can only be secured in South Africa under the Union Jack, as the symbol of political and religious liberty" ("The Boers" 593). Of course clergy had a long history of calling on Britain to use its "superior" civilization to "protect" black Africans. But Wirgman's argument is a most unusual employment of the discourse of evolution to defend the British cause in the Boer War. "Survival of the fittest" means that Britain is most fit to protect the liberty of peoples unfit to survive on their own. Here the Darwinist contest for survival, usually seen as between a European power and an indigenous people, is transformed into a contest between European races for the advantage of an indigenous people.

John Macdonell, the chair of the government-appointed South African Native Races Committee, also sees the situation in South Africa in evolutionary terms:

Whatever be the issue of the war in South Africa, it will probably leave behind it a struggle not less enduring or grave: a struggle between the white races and the coloured; between a minority of about three-quarters of a million and a majority of about four millions; between a vigorous modern industrial civilisation and primitive communities falling into decay: an economic struggle of a large and hitherto unknown scale. ("The Question of the Native Races" 367)

Macdonell sees Africans as degenerate, lapsed into a state lower than one which they had previously achieved. Macdonell asserts that black people were much more contented without white people around, hinting that perhaps it was contact with white people that had caused the African's decay. The Boers, as a nation of Europeans, are not living up to their obligations to black Africans because they do not share the British "fundamental principles – in particular as to the rights of the weak, the duties of the strong" ("The Question of the Native Races" 367).

While Patrick Brantlinger attributes the increasing racial intolerance in late nineteenth century Britain to issues of class mobility, Macdonell links the new racism directly to science:

Anyone reading the early history of the anti-slavery movement, or the formation of the Aborigines' Protection Society, must be struck by the change in the public conscience towards slavery and the welfare of uncivilised races – a change so signal that it must be doubted whether if the work of emancipation had still to be done there exists the enthusiasm to carry it through... The creed of the Eighteenth Century that all men are equal is discredited. Many are convinced of the contrary; and the teaching of Darwin as generally understood seems to have placed on a scientific basis the pretensions of civilised races to dominate the black races... The Dutch farmer, quoting Deuteronomy in justification of high-handed acts; the mine-owners, demanding measures to secure cheap labour; and the man of science, citing Darwin, are here in apparent accord. ("The Question of the Native Races" 367)

But Macdonell is not shy about making the declarations about racial type that characterized Victorian anthropology: the British are "an aggressive industrial civilisation" coming into contact with black races with "many-sided aptitudes: ... people who do not readily take to regular toil, but, possessing considerable physical strength and no small ingenuity, are capable of performing many kinds of work admirably" ("The Question of the Native Races" 368).

J. T. Darragh, writing in January 1902 from South Africa for the *Contemporary Review*, stresses the importance of the question, "How is the superior race to treat the inferior justly and fairly, without treason to the civilisation of which it is at once the beneficiary and the trustee?" ("The

Native Problem" 87). The writers in the British reviews or quarterlies, including Schreiner, never deny that the African was or should be the working class of South Africa or that Britain had a civilizing role to play in relation to the African. Darragh condemns "stay-at-home negrophilists" whose ideal is "non-interference" with the lives of Africans. African labor is necessary, he argues, and so Africans must be taught the importance of work and the value of private property. Schreiner, too, believes in the obligations of European cultures to Africans. After the Boer War, in *Closer Union* and in her unfinished novel *From Man to Man*, she calls for European responsibility toward Africans in a language less condescending and evolution-centered than some of her earlier writings.

While the position Schreiner assigns to the Boer in an English South Africa arises from an evolutionism that ultimately erases the Boer as a national and cultural identity, the positions within the new South Africa that Schreiner assigns to Africans are more problematic still. Although the language of evolution was commonly used in discussing Africans in the late nineteenth century,[14] and although Schreiner herself uses that language when it is convenient to explain some aspects of Boer-African history, she relies much more heavily on political economy than evolution in her analysis of Africans' place in South African society. At the time of the Boer War, black South Africans were foremost an economic issue for Schreiner.

The Political Situation, which Schreiner wrote with her husband, who delivered it at the Town Hall of Kimberley on 20 August 1895, is directly engaged with South African politics, addressing specific Cape legislation. In constructing Africans as a working class comparable to European working classes, Schreiner calls for rights at the same time as she reassures her readers that she is not ignoring the question of race. She argues against compulsory labor for Africans, made necessary by taxation (*Political Situation* 12–14). "In South Africa," she declares, the "Labour Question" inevitably "assumes gigantic importance, including as it does almost the whole of what is popularly termed the Native Question; the question being indeed only the Labour Question of Europe complicated by a difference of race and colour between the employing and propertied, and the employed and poorer classes" (*Political Situation* 108–9). She offers two alternatives for white attitudes toward African workers:

the one held by the Retrogressive Party in this country regards the Native as only to be tolerated in consideration of the amount of manual labour which can be extracted from him; and desires to obtain the largest amount of labour at the cheapest rate possible; and rigidly resists all endeavours to put him on an equality with the white man in the eye of the law. The other attitude, which I hold must inevitably be that of every truly progressive individual in this country, is that which regards the Native, though an alien in race and colour and differing fundamentally from ourselves in many respects, yet as an individual to whom we are under certain obligations: it forces on us the conviction that our superior intelligence and culture render it obligatory upon us to consider his welfare; and to carry out such measures, not as shall make him merely useful to ourselves, but such as shall tend also to raise him in the scale of existence, and bind him to ourselves in a kindlier fellowship. (*Political Situation* 109–11)

The return of evolutionary language here reassures Schreiner's readers that she is not discounting "racial" difference that would make Africans inferior to Europeans. She can argue for "equality with the white man in the eye of the law" without being accused of arguing that Africans were equal to Europeans in "intelligence and culture."

Schreiner goes on to link the plight of African workers with that of workers worldwide, declaring that the person who takes up the attitude supportive of African workers "will find himself in accord, not merely with the Progressive Element in this country, but with the really advanced and Progressive Movement all the world over. In fact, I go so far as to think that the mere subscription to the latter mode of regarding the Labour and Native question would constitute an adequate test in this country as to a man's attitude on all other matters social and political" (*Political Situation* 111). To be politically progressive in South Africa is to advocate rights for African workers.

Whether Schreiner employs it consciously or not, the strategy is fascinating. Schreiner pulls out the evolutionary references only where necessary to deflect opposition to the political point. If she is to make a strong case for economic and political rights, she cannot risk losing the argument by allowing her reader to think that she is arguing for immediate social equality as well. At the same time, her long-term vision clearly includes such a possibility. In *Closer Union*, in 1909, Schreiner appeals to white self-interest to ask South African citizens to think of a new kind of future: "As long as nine-tenths of our community have no permanent stake in the land, and no right or share in the government, can we ever feel safe? Can we ever know peace?" (52). She wants white South Africans to consider that their own humanity depends on the extent to which they allow for the humanity of African workers: "We cannot hope ultimately to equal the men of our own race living in more wholly enlightened and humanised communities, if our existence is passed among millions of non-free subjected peoples" (*Closer Union* 53).

Schreiner declares that the state is a white state but must win the loyalty of blacks and must provide opportunities for Africans to "take their share in the higher duties of life and citizenship, their talents expended for the welfare of the community and not suppressed to become its subterraneous and disruptive forces" (*Closer Union* 49). Indeed, her predictions in *Closer Union* are chilling in their accuracy:

if we force him permanently in his millions into the locations and compounds and slums of our cities, obtaining his labour cheaper, but to lose what the wealth of five Rands could not return to us; if uninstructed in the highest forms of labour, without the rights of citizenship, his own social organisation broken up, without our having aided him to participate in our own; if, unbound to us by gratitude and sympathy, and alien to us in blood and colour, we reduce this vast mass to the condition of a great seething, ignorant proletariat – then I would rather draw a veil over the future of this land. (*Closer Union* 50)

Schreiner's political analysis, which she opposes to the personal reflections of her articles on the Boers, stresses the African's position and the necessity for twentieth-century South Africa to stop treating African workers as a subordinate race and start treating them as a working class with rights commensurate with working classes everywhere, including the right to class mobility. Although she never goes so far as to advocate miscegenation, she hints that the South Africa of the distant future would be plagued no more by the Native Question because Africans will have been "raised" in the scale of existence to a place alongside Europeans.

The turn-of-the-century racial problem, Schreiner indicates, is the failure to acknowledge that distinctions between black and white peoples "form a barrier so potent that the social instincts and the consciousness of moral obligation continually fail to surmount them" (*Political Situation* 296). Schreiner asserts that "only in the case of exceptional individuals gifted with those rare powers of insight which enable them, beneath the multitudinous and real differences, mental and physical, which divide wholly distinct races, to see clearly those far more important elements of a common humanity which underlie and unite them, is the instinctive and unconscious extension of social feeling beyond the limits of race possible" (*Political Situation* 296). She does not include herself among these exceptional individuals, for she is aware of her shortcomings in relations with Africans. Scientific, evolutionary differences, the "real differences ... which divide wholly distinct races," overcome her politics. A social problem, racism, arises from a "real" condition, the "limits of race." The biological differences

Schreiner sees between races need not be a social problem if only people can look beyond them, to "a common humanity." Schreiner's is a classic liberal position – reaffirming a biological determinism that describes differences between races, yet calling for a color-blindness that would ignore those differences.[15] Schreiner's acknowledgment of racial barriers is at least in part a defense of the Boers, an argument that all European-descended peoples are limited in their dealings with Africans. Given those limitations, Schreiner asks, why should we trust British capitalists any further in their dealings with Africans than Boer farmers? Here, where the concept of race is used to link white peoples rather than to separate them, race is nevertheless used in defense of the Boer.

In *Thoughts on South Africa*, Schreiner uses the category of race to describe the distinctions among Italians, Swedes, and French (21) as well as to describe what she also referred to as "colour" – the differences between white European peoples and Asians or Africans, in her essay on "The Psychology of the Boer" (*Thoughts* 296–98). Schreiner's assertions about the differences between African and European peoples are, in fact, set out largely in social or economic terms rather than biological, once she has moved away from the extremely science-flavored dis-cussions of the Bushman and begins to discuss the African peoples whom she sees as more equivalent to Europeans, the Zulu, "Bantus," or "Kaffirs." These new social and economic terms seem to arise more from her socialism than her evolutionism. In "The Problem of Slavery," she describes the Bantu repugnance for the concept of private property, noting that "[t]he idea which to-day is beginning to haunt Europe, that, as the one possible salve for our social wounds and diseases, it might be well if the land should become the property of the nation at large, is no ideal to the Bantu, but a realistic actuality" (*Thoughts* 113). Although she could posit this aspect of African society as a model for European society, her overall prediction for South Africa was a more traditional economic structure.

The "Native Question," Schreiner wrote, was "indeed only the Labour Question of Europe complicated by a difference of race and colour between the employing and propertied, and the employed and poorer classes" (*Political Situation* 109). The question was the key to the future of South Africa, but whites would determine that future.

The issue of the role of cheap black labor in South Africa served as a huge wedge between white and black in that country, whether the white be Briton or Boer. As South African radical historians Jack and Ray

Simons have pointed out, "racial and national cleavages distorted class alignments" in the diamond town of Kimberley and on the Witwatersrand at the turn of the century (*Class and Colour* 56). The class affinities that should have united white and black manual laborers never arose, partly because different wage structures pitted them against each other. In addition, the white ethnic groups were not able to achieve class solidarity, as English mineworkers organized separately from Afrikaners; and neither white group expressed any identification with African laborers.

The rival nationalisms of the Afrikaners and the British in South Africa made for a complicated system of racial oppression against Africans. Both white groups were content to have "coloured," Asian, and black African workers perform most manual labor, whether it was in the mines, on the railroads, on the farms, or in the home, for wages so low as to be unacceptable to white workers. Color complicated the issue of class. British South African women looking for white domestic help complained that the young working-class women emigrating from Britain to work in South Africa could not get along with colored or black fellow-servants or were unwilling to work as hard as these other servants. No working-class solidarity emerged in the mines or the kitchens between black and white laborers.

Schreiner's "personal" essay "The Problem of Slavery" contains more on Africans than any of her other pre-Boer War writing, although Schreiner presents it as an essay not about "natives" but about the Boers. In "The Problem of Slavery," Schreiner differentiates among the many African peoples in South Africa, as she had differentiated among the Dutch, Huguenot, and English whites in the region in her essay on "The Boer." She is careful to point out that the black peoples in South Africa were not slaves:

It would have been as easy for the early Boers to catch and convert into beasts of draught the kudus and springbucks, who kick up our African dust into your face, and are off with the wind, as to turn into profitable beasts of burden our little, artistic Bushmen, or our dancing Hottentots; and our warlike Zulu Bantus from the East Coast would hardly have been more acceptable as domestic slaves than a leash of African lions. Then, as now, when submissive slaves are desired in South Africa, they have to be imported: we do not breed them. (*Thoughts* 116)

Schreiner asserts the superiority of the various South African peoples over the Central Africans who were the staple of the European slave trade, and she uses the language of evolution (or agriculture), to support her arguments: "we do not breed them."[16] In her discussion of South African society, African groups are considered separately when convenient and together when convenient. In this essay about the Boers, it is politically expedient to discuss the separate African peoples in making a case for the maintenance of South Africa as independent. But as she glorifies the social structures of South Africa in her essays, Schreiner must also take account of the recent profound changes in those social structures, such as the near-total disappearance of the Bushman (San) people in South Africa.

THE BOERS AS AN AFRICAN RACE

To account for the loss of the Bushman, Schreiner needs a discourse of evolution, invoked to justify the actions of the *Boers*. One African group evolves away in a social Darwinist encounter with a superior people. Evolution can account for the place of the Boers in South Africa in the present and will take care of the place of the Boers in South Africa in the future. Schreiner's first loyalty is to the future white South Africa. She must win sympathy for the Boer in Britain and create a climate in which Britons would look forward to a future South Africa with blended Briton and Boer. To that end, the elimination of the Bushman must be justified. Later we will see Schreiner switch terms in her discussion of Africans, defending them against white economic exploitation. But that defense can only be made against a generic white South African, not against the Boer. The Boer is not a political entity but a racial one; the African is a racial entity only when necessary to account for Boer excesses such as the slaughter of the Bushman.

The loss of the Bushman had to be accounted for in Schreiner's account of South Africa, and the language of evolution accommodates it well. Whereas Arnold located art and spirituality in the Celt, Schreiner locates it in the African Bushman. The Boer did not have the aesthetic sensibility necessary for Schreiner's future South Africa, so art came by way of the Bushman. The modern South African poet, she argues, owes a debt to the artistic Bushman. But this debt need never be repaid, since, conveniently, the Boer has destroyed all Bushman communities in South Africa.

Schreiner's "The Wanderings of the Boer" (1896) lined up the Boers alongside black Africans as the legitimate owners of South Africa. Of the Boers Schreiner wrote, "[T]hese men, and the women who bore them, possessed South Africa as no white man has ever possessed it, and as no white man ever will, save it be here and there a stray poet or artist. They possessed it as the wild beasts and the savages whom they dispossessed had possessed it" (*Thoughts* 160). In this passage, Schreiner appears to deny the Boers the status of "white." The Boers possess South Africa as "no white man ever will" possess it. The Boers have the right to the land because "they grew out of it; it shaped their lives and conditioned their individuality. They owed nothing to the men of the country and every-thing to the inanimate nature around them" (*Thoughts* 160). But in constructing the Boers as a species of South African flora or fauna, Schreiner sets them up in opposition to the categories of poet, artist, and native. White men can possess South Africa if they are poets or artists, but the Boers are neither. Their title to the land is organic, like the title of "wild beasts" or "savages."

While Schreiner recognizes the British aversion to the Boers, she attempts to romanticize them in the terms available to her, the new nationalism of blood and land. The Boer is inextricably linked to the land of South Africa, Schreiner argues, having earned title to it in a "fair fight" with Africans (the Boers used no superior technology, no maxim guns). The Boer victory was, therefore, a triumph of the fittest. By placing Boer and black South African on a similar level, able to engage in a "wild, free fight on even terms" (*English-South African* 26), a "merci-less, primitive fight," "fair and even" ("The Wanderings of the Boer" in *Thoughts* 152), yet allowing that the Boers won the fight, Schreiner constructs the Afrikaner-African struggle as an example of evolution in action. Boer must have been further up the evolutionary scale than Africans because the Boers, in a kind of "natural selection," had won. Evolutionary discourse here conveniently allows Schreiner to ignore Boer policies of repression of Africans in political and domestic contexts. She casts Boer-African battles as biological instead of political, although we know from *The Political Situation* and other writings that she was quite capable of seeing black-white relations as problems of economics and politics.

The battles Schreiner describes in *An English-South African's View of the Situation* and those in "The Wanderings of the Boer," although presented in similar terms, are actually against two different African enemies. In *An English-South African*, the "free, even stand-up fight" of Boer against Zulu is a battle in which "[t]he panther and the jaguar rolled on the ground, and, if one conquered instead of the other, it was yet a fair fight, and South Africa has no reason to be ashamed of the way either her black men or her white men fought it" (*Thoughts* 26). The Zulu people are dispossessed of their land, but they remain in South Africa. The image of the fierce, proud Zulu warrior had remained strong in Britain after the Zulu Wars, and a defeat of the Zulu would carry weight in Britain, marking the Boers as great fighters. A Boer victory in a "fair fight" with the Zulu is a triumph, showing that the Boers are destined to control South Africa. And although the defeat of the Zulu is significant, the Zulu survives to become part of the South Africa of the future. The Zulu are defeated militarily and suffer only the usual consequences of that – they lose their land and are subordinated to those who defeated them.

In both her descriptions of the Boer battles with Africans, Schreiner uses the language of evolution, but she describes the defeat of the Zulu in scientific *metaphor*, while she portrays the disappearance of the Bushman as true natural selection, a triumph of the fittest. Schreiner's goal is to justify Boer title to the land of South Africa, and she does so in evolutionary terms, even though those would certainly not have been the terms Boers would have chosen. In "The Boer" she explains that "[t]he primitive Boer believes he possesses this land by a right wholly distinct from that of the aborigines he dispossesses, or the Englishmen who followed him; a right with which no claim of theirs can ever conflict" (*Thoughts* 84). This claim is, of course, a religious one: "Its only true counterpart is to be found in the attitude of the Jew toward Palestine" (*Thoughts* 84). A Boer claim to South Africa by virtue of its being the Promised Land would not go far with British colonial officials or the British public. So it is not surprising that Schreiner turns to the evolutionary argument for Boer rights to South Africa.

THE HERITAGE OF THE BUSHMAN

In "The Wanderings of the Boer," Schreiner describes the battle between Boer and Bushman, in which the Bushman's "little poisoned arrow" is "inevitably" wiped out by the "great flint-lock gun," although the Boer-Bushman battle "seems to have been, on the whole, compared to many modern battles, fair and even" (*Thoughts* 152). Perhaps the elimination of the Bushman need not have happened, Schreiner says, but "the fore-trekkers were not missionaries, nor thirsting to sacrifice themselves for the aborigines," and, "the Bushman, being what he was, a little human in embryo, determined to have his own way, the story could take its course in no other direction than that in which it did!" (*Thoughts* 152–53): a more advanced race physically replaces one "a million centuries of development" behind its "kinsman" (*Thoughts* 153).

Schreiner is reluctant to criticize Boer treatment of Africans because she wants the British to see the Boers as partners in the future South African nation, and the language of evolution provides her with a handy mechanism with which she can justify Boer genocide against the Bushmen.

Lest the philanthropic English blame the Boers for killing off the Bushmen, Schreiner brings the problem into her reader's middle-class home:

It is easier yet for the fair European woman, as she lounges in her drawing-room in Europe, to regard as very heinous the conduct of men and women who destroyed and hated a race of small aborigines. But if, from behind some tapestry-covered armchair in the corner, a small, wizened, yellow face were to look out now, and a little naked arm guided an arrow, tipped with barbed bone dipped in poison, at her heart, the cry of the human preserving itself would surely arise; Jeames would be called up, the policeman with his baton would appear, and if there were a pistol in the house, it would be called into requisition! The little prehistoric record would lie dead upon the Persian carpet. (*Thoughts* 154)

This scenario reveals Schreiner's ambivalence about the destruction of the Bushman. She must justify it to her readers, yet she cannot fully approve. The woman she describes in her hypothetical self-defense plea is not entirely sympathetic. The upper-class woman in the story lounges around in drawing rooms and calls on servants to do her dirty work for her – just the kind of "sex-parasite" Schreiner's *Woman and Labour* seeks to eliminate in favor of productive, self-supporting women.

By awarding the Boer moral title to the land, gained in a tooth-and-claw evolutionary battle, Schreiner legitimizes the Boer right to govern in republics threatened by Britain. This justification of Boer land rights comes at the same time as Schreiner is declaring, in *The Political Situation* (1896), that the "Native Question" is the most politically significant issue in South Africa. It was hard to praise the Boer on that issue, as Schreiner knew. Describing the Boers in evolutionary, biological terms allows Schreiner to avoid describing them in terms of their historical behavior towards Africans in South Africa, whether it was land-grabbing, denial of political rights, or use of the strop on farmworkers. In both of her descriptions of the Boer-African "fair fights," Schreiner emphasizes that South Africa need not be "ashamed" of either party in the fighting – that is, South Africa need not be ashamed that the Boers have dispossessed or destroyed Africans. Only an evolutionary argument could have allowed Schreiner to make such a case.

Although Bushmen have been physically eliminated from Schreiner's vision of South Africa, they are not totally absent from the new nation-race. While lamenting the loss of the Bushman as a human "species," Schreiner immortalizes the Bushman through his art (the Bushman artist is always male in Schreiner's writings). In the "Plans and Bush-man-paintings" chapter of *The Story of an African Farm* and in "The Wanderings of the Boer," the Bushman lives on after virtual extinction through his cave-paintings that remain. Schreiner's eulogy in the essay is worth quoting at length:

> Ring round head, ears on pedestals, his very vital organs differing from the rest of his race – yet, as one sits under the shelving rocks at the top of some African mountain, the wall behind one covered with his crude little pictures, the pigments of which are hardly faded through the long ages of exposure, and, as one looks out over the great shimmering expanse of mountains and valleys beneath, one feels that the spirit which is spread abroad over exist-ence concentrated itself in those little folk who climbed among the rocks; and that that which built the Parthenon and raised St. Peter's, and carved the statues of Michael Angelo in the Medici Chapel, and which moves in every great work of man, moved here also. That the Spirit of Life which, incarnate in humanity, seeks to recreate existence as it beholds it, and which we call art, worked through that monkey hand too! And that shelving cave on the African mountain becomes for us a temple in which first the hand of human-ity raised itself quiveringly in the worship of the true and the beautiful. (*Thoughts* 153–54)

Waldo, the artist-figure in *The Story of an African Farm*, elaborates on the artistic inclination of the Bushman, who "did not know why he painted, but he wanted to make something, so he made these. He worked hard, very hard, to find the juice to make the paint; and then he found this place where the rocks hang over, and he painted them. To us they are only strange things, that make us laugh; but to him they were very beautiful" (49). The Bushman connects South Africa to a transcendent spirit of art. As the Bushman is more in touch with the land, with nature, than the "civilised" European, so is the artist or poet closer to the land, and "the artist or thinker who is to instruct mankind should not live too far from the unmodified life of nature" (*Thoughts* 160), according to Schreiner.[17] The poet or artist, whose claim to the land is aesthetic, is closely allied with the African, the "artistic Bushman" and "dancing Hottentot," if not the "warlike Bantu." But if the non-African artist has a mystical tie to the artistic Bushman, this tie can only be metaphorical and spiritual, since, in Schreiner's construction of South Africanness, the Bushman is *only* art, no longer a human to be reckoned with.

The Boer elimination of the Bushman, according to the "fair fight" model, was only proper, in evolutionary terms, but Schreiner's vision for South Africa had to include the spirituality represented by the Bushman. Such racial traits as the Boer affection for the land can be passed on directly, because the South African of the future would be a physical mix of Boer and Briton. Art, however, is African, not Afrikaner, and so cannot be inherited by the white South African: One of Schreiner's biggest fears for South Africa, expressed in "The Problem of Slavery," is miscegenation, the social problem presented by the "Half-caste" (*Thoughts* 146). Thus art, or spirituality, must move into the realm of the mystical.

Schreiner links the non-African artist with indigenous Africans by virtue of their respective ties to nature. Although she grants the Boers no artistic abilities, Schreiner does see the Boers as having the special appreciation for the land that comes from having "possessed it as no white man ever had possessed it." In the Boer "the intellectual faculties are more or less dormant through non-cultivation" (*Thoughts* 174), but the Boer appreciates nature. Handicapped by the Taal, the Boer "has no language in which to re-express what he learns from nature, but he knows her" (*Thoughts* 187). The Boer cannot be a poet, but "[n]o one with keen perception can have lived among the Boers without perceiving how close, though unconscious, is their union with the world around them, and how real the nourishment they draw from it" (*Thoughts* 188). Schreiner's language, of the "unconscious" connection to nature, is the language of western writing about "savages." The Boers are not yet civilized enough to understand their own connection to the land. Their aesthetic, spiritual, and intellectual limitations meant that the Boers were not the ideal inheritors of the land of South Africa. But their love for the land and their strong religious faith, Schreiner proposed, were elements worth absorbing into the South African of the future.

MISCEGENATION

Because Schreiner traces the artistic impulse in South Africa to Bushmen and not Boers, it cannot be passed on to future South Africans through intermarriage, as the Boer love for the land would be inherited. Schreiner sees no Bushman blood in the veins of her "blended" South African. Any miscegenation is seen as a social evil, but on a scale of civilization, the Bushman ranks at the bottom. Art is thus doubly removed from white South Africa – Bushmen cannot be allowed to interbreed with Boers or British, and, in any case, the Bushmen are all gone. Art, or spirituality, must move into the realm of the mystical because miscegenation cannot be permitted.

Miscegenation was perhaps the most difficult racial issue for Schreiner, as it was for many liberal white South Africans. The issue cropped up again and again in Schreiner's political journalism and her fiction – for her, it was one of the greatest evils of South Africa. Her essay on "The Problem of Slavery," originally printed in 1896, declared that the first social duty of South Africa was to *"Keep your breeds pure!"* (*Thoughts* 146). Interbreeding of Europeans and Africans in South Africa, she declared, had produced a huge social problem – the mixed-race South African.[18] Schreiner's faith in Victorian science appeared to be at odds with her progressive politics in her assessment of the position of the "Half-caste." She eventually concluded that "there *do* exist in the social conditions of the Half-caste's existence, in almost every country in which he is found, causes adequate, and more than adequate, to account for all, and more than all, the retrograde and anti-social qualities with which he is credited" (*Thoughts* 139). Therefore, despite the existence of "certain circumstances which suggest the possibility of the crossing of widely discovered varieties producing a tendency to revert to the most primitive ancestral forms of both" (*Thoughts* 139), not enough evidence existed to prove that this would produce a biological reason for the problems of the mixed-race South African. "Half-castes" were as likely to be "anti-social" (criminal, amoral) because of the discrimination they suffered at the hands of both white and black communities. Schreiner's impulses to look for evolutionary reasons for the position of the "Half-caste" clashed with her impulse to look for political reasons for that position, but she eventually acknowledged the large role of social factors. Rather than call for improvements in the status of mixed-race South Africans, however, Schreiner simply advocates racial "purity" as a solution.

In her writing on miscegenation Schreiner's feminism and her racial politics come together in an uneasy alliance, for Schreiner had good feminist reason to deplore miscegenation: the white man's sexual exploitation of the black woman. It is on this topic that Schreiner develops most clearly the connections between her feminism and her anti-racism, both in her polemical non-fiction and in her fiction. One of the strongest features of Schreiner's anti-imperialist allegory, *Trooper Peter Halket of Mashonaland*, is its treatment of white men's sexual exploitation of black women.

The plot of *Trooper Peter* has the eponymous hero, a soldier in the employ of Rhodes' Chartered Company, accidentally stranded in the veldt for a night. He is visited by a mysterious stranger, a linen-garbed Jew with wounds in his hands and feet, and the two talk all night. Inspired by the memory of his mother at home in England, Peter decides to spread the stranger's message of love. His new resolve is tested the next day back in camp, when he is ordered to shoot an African captured by his troop. Freeing the man instead, he is shot by his commanding officer.

One of the most startling passages in *Trooper Peter* is Peter's description of the domestic life of the British adventurer in southern Africa:

"I had two huts to myself, and a couple of nigger girls. It's better fun," said Peter, after a while, "having these black women than whites. The whites you've got to support, but the niggers support you! And when you're done with them you can just get rid of them. I'm all for the nigger gals... One girl was only fifteen; I got her cheap from a policeman who was living with her, and she wasn't much. But the other ... belonged to the chap I was with. He got her up north. There was a devil of a row about his getting her, too; she'd got a nigger husband and two children; didn't want to leave them, or some nonsense of that sort." (55, 57–58)

Like Rebekah's husband, Frank, in Schreiner's unfinished novel *From Man to Man*, Peter takes for granted the white man's sexual privilege. In *From Man to Man*, Rebekah takes in her husband's mixed-race child and raises the girl, Sartje, with her own children. As Anne McClintock has pointed out, black women are granted no agency in Schreiner's fictional portraits, and, indeed, black mothers are bad mothers (*Imperial Leather* 272–73). Schreiner devotes little fictional attention to African women – *Trooper Peter* and *From Man to Man* focus on criticizing white male privilege rather than exploring the condition of being an African woman. But they reveal the connections Schreiner saw between racial and sexual exploitation. Unable to write as directly about black South Africans as she had about the Boers, Schreiner was nevertheless able to write sympathetically about the exploitation of African women as women. Schreiner does not, however, discuss the oppression of African women as just another example of sexism; she is careful to discuss black women's oppression as double jeopardy – as racial as well as sexual oppression.

Schreiner resigned from the South African Women's Enfranchisement League over that organization's refusal to call for the vote for African women, although she did advocate an education qualification that would have disenfranchised most blacks and some whites (First and Scott *Olive Schreiner* 261–62). She called for whites to "raise" Africans in the "scale of existence," but she also believed in a certain amount of determinism. In *Woman and Labour*, she explained that "the development of distinct branches of humanity has already brought about ... a severance between races and classes which are in totally different stages of evolution" (248). This is the classic conversion of Darwinism to social Darwinism: separations between races and even between classes are determined by evolution. The resulting gaps are so wide that some groups simply could not intermix sexually:

> Were it possible to place a company of the most highly evolved human females – George Sands, Sophia Kovalevskys, or even the average cultured female of a highly evolved race – on an island where the only males were savages of the Fugean type, who should meet them on the shores with matted hair and prognathous jaws ... so great would be the horror felt by the females towards them, that not only would the race become extinct, but if it depended for its continuance on any approach to sex affection on the part of the women, that death would certainly be accepted by all, as the lesser of two evils ... A Darwin, a Schiller, a Keats ... would probably be untouched by any emotion but horror, cast into the company of a circle of Bushman females with greased bodies and twinkling eyes, devouring the raw entrails of slaughtered beasts. (*Woman and Labour* 248–49)

It is difficult to reconcile these Bushman women with Schreiner's earlier image of the Bushman as a romantic, solitary painter, prototype for the modern artist and poet. But to establish the Bushman's sexual incompatibility with modern Europeans was essential to Schreiner's project of locating artistic spirituality in that people. Schreiner reinforces the prohibition against sexual contact between white South Africans and Bushmen by asserting an almost physical incompatibility between them that lies within the aesthetic sense of the white man.

Honest hard work and strong family ties come from the Boers, while the benefits of European civilization come from the English. These two can blend sexually. But the mystical, spiritual, artistic feeling that must also contribute to the new South Africa cannot be found in either the plodding Afrikaner or the sophisticated Briton.

EVOLUTION AND FEMINISM

Just as Schreiner's projected ideal South African society needs the idea of Africans in order to function, but cannot directly include the African, so her writing on feminism exploits images of African women without allowing feminism to be available to African women. In "The Boer Woman and the Modern Woman's Question," one of her pre-Boer War essays on South Africa, and later in *Woman and Labour*, Schreiner recounted a conversation she had had with a "Kafir woman still in her untouched primitive condition." Although the woman lamented the condition of the women of her "race," she offered, Schreiner said, "not one word of bitterness against the individual man, nor any will or intention to revolt; rather, there was a stern and almost majestic attitude of acceptance of the inevitable; life and the conditions of her race being what they were" (*Woman and Labour* 14). This conversation, Schreiner recalled, was her first encounter with the idea she later came to regard as "almost axiomatic," that "the women of no race or class will ever rise in revolt or attempt to bring about a revolutionary readjustment of their relation to their society, however intense their suffering and however clear their perception of it, while the welfare and persistence of their society requires their submission" (*Woman and Labour* 14). The account of the conversation is one of the few instances in Schreiner's writing of a direct exchange between a white and a black person. Schreiner's approach is distinctly anthropological, but it is nonetheless significant that it is in a discussion of gender issues that she is finally able to write about a black person. Very real boundaries prevented Schreiner from writing sympathetically about individual black Africans in her essays on South African politics, but those boundaries do not appear to have posed as much of a problem in her writing about women. The problem occurs because the African woman can be only an object lesson to the European; feminism cannot help the African woman because her race is not ready for it, but European races have evolved to the point at which feminism is possible and, indeed, necessary.

In her article on Boer women, Schreiner referred to "The Woman's Movement of the nineteenth century" as "in its ultimate essence . . . *The Movement of a Vast Unemployed*" (*Thoughts* 209). The problem with modern European women's social position was both social and economic:

In primitive societies woman performed the major part of the labours necessary for the sustenance of her community, as she still does in Africa and elsewhere, where primitive conditions exist . . . Undoubtedly woman suffered, and often suffered heavily, in those primitive societies, but she must always have been clearly conscious, as was the Bantu woman quoted, of the inevitableness of her position . . . Her labour formed the solid superstructure on which her society rested. (209–10)

With industrialization, however, men took over the production of most goods, and now, for example, "beer, the right brewing of which was our grandmother's pride, is exclusively the manufacture of machinery and males, who, for absorbing this branch of the female's work, are often rewarded with knighthoods and peerages" (212). In addition, women were no longer required to spend the better part of their lives bearing children. As Schreiner constructed her argument, the outcomes of this new social ordering could be either "sex parasitism," in which women remained entirely dependent on male labor and lost any social and economic function except as sexual servicers of men, or "the Woman's Movement," "essentially a movement based on woman's determination to stand where she has always stood beside man as his co-labourer . . . benefiting not herself only, but humanity" (216–17).

The European women's movement, Schreiner argued, was "impossible in the past and inevitable in the present to women within whom the virility and activity of the Northern Aryan races is couched" (217). Thus Schreiner relied on distinguishing her own stock, the "Northern Aryan races," from other white peoples as well as from Africans in order to assert the inevitability of the women's movement. She went on to assert that the movement was as yet unnecessary for Boer women, even though they belonged "by descent to the most virile portions of the Northern Aryan peoples" (217). For the Boer woman, "the conditions of woman's life and work have not changed; she still has her full share of the labours and duties of life" (217). Feminism, for these simple economic reasons, was not yet on the cards for the back-country Boer, as it was not for African women. But while Schreiner asserted that it was only a matter of time before the South African economy would change and Boer women would initiate a movement of their own, she never made such a claim for African women.

To argue on evolutionary grounds for a white women's movement, Schreiner had to be able to compare the African woman to the new European woman. The African woman not only still worked beside her man; she also suffered under his rule. To show that the European woman was ready to rise to equality with her man, Schreiner required the example of the African woman, who was not "ready," in terms of social evolution, to challenge the authority of her man because her submission was necessary for the survival of her "race." At the time of the Boer War, Schreiner was still working out her relationship to social Darwinism. In her twentieth-century writings she would move closer

toward a view of total equality among the races in South Africa. But as
of the war, she remained limited by social Darwinist frameworks of the
hierarchy of races[19] and so was, for the most part, unable to look at
African women's situation except as a justification for the white
women's movement. While she did not romanticize the oppression of
the African woman, neither did she believe it could be redressed.

Schreiner saw her writing as part of a strategy for social change – her
novels and allegories as well as her journalism and polemic. *The Political
Situation* was delivered as a speech aimed at forming a political party,
and she intended the essays of *Thoughts on South Africa* and the pamphlet
An English-South African's View of the Situation to help prevent the Boer War.
Woman and Labor, The Story of an African Farm, and Schreiner's idiosyn-
cratic "dreams" meant much to British feminism. To be sure,
Schreiner's brief references to racial interaction in her fiction had, as
Richard Rive characterized them, "an air of condescension, patroniz-
ation, [and] custodianship" that defines the word "liberal" (Birbalsingh
"Interview with Richard Rive" 38). But her non-fiction about race, both
in the context of the Boer War and afterwards, reveals a position that
demands a more complex evaluation.

   While Schreiner's writings about women are now taking their place
in a feminist canon, the time has come to recognize also her complicated
analysis of race and ethnicity. Schreiner's writing has been broken down
into two bodies: her political, anti-imperialist and "pro-native" work,
including her journalism and *Trooper Peter Halket of Mashonaland*; and her
feminist writing, including her allegories and her novels as well as
Woman and Labour. But Schreiner's analysis of the position of African
women reveals that she recognized the connections between sexism and
racism. Although her inclination to rely on evolutionary theory sometimes skews her analysis of racial oppression, that very theory enables
her to formulate one of the first thorough critiques of white patriarchy. If
we want to arrive at an assessment of the value and influence of
Schreiner's writing, we must forget neither its limitations nor its insights.
As she interpreted South Africa to Britain, Schreiner presented a picture
of a white country divided by its very nature, with a future, she felt, that
could only lie with unity. Boers could not exist without Africans, nor
English without Boers.

   To try to tease out turn-of-the-century British or English South
Africans' views of Africans from their views of Afrikaners is to misunder-
stand the meaning of race in the late-Victorian context. Schreiner – a

British intellectual who lived only a few years in Britain, a rural South African who called Britain "home" – was a product of the British Empire at the end of the century. Her journalism about race and Empire was some of the first writing from South Africa to be taken seriously in Britain, as a threat by some and as a vision by others. Her complicated readings of the roles of the English, African, and Afrikaner in a new South Africa are among the most nuanced of the 1890s. In positing a future united nation of South Africa rather than a collection of Boer republics and British colonies, Schreiner had to create that nation on a racial basis. The "blended" white race of the united South Africa would evolve from the union of the two distinct white racial elements of nineteenth-century South Africa. The language that discusses race in terms of nation and vice versa allows Schreiner to envision her twentieth-century South Africa without strife between Briton and Boer: the two races simply evolve into one race.

This same racial thinking, however, with its emphasis on biologism and its concurrent fears of miscegenation, prevented Schreiner from positing a new South Africa that would blend the groups twentieth-century readers most readily think of as races – that is, blacks and whites. In Schreiner's future South Africa, black and white groups are linked by economics, while white and white groups become linked by evolution. Schreiner's vision of the fusion of Boer and Briton relies on evolutionary discourse about race and ethnicity when it discusses the social identity of the nation, while it relies on political definitions of race as class when it discusses the political and economic future of the nation. Schreiner carefully threaded her way through the complexities of racial definition at the turn of the century to arrive at a position that allowed her to advocate for the Boer, excusing Boer crimes against Africans while still calling for the rights of Africans in a new South Africa. This paradoxical position was possible because for Schreiner the evolution of Boer and Briton would create a South African who was *not* a Boer, who had evolved beyond the limitations of the Boer, be they spiritual, aesthetic, or political. Evolution allowed her to be rid of the Boer and politics allowed her to keep the African. Schreiner's progressive political agenda meant that she could use the period's unstable definitions of race to make the Boers a race, make Africans a class, and see a future for South Africa in which a blended white people worked to replace African civilizations with copies of European ones. The limitations of Schreiner's position on race or class are evident; nevertheless, her vision of a bloody future for her nation if it did not take her advice proved all too accurate. Instead of de-emphasizing racial separations, as Schreiner advocated, South Africa under segregation and then apartheid reinforced racial divisions. Whether or not definitions of race are ever clear-cut, separation according to such definitions has proved, as Schreiner warned, ultimately destructive.

CHAPTER 6

The imperial imaginary – the press, empire, and the literary figure

Although Olive Schreiner was the South African writer most famous in Britain, the novels of South Africa that England loved best were H. Rider Haggard's. Through Schreiner and Haggard, 1880s and 1890s Britons derived a sense of southern Africa, and two more different versions of the region would be difficult to imagine. Schreiner used essays, allegory, polemic, and fiction to try to paint a portrait of a South Africa that Britons would respect for its differences yet want as a somewhat autonomous member of the empire, perhaps equivalent to Canada. *The Story of an African Farm*, for all of its spirituality and experimentation, is at heart a Victorian realist novel, set in an Africa about which Britons were increasingly eager to learn. The novels of Rider Haggard, however, treated the reading public to a very different southern Africa. "King Romance" filled his southern Africa with adventure, passion, guns, and spears. But with the coming of the Boer War, Britons looked beyond these writers associated with southern Africa. For an imperial war, the services of the laureate of empire were needed. This chapter moves from the African expert Haggard to the imperial bard himself, Rudyard Kipling, and explores the effects of the British public's desire for a single, Kipling-shaped, sense of empire.

Both Olive Schreiner and Arthur Conan Doyle were able to contribute to public debate about the Boer War because of their positions as prominent literary figures. Doyle had made his name through Sherlock Holmes and historical romances; he had no direct connection to empire before the war. Schreiner was a South African, but beyond that, she had no particular political or economic expertise to allow her to command respect for her views on what she called "The Political Situation." And, of course, Doyle and Schreiner were only two among many literary figures who wrote in the periodical press about the war. The new journalism of the late-Victorian period offered new political platforms for authors, both those associated with high culture and those who were more mass-market. The period at the end of the flourishing Victorian era of reviews and magazines was perhaps the height of literary figures' involvement in public debate on political issues in Britain, and imperialism was a topic that became linked especially with writers of popular fiction, such as Haggard, Doyle, and especially Kipling. In this period, jingoism came to be associated with the working classes, especially the jingoism of popular culture, such as the music halls. A similar connection between popular fiction and those same groups played a part in the attribution of authority on the topic of imperialism to popular literary figures. Consequently, later historians and cultural critics have not been shy about apportioning blame for Victorian jingoism to such figures as Haggard and Kipling, based on what is seen as a glorification of empire in their fiction and poetry. This chapter will explore how such literary figures contributed in various, sometimes contradictory ways, to the public exchange of ideas on imperialism and the Boer War, through poetry, fiction, propaganda, and speechmaking. The historical and cultural reasons why they should have been offered such exposure for their views, and the consequences of those views, make for a complicated picture of the place of the literary figure in public discourse on imperialism. The late-century linking of authors and empire was not a simple question of the inclusion of imperial themes in fiction. Empire, at the turn of the century, was not simply a setting, a way of providing an adventure plot. Instead, the link between author and empire during the Boer War arose very directly in the context of the popular press, as the public face of imperialism came to depend more and more on a connection to the imagination.

Fiction had long included empire in its material, "imaginatively collaborat[ing] with structures of civil and military power," as Deirdre David has explained (*Rule Britannia* 13). In according authority to imaginative writers on questions of empire, the Victorian press and reading publics were acknowledging the importance of fiction to the fact of empire – the necessity of cultural support for the political/economic/military venture of war. Imagination was of necessity an important ingredient in British public perceptions of imperialism. As Laura Chrisman has pointed out in her analysis of Rider Haggard's adventure fiction, "For a community whose experience of actual imperialism was profound and asymmetrical (people were both British subjects and objects of the political and economic complex), the fantasies produced by this popular form may well have seemed to promise more 'knowledge' of the race's destiny than journalistic reports from the Boer War front" (56). What would be more natural than to trust such adventure-authors, to read not only their fiction but their own "journalistic reports" in search of the (imaginative) truth about empire? No public policy issue of the time relied so heavily as did imperialism on the British public imagining both faraway places and a prosperous future. To that necessity for imagining, we may add the urgency of war, and of the Boer War in particular: the impact of the late-nineteenth-century news technologies meant that British readers eagerly awaited news from the imperial front every day.

The Boer War, the first major imperial war against a white settler population, required that the British people be able to imagine the value to Britain of a strange landscape most of them would never see, positing a future of wealth and "freedom" for white British-descended people in that land. Perhaps more than any other imperial conflict, this war relied on an imperial imaginary – the myths of British imperialism as they interacted with its material conditions. As Edward Said notes, "Neither imperialism nor colonialism is a simple act of accumulation and acquisition. Both are supported and perhaps even impelled by impressive ideological formations" (*Culture* 8). In that imperial imaginary, created and sustained by the literature of imperialism in conjunction with the press, the literary figure is key. The Boer War brought imperialism into the public eye in a new way, as the British fought with a white settler nation for lands where the indigenous population was African. The "impressive ideological formations" that supported such a war included the popular press, of course, but they also included the literary – and in a much more direct way than in the imperial allusions to which Said refers in, say, *Mansfield Park*. The conjunction of popular press power and the increased visibility within popular culture of the imperial project by the end of the nineteenth century meant that literary figures who were by then directly addressing empire in their fiction were called upon to address imperial questions in the press as well. We have inherited a picture of jingoism as a working-class phenomenon, but after the success of the imperial romance adventures of Rider Haggard, and with the advent of the cross-class phenomenon of Rudyard Kipling, the popular press and jingoism reached wider audiences. Imperial enthusiasm, as shown on Mafeking Night, could include all social classes. Although literary figures certainly had been accorded authority in the press on political and social issues before the turn of the century, the literary figures who became associated with imperialism during the Boer War held a new authority that came from the powerful combination of the new literacy of the lower classes, the new penny and halfpenny news-papers, the imperial experience of the individual writers, and the new controversies associated with imperial policy as a result of the concen-tration camps and other unsettling aspects of this particular war.

Early- and mid-Victorian literary figures had published in many different kinds of periodicals, prestigious and popular, conservative and radical, on political controversies of many sorts, from the woman question to the Jamaica Rebellion to copyright law.[1] As Joanne Shattock and Michael Wolff have observed, the periodical press flourished to an unprecedented extent in the Victorian age, and "[t]he press, in all its manifestations, became during the Victorian period the context within which people lived and worked and thought, and from which they derived their (in most cases quite new) sense of the outside world" (*Victorian Periodical Press* xiv–xv). This became even more the case as literacy rates increased and newspaper prices fell, until the turn of the century's burgeoning of the halfpenny newspapers. Imperialism's pres-ence in popular culture, outlined by such cultural historians as John MacKenzie and Anne McClintock, was bolstered by the association of popular literary figures with empire. In most cases, the literary figures were able to provide the authority of experience alongside the romance of the imaginative.

When the author in question had credibility through experience of empire, the combination of credit for the authority of the imagination (this author is worth reading) and the authority of experience (this person has lived in that mythical place, the empire) was formidable. Kipling, of course, had his Indian experience; on the basis of his popularity and his journalistic experience he was asked by Lord Roberts to edit a troop newspaper in Bloemfontein and even allowed to partici-pate in a battle against the Boers. Arthur Conan Doyle served as a physician in a field hospital during the war and was knighted for his pro-British propaganda. H. Rider Haggard had been an imperial ad-ministrator in southern Africa during the first Boer War in 1881, and Olive Schreiner was South African and came to be treated in the press as representative of a particular strand of South African thinking.

Any author who would be known to the general public as an author can be seen as a "literary figure," and such a definition allows for a broad group to be included. As Regenia Gagnier points out, although authorship was being institutionalized and professionalized in the late nineteenth century, "literary hegemony, or a powerful literary bloc that prevented or limited 'Other' discursive blocs, did not operate by way of the institutional infrastructure, rules, and procedures of the ancient professions of law, medicine, and clergy" (*Subjectivities* 31). Instead, market conditions alone seemed to determine who counted as an author, and status as an author often conveyed a right to write about the war, in one's usual genre (such as Algernon Swinburne's fierce anti-Boer poetry), or in propaganda publications or essays (such as the romance novelist Ouida's essay attacking the Colonial Secretary, Joseph Chamberlain).[2]

RIDER HAGGARD'S SOUTH AFRICA

Certainly the writer who first comes to mind as spokesperson for empire at the turn of the century is Kipling. But Kipling was not the first literary figure to build a reputation on the empire: H. Rider Haggard, who would be eclipsed by Kipling shortly after the younger man arrived on the literary scene, had already made a reputation for himself as the premier African adventure writer by the early 1890s.[3] Martin Green has pointed out that "the adventure tales that formed the light reading of Englishmen for two hundred years and more after *Robinson Crusoe* were, in fact, the emerging myth of English imperialism. They were, collectively, the story England told itself as it went to sleep at night" (*Dreams of Adventure* 3). The adventure stories of Rider Haggard, many of them set in the southern Africa he knew from his days as a colonial administrator, were part of the myth of English imperialism, to be sure. But Haggard himself became part of that myth as well, part of the public discourse of imperialism that helped to sustain it as both an ideological and a material phenomenon. As Patrick Brantlinger points out, British literary figures had been writing about empire throughout the nineteenth century, both in fiction and in non-fiction. Brantlinger cites Trollope's travelogues of his visits to the British colonies in the 1870s, and his letters to the *Liverpool Mercury* on colonial issues (*Rule of Darkness* 4–6), for example. But as the myth (or myths, for certainly India and Africa and the Far East generated different myths) of imperialism grew, peaking with the New Imperialism of the latter part of the century, the involvement of literary figures in the public discourse of imperialism likewise grew. Kipling's poetry, Doyle's propaganda, Haggard's history, all worked in support of imperial ideology during the Boer War, while Olive Schreiner's essays and letters attempted to intervene against the war. The presence of these specifically literary celebrities marks the need for turn-of-the-century imperialism to invoke the imaginary in

support of a project that needed public support. The work of the
pro-empire literary figures could not be enough, however, to secure
imperial hegemony, and an examination of the roles of Haggard and
Kipling in the public discourse of imperialism during the Boer War
reveals the faultlines in their own presentations of the imperial ideal.

H. Rider Haggard went to South Africa in 1875 as a nineteen-year-
old attached to the service of his father's acquaintance Sir Henry
Bulwer, the new Lieutenant-Governor of Natal. The young Haggard
worked at Pietermaritzburg for Bulwer, in charge of entertaining, setting up household staff, and other secretarial duties. When Sir
Theophilus Shepstone offered Haggard the chance to accompany him
on his mission to annex the Boer territory of the Transvaal in 1876, the
young man eagerly accepted. Shepstone was charged with convincing
the Boers to accept annexation so they would be under British protection from possible Zulu invasion, and Haggard was thrilled to be the one
to raise the Union Jack over Pretoria once the annexation was com-
pleted. The annexation was never popular with the Boers, who felt that
they had been tricked into it by Shepstone, whose promises of self-
government proved false. Boer resistance mounted, and by the end of
1880, full-scale rebellion had broken out. The British, still smarting from
the 1879 Zulu War, fared even worse against the Boers, whose military
skills they mightily underestimated. The peace settlement negotiated
through the spring and summer of 1881 was humiliating for the British,
who granted Boer self-government under British suzerainty. Haggard,
disillusioned, left for Britain with his wife and small son.

Haggard's years in South Africa, first as a colonial administrator and
then as an ostrich farmer, were also his first years as a writer. His first
published articles were descriptions of the politics and history of "The
Transvaal," (*Macmillan's Magazine* May 1877) and the spectacle of "The
Zulu War Dance" (*The Gentleman's Magazine* August 1877). In 1882 he
paid £50 to Trübner's to publish his *Cetywayo and his White Neighbours*, the
book about southern Africa from which he would in 1899 excerpt *The
Last Boer War*. The book received mixed reviews but resulted in Haggard
being established as an authority on southern African matters. He
contributed a series of articles to the *South African* and wrote letters to
newspapers about African affairs (Ellis *H. Rider Haggard* 92). But Haggard's first real success on an African theme was, of course, *King Solomon's
Mines*, which catapulted him to fame in 1885. His tales of African
adventure included *Allan Quatermain* (1887), *She* (1887), *Nada the Lily* (1892),
and many others. Most of Haggard's African fiction is concerned with

white people's interactions with African peoples, but white explorers rather than settlers – 1870s southern Africa rather than turn-of-the-century South Africa. Haggard's popularity contributed to new interest in the empire, as Wendy Katz notes, citing a 1926 review of Haggard's autobiography that declared that Haggard's "South African romances filled many a young fellow with longing to go into the wide spaces of those lands and see their marvels for himself" (quoted in Katz *Rider Haggard* 1), as, presumably, did the works of other, lesser, imperial adventure novelists.[4] Imperial adventure fiction was part of the cultural milieu described by John MacKenzie in *Propaganda and Empire* – a non-stop cultural undercurrent of empire in advertisements, fiction, art, and other artifacts of everyday life. Haggard's fiction has been seen as contributing to the ideological hegemony of imperialism at the end of the century (Katz *Rider Haggard*, Low *White Skins/Black Masks*, David *Rule Britannia*, McClintock *Imperial Leather*, Chrisman "Imperial Unconscious?", Bristow *Empire Boys*, Gilbert and Gubar *No Man's Land*), but his contribution went beyond *King Solomon's Mines* and *She*. Haggard was also active in the Anglo-African Writers' Club, edited the economic journal *African Review*, and published non-fiction about African affairs.

Haggard's success as an imperial adventure-writer was what gave him a platform from which to preach, and Haggard had his say on many different topics, including the Salvation Army and agricultural reform. By the Boer War, having made his name creating an imaginary Africa, Haggard had earned the right to write about the real Africa. Rider Haggard's role in the creation of late-Victorian Britain's image of southern Africa is akin to Kipling's role in the creation of an image of India. Young Haggard had pleaded the case for the empire in the early 1880s, when it seemed that few at home supported the goals of colonialism:

How common it is to hear men whose fathers emigrated when young, and who have never been out of the colony, talking of England with affectionate remembrance as "home"!

It would, however, be too much to suppose that a corresponding affection for colonies and colonists exists in the bosom of the home public. The ideas of the ordinary well-educated person in England about the existence and affairs of these dependencies of the Empire are of the vaguest kind ... there are few subjects so dreary and devoid of meaning to nine-tenths of the British public as any allusion to the Colonies or their affairs.[5]

Haggard himself would soon be a major factor in remedying that situation. *King Solomon's Mines* (1885) sold 12,000 copies in its first twelve months alone, garnering rave reviews (Ellis *H. Rider Haggard* 101). *She* (1887) was an even bigger sensation and made its author's reputation as a master of the imperial romance. Peter Berresford Ellis quotes W. E. Henley's assessment of the impact of Haggard's African romances, after almost a century of the realist novel: "Just as it was thoroughly accepted that there were no more stories to be told, that romance was utterly dried up, and that analysis of character ... was the only thing in fiction attractive to the public, down there came upon us a whole horde of Zulu divinities and sempiternal queens of beauty in the Caves of Kôr" (*H. Rider Haggard* 119). The genre of romance was resurrected via Africa; colorful battles, tortures, wild animals as the setting for human relationships that operated on a strictly surface level. The appeal was certainly the exotic – as one American reviewer noted, "Not very many of one's personal friends, it must be admitted, belong to a Zulu 'impi'" (K. Woods "Evolution" 351).

Haggard's position as king of imperial literature was taken by Kipling in the mid-1890s, but Haggard continued to write and to sell. When the second Boer War loomed in summer of 1899, Haggard felt he could make a real contribution to the war effort by lending some historical analysis. This conviction came from his knowledge and experience of southern Africa, not from his adventure-writing. Haggard had written *Cetywayo and his White Neighbours* in 1882, immediately upon his return to England. Thinking about his analysis of the 1881 conflict must have frustrated him as he watched the build-up to war in 1899, and Haggard's publication of the relevant portions of *Cetywayo and his White Neighbours* as *The Last Boer War* is an "I told you so" aimed at the British colonial administrators who failed to learn from the experience of Haggard's southern African chief Sir Theophilus Shepstone.

The "Author's Note" to Haggard's *The Last Boer War* explains the value in 1899 of reading a history of the Boer War of 1881. Haggard asserts that "any who are interested in the matter may read and find in the tale of 1881 the true causes of the war of 1899" (vi). Haggard's aim in republishing the book is to justify the second Boer War while blaming the British government for not learning the lessons of the first. The message is this: had Britain taken a tough line with the Boers in and after 1881, there would have been no need to do so in 1899. The problem in South Africa, says this romance-writer and former colonial functionary, is one of character. The Boer is lazy, corrupt, sneaky, and wants most of all "to live in a land where the necessary expenses of administration are paid by somebody else" (ix). The Briton, however, has different priori-

ties in ruling southern Africa: "a redistribution of the burden of taxation, the abolition of monopolies, the punishment of corruption, the
just treatment of the native races, [and] the absolute purity of the
courts" (x). It is a list reminiscent of Ignosi's promises that he will rule
Kukuanaland justly and fairly in *King Solomon's Mines*: "When I sit upon
the seat of my fathers, bloodshed shall cease in the land. No longer shall
ye cry for justice to find slaughter . . . No man shall die save he who
offendeth against the laws. The "eating up" of your kraals [taxation]
shall cease; each shall sleep secure in his own hut and fear not, and
justice shall walk blind throughout the land" (192). What Ignosi learned
from his years of living with white men in southern Africa was the best of
the values of the white man, that is, the Briton. Restored to his throne in
Kukuanaland, he is, as Deirdre David notes, "a leader uncannily
schooled in the ideals of new imperialism, which he will implement
without the presence of white Europeans" (*Rule Britannia* 191). This
vision of African self-rule in *King Solomon's Mines* exists strictly in fiction
for Haggard, however. The real question for southern Africa, as *The Last
Boer War* testifies, is this: which white race should control South Africa,
its land and its (black) people – the lazy, backward whites or the
progressive, fair-minded whites?

Haggard believed in the importance of the literary figure in the effort
to sustain public enthusiasm for empire. In introducing Kipling to the
Anglo-African Writers' Club in May 1898, Haggard predicted the
importance of the younger writer to an imperial war:

Wait till a great war breaks upon us – and I wish that I could say that such an
event was improbable – and then it is when wheat is a hundred shillings a
quarter, and you have tens of thousands of hungry working men, every one of
them with a vote and every one of them clamouring to force the Government of
the day to a peace, however disgraceful, which will relieve their immediate
necessities, then it is, I say, that you will appreciate the value of your Kiplings.[6]

Haggard understood the significance of the literary figure in the ideology of imperialism. Who but a Kipling could convince hungry working
men that the empire was more important than the price of bread?
Nevertheless, when Haggard claimed authority for himself in imperial
debates, it was not as a writer of imperial fiction – it was primarily as an
expert on African affairs. In a letter he wrote to *The Times* on 1 July 1899,
he identified himself thus:

As one of the survivors . . . of those who were concerned in the annexation of
the South African Republic in 1877, as a person who in the observant day of

youth was for six or seven years intimately connected with the Transvaal Boers, and who, for reasons both professional and private, has since that time made their history and proceedings a special study, I venture through your columns at this crisis in African affairs, perhaps the gravest I remember, to make an earnest appeal to my fellow-countrymen.[7]

Haggard invokes his experience in South Africa as well as his "special study" of the Boers to back up his claims to the attention of readers. But it is not only as an African veteran that he appeals; he also makes a modest allusion to his "profession," with which, he can assume, every *Times* reader will be familiar.

In a later letter about the war, Haggard is more direct about the authority of literature; he states, "Within the last year I have addressed the public thrice upon matters connected with the Transvaal."[8] Those three occasions, he notes, were a letter to *The Times*, a speech to the Anglo-African Writers' Club, and the publication of his latest novel, *Swallow, a Tale of the Great Trek*. The three genres work together to influence "the public" to whom Haggard refers, and he weights the novel equally with the others. Perhaps fiction would be taken seriously as a form of public address on political matters of other sorts – certainly literature had intervened in public matters before the Boer War – but the conjunction of speechwriting, history-writing, journalism, and novel-writing we find in Rider Haggard was a combination in which the imaginary and the empirical reinforced each other. Haggard's presentation of himself as an Africanist depends, in the end, as much on his fiction as on his historical and political knowledge. What is curious, however, is the very different versions of the Transvaal presented in Haggard's Boer War fiction and non-fiction.

SWALLOW

Swallow, a Tale of the Great Trek is not at all a tale of the Great Trek, although it does focus on Boers. Only a tiny part of its action-packed plot hinges on the Trek, but, amidst the trials and tribulations of the rather characterless main character, the novel does in fact reinforce a message about Boer resentment of English arrogance. The driving force behind the action is the sexual threat posed by a mixed-race Boer farmer ("Swart Piet") toward a pure Boer girl who is in love with her foster-brother, a shipwrecked Scottish boy raised by her parents after being rescued. The complicated plot involves four generations of the family (including three different women named Suzanne), hairbreadth escapes on horseback, Zulu wars, the Great Trek of the 1830s, and a fair bit of the supernatural. The novel includes sympathetic portraits not only of individual Boers but also of the Boers as a people who had suffered at the hands of the English. The narrator is an old Boer vrouw, who tells us the story of her daughter, who was nick-named "Swallow" by Africans. The sharp-tongued narrator is a strong character but, as Katharine Pearson Woods noted in her *Bookman* review, the story features only one other "sharply outlined" character – Sihamba, the African "doctoress" who is saved by Swallow and then in turn repeatedly rescues Swallow and her lover, then husband, Ralph Kenzie.

Swallow gives a sense of Haggard's understanding of various peoples of southern Africa: Boers, Zulu, "Red Kaffirs," as well as other African peoples. Whereas, as we shall see, Kipling never really got a feel for either Boers or Africans, Haggard, who lived much longer in southern Africa, was adept at sketching the national character attributed to different groups as well as adding variations. The beginning of the novel sympathetically outlines the Boer reactions to the early-nineteenth-century Slagter's Nek incident, when Boer rebels were hanged and then re-hanged by the English after their ropes broke: "Petitions for mercy availed nothing, and these five were tied to a beam like Kaffir dogs yonder at Slagter's Nek, they who had shed the blood of no man" (5). Later the story explains the motives of the trekboers, who left behind British rule and set off beyond the Vaal River to establish a new homeland: "in those times there was no security for us Boers – we were robbed, we were slandered, we were deserted. Our goods were taken and we were not compensated; the Kaffirs stole our herds, and if we resisted them we were tried as murderers; our slaves were freed, and we were cheated of their value, and the word of a black man was accepted before our solemn oath upon the Bible" (228). Such sympathy towards the Boers seems far afield from the sentiments Haggard had expressed in the *South African* on 5 October 1882: "[I]f a Boer were asked to define his idea of a perfect Government, he would reply, "A Government to which it is not necessary to pay taxes'... Where then is the money to come from? Ask the Boer again, and his response will be a ready one – from the natives."[9] With hostilities with the Boers already building in early 1899, a novel sympathetic to them was not particularly well timed; it was published in the same year as Haggard's *The Last Boer War*, which was much less sympathetic. But behind *Swallow*'s romance plot and likeable Boer narrator, the book leaves the reader feeling that British control of southern Africa is inevitable, if perhaps sad for old-style Afrikaners. Vrouw Botmar says,

> to this day I am very angry with my daughter Suzanne, who, for some reason or other, would never say a hard word of the accursed British Government – or listen to one if she could help it.
>
> Yet, to be just, that same Government has ruled us well and fairly, though I could never agree with their manner of dealing with the natives, and our family has grown rich under its shadow. (335)

The more sensible and liberal-minded Suzanne was more pro-British than her mother and her father (whose own father had died at Slagter's Nek). And even Vrouw Botmar herself has to admit that the British have been fair to the Boers, even while being excessively generous to Africans.

In its sentiments about the Boers, *Swallow* is not far from what Olive Schreiner was saying in her essays on the Boers earlier in the 1890s. Both writers romanticized old-fashioned, rural Boers while projecting that the future of southern Africa would be more English. Schreiner tended to make excuses for Boer maltreatment of Africans, while Haggard does not let the Boers off the hook so easily – Haggard's Boers resent that the fair and progressive English government is so extreme that it wants to be fair to "the natives" as well. Schreiner focuses on the South African situation of her day, while Haggard's southern African fiction is set firmly in the past. He resisted *The Times*'s efforts to get him to serve as a war correspondent and decided against writing a series for the *Daily Express* on South Africa after the war, after initially agreeing to do it (Ellis *H. Rider Haggard* 158). Haggard was not going to be drawn into direct analysis of the war itself.

Haggard set his views on the politics of the South African situation before the British public and left it for them to decide. But those views were not simplistic, and the message of *Swallow* is somewhat difficult to reconcile with his non-fictional writings on Boer War South Africa. The Boers of *Swallow* bear little resemblance, for example, to those in the letter Haggard wrote to *The Times* on 1 July 1899: "The average up-country Transvaal Boer ... is more ignorant than the average ante-Board-school English peasant. But to his ignorance he adds much fierce prejudice and a conceit that is colossal."[10] Again we are reminded of Schreiner, who expresses sympathy for the Boers in one place while describing them as backward, prejudiced peasants in another. Both writers would like to see more understanding of South Africa by the British public, but Haggard's view is that only with tight British control can South Africa become an economically and politically successful region. Haggard blames the British government for "many blunders"[11] committed in the administration of areas of southern Africa, and it is there that we can reconcile the politics of *Swallow* with Haggard's other writings. From Slagter's Nek on, British misunderstanding of the Boers had caused resentment and alienation, and resulted in needless confrontation in a region that, in Haggard's view, should have been under strong but humane British control all along. Haggard refuses to go along with the pro-Boers who attribute the move toward war to a defense of mining capitalists, but asserts instead that the war is also important to "our national repute amidst the natives of South Africa," who are "watching very keenly."[12] In his sense of the history of African-imperial relations Haggard was well beyond any other literary figure of the period, and well beyond many political figures as well. As Norman Etherington points out, Haggard understood the nuances of many kinds of relations in the region – *Swallow*, Etherington notes, gives a detailed portrait of the chaos that resulted for small tribes caught in "the crushing" that followed the rise of the Zulu monarchy (*Rider Haggard* 68). This detailed description of the history of Africans in the region, for Etherington, "rather than the fragmentary references to the Great Boer Trek, makes *Swallow* one of the best historical romances to come out of South Africa" (*Rider Haggard* 68). Nevertheless, it is the Boer story that frames all in *Swallow*, and it is unlikely that the forced migration of smaller African tribes was the aspect of the novel to which Haggard was referring when he called *The Times* readers' attention to the story. Haggard presented the story in terms of its relevance to Boer-British relations, with African history relevant insofar as it helped to motivate Boer and British actions.

Swallow ends in the 1880s, with a postscript from the transcriber of the tale, the narrator's great-granddaughter, Suzanne Kenzie. The basic romance of the story has been a South African one, the obstacles to the happiness of a Boer girl and her Scottish lover, but we finish the tale in a castle in Scotland. Suzanne has fallen in love with an English officer called Lord Glenthirsk, who turns out to be descended from the nobleman who wrongfully inherited Ralph Kenzie's title when it was believed that he had died in the Transkei. Together the lovers discover that Suzanne is the rightful heir, and all ends happily with Lord Glenthirsk becoming plain old Ralph Mackenzie and Suzanne Baroness Glenthirsk. This Suzanne and Ralph relive the love of three generations before, although this time it is the woman who ends up with the title and the riches. All is righted, as the title is returned to the correct line, and

Vrouw and Heer Botmar's "sin" in not forcing the first Ralph to return
to Scotland to claim his title is erased.

Swallow's conclusion in Scotland does not detract from the South
Africanness of the main tale, but it does remind readers of the important, indisputable links between Britain and South Africa – even Afrikaner South Africa. Never is this "Tale of the Great Trek" far away
from a Briton or British interests. The final reconciliation is hardly a
straightforward one of Boer and Briton: it links a Scotsman with a
woman who is more British than Boer, born to the second-generation,
half-Scottish Ralph Kenzie and "an Englishwoman of good blood"
(*Swallow* 335). Vrouw Botmar herself is a remnant of the past, and her
great-granddaughter turns out to be no Boer but a Scottish Baroness.
Ultimately Haggard and Schreiner appear to agree that the old Boer,
while admirable in many respects, must give way to a new, Anglicized
South African if South Africa is to progress.

ENTER KIPLING

Rider Haggard stepped away from writing about the political situation
in South Africa once the war started, perhaps feeling that he had set
before the public all that he could contribute on the topic. His friend
Rudyard Kipling, no authority on South Africa but an authority of sorts
on "empire," took a much different approach. The Boer War's intersec-
tion with the New Journalism produced a natural place for Kipling. The
Daily Mail published his sketches from a hospital train and the shame-
lessly sentimental "The Absent-Minded Beggar," *The Times* published
his polemical articles on South Africa, the *Daily Express* his Boer War
fiction, and the army his contributions to the *Bloemfontein Friend*. The
imperial imaginary demanded the participation of empire's prime
spokesperson in this troubling imperial war. But while Kipling produced
much poetry, fiction, and polemic about the war, he was unable to
produce what was in effect being demanded of him from all sides – a
coherent, unified empire.

Edward Said focuses on imperialism's place in the works of "Ruskin,
Tennyson, Meredith, Dickens, Arnold, Thackeray, George Eliot, Carlyle, Mill – in short, the full roster of significant Victorian writers"
(*Culture* 126), and on the ways the British imperial identity affected the
world view of such figures as they came to "identify themselves with this
power" (127) that was imperialism. Significant writers, for Said, are not
the writers being read by the masses in the circulating libraries, such as

the sensation novelists, or in the newspapers and cheap periodicals. Of course, Kipling is included in Said's analysis, for he is the primary cultural figure associated with imperialism. Said notes that "high or official culture," represented by the major writers he lists, nevertheless "managed to escape scrutiny for its role in shaping the imperial dynamic and was mysteriously exempted from analysis whenever the causes, benefits, or evils of imperialism were discussed"; "culture participates in imperialism yet is somehow excused for its role" (128).

Said's assertion that "culture" gets away without blame for British imperialism is evidence of the ways in which both critiques of imperialism and analyses of literature have been severely limited by their working definitions of the relevant terms. As early as 1899, J. A. Hobson explicitly cites the importance of cultural factors for the maintenance of an ideology of imperialism and jingoism, but Said does not consider the critique of Hobson to be a valid critique of "culture" because the culture Hobson analyzes includes the press, the church, and the schools rather than high literature. A focus on culture that means only high culture or only literature can look at Haggard or Kipling or Schreiner or Doyle only in terms of their fiction. But to look at the public discourse of imperialism more broadly is to take in these figures' journalism, speeches, and essays as well as their literature, and to consider their writings as part of an overall cultural support for the imperial project. Public debate about the war relies on a host of discourses of militarism, morality, gender roles, patriotism, and racial categories – discourses that are in use in imperial ideology but that also exist beyond its borders.

Unlike Olive Schreiner, who was his public counterpart on the other side of the Boer War question, Kipling published little non-fiction about the war: just two *Times* articles for the Imperial South Africa Association and a series of four newspaper articles about a hospital train. He did produce fiction and poetry during the war (most notably *Kim*, which he finished early in 1900), yet Kipling, the most important public spokesperson for empire at the turn of the century, was considered to have failed in literature when it came to South Africa. His stories and poems throughout the 1890s had chronicled the empire, stirring British interest and pride in (mostly Eastern) places to which the average Briton would never travel. Because of his association with empire, Kipling's public seems to have felt that he should have been an authority on all aspects of the empire, and in this first large imperial war, Kipling seems to feel an obligation beyond any other literary figure (save perhaps Doyle) to support the war and the troops fighting it.

Eric Stokes, in "Kipling's Imperialism," outlines the varying theories about the "rabid imperialist" phase in Kipling's writing – most critics locate it smack in the middle of the Boer War. Some exempt *Kim* (1901) from the charges, but many agree that Kipling's Boer War fiction and poetry mark the triumph of Kipling the ideologue over Kipling the artist. Kipling's writing on the Boer War, however, cannot be seen strictly in terms of either his own political positions or the "quality" of his literature. His Boer War output must be seen in relation both to the earlier part of his career and to the careers of other writers during that war. While Kipling's writing about the Boer War certainly supports the British side, especially the soldiers who were doing the fighting, most of the writing appears to have been done not out of rabid imperialist sentiment but out of a sense of obligation to the British public and to Tommy Atkins – an obligation that arose from Kipling's place in the public eye. Kipling had become a symbol not of the British Empire but of Britons out in the empire. He was therefore the logical chronicler of the Boer War and of this new South African part of the empire, where he already had a summer home. Given the historical conditions[13] that had produced a Kipling-crazy public at the time of the mass-market newspaper and the climax of the New Imperialism, where else could Kipling have been during the Boer War than writing for newspapers about and in South Africa?

This moment of the popular press and popular imperialism is a moment when new and newly divided publics replaced a more unified concept of the Great British Public. The new halfpenny press reached a different public than that reached by *The Times*, although information was shared between the types of newspapers. The halfpennies arose at the same time as the new spirit governing the book-publishing industry, with the rise of the literary agent and authors' associations, the drive to protect copyright internationally (a movement spear-headed by Kipling), and a new emphasis on advertising. During the Boer War, many aspects of the popular newspapers were drawn into the metaphor of the war: advertisements boasted that Lord Roberts had spelled out "Bovril" (a brand of beef extract) in the British army's troop movements across South Africa; tobacco ads featured British soldiers, the newspapers profiled leading military figures in their new "soft news," or feature sections. The literary world supported the imperialism of the Boer War primarily through the newspapers, the most timely place for publication. Literary figures such as Kipling and Haggard, who had both published in the daily press in the past, were naturally called on to do so again during the war. But where Haggard was seen as a chronicler of South Africa, it was a South Africa of the past. More important would be the support of the present-day chronicler of empire, Kipling. The difference in the roles of Haggard and Kipling during the war is a difference in positioning – Haggard refused requests to write about the war; despite his support of imperial acquisition of the Boer republics, he did not write in service of the war. Kipling, on the other hand, was not seen as a regional writer, a writer of tales of India. Instead he was a writer of empire – perhaps this was so because, unlike Haggard, he did not write exotic romance but poetry and a kind of witty realist fiction (mixed, of course, with romance). At any rate, it was Kipling more than Haggard of whom imperialist fiction in the service of the war was expected, and what Kipling produced must be seen in that context.

Kipling's 1897 "Recessional," sung by 10,000 British soldiers outside the Boer parliament building, the Volksrad, in a victory celebration during the war (Parry *Poetry of Kipling* 79), had reminded Britons, "Lest we forget – lest we forget!"[14], of the moral duty behind imperialism. But that Jubilee poem had disapproved of the very sentiment that Kipling is most often charged with stirring up in his most famous Boer War poem, "The Absent-Minded Beggar." The most unpoetic of Kipling's Boer War verse, by the poet's own admission, "The Absent-Minded Beggar" raised a quarter of a million pounds for the families of soldiers through a fund set up by the *Daily Mail*, which published the poem in October 1899. Kipling admitted to selling his name "for every blessed cent it would fetch" (quoted in Pinney *Letters* 11) by writing the sentimental ballad, which Arthur Sullivan set to music "guaranteed to pull teeth out of barrel organs" (Kipling *Something of Myself* 122), and the poem's music-hall popularity came to symbolize Victorian jingoism:

> He's an absent-minded beggar, but he heard his country call,
>   And his reg'ment didn't need to send to find him!
> He chucked his job and joined it – so the job before us all
>   Is to help the home that Tommy's left behind him!   (458)

The poem is that affectionate chiding Kipling does so well; Tommy Atkins has gone off to war for the sake of his country, but he is "an absent-minded beggar" and can't look after both his country and his family, with "the house-rent falling due" and no wage to pay it. As Ann Parry reminds us in *The Poetry of Rudyard Kipling*, "The Absent-Minded Beggar" was not the simplistic jingoism it is often seen to be (92); it attempts to cross social classes in its appeal for every citizen, rather than simply "killing Kruger with your mouth," to act responsibly and "Pass the hat for your credit's sake,/and pay-pay-pay" (457).

The Boer War, according to Kipling, was poorly directed, and the British soldier was treated badly, both in South Africa and on his return home. Kipling rapped the knuckles of the nation after the peace was signed with "The Lesson," in which he declared:

> It was our fault, and our very great fault, and *not* the judgment of Heaven.
> We made an Army in our own image, on an island nine by seven,
> Which faithfully mirrored its makers' ideals, equipment, and mental
>   attitude –
> And so we got our lesson: and we ought to accept it with gratitude.   (297)

"The Lesson" addresses a serious topic, making something useful out of a long, expensive, and ultimately unrewarding war. Kipling does not make the Boers into the kind of romantic, worthy opponents that Arthur Conan Doyle had constructed; the lesson bestowed by the war is not attributed to the Boers directly. Indeed, the Boers do not appear in the poem at all, although readers knew that it was Boer commando tactics that had stretched the war out for so long. The Boers fought a tenacious guerrilla war, often attacking in small groups and then escaping to attack another day rather than staying around for more standardized, European-style battles. Military critics spent much of the early part of the war trying to convince the War Office to copy the Boer tactic of mounting their riflemen rather than using cavalry with swords and pistols, and footsoldiers with rifles:

> We have spent two hundred million pounds to prove the fact once more,
> That horses are quicker than men afoot, since two and two make four;
> And horses have four legs, and men have two legs, and two into four goes
>   twice,
> And nothing over except our lesson – and very cheap at the price.   (298)

We must learn this lesson as we learned our lessons in school: by rote, by repeating it to ourselves in singsong. "The Lesson" seems simple enough after you have learned it: "two and two make four." But until it is taught, by the Boers or by Kipling, it cannot be learned.

In 1899, the newspapers were the place for teaching lessons to the Great British Public. As Ann Parry notes, "When *The Times* received from Kipling a poem with the note that he required no payment, it was understood that in his view he was speaking on an issue of national importance and an editorial on the same subject usually followed. No other political poet has ever had the means, or sufficient reputation, to appeal to the nation in this way" (*Poetry of Kipling* 80). Kipling's access to the press, and not just to *The Times*, was certainly extreme, but it was by no means unique. Haggard, Doyle, Schreiner, Swinburne, Hardy, and other Victorian literary figures were also publishing letters, articles, and poetry about the Boer War in the dailies.

Certainly, Kipling took his role as public spokesperson for imperialism seriously. As did Doyle and Haggard, he wrote for the daily press and gave pro-empire speeches. And just as his fellow adventure-writers gently chided the nation to take military preparedness more seriously, Kipling, too, berated Britons for insufficient enthusiasm about imperial defense. While Doyle and Haggard wrote letters to the papers and created relatively little stir, however, Kipling put his suggestions in poetry, riling his readers mightily. Many members of the Great British Public felt a bit annoyed, for example, by Kipling's "The Islanders," published in *The Times* on 4 January 1902 (p. 9). It hardly seemed fair to be told by your beloved imperial poet that you were "Idle – openly idle" and that, when it came to soldiers, "Ye set your leisure before their toil and your lusts above their need," valuing "the flannelled fools at the wicket or the muddied oafs at the goals" above those who were willing to die in the service of their country. "The Islanders," an argument for compulsory military service, appeared in *The Times* when Kipling was already on his way back to the Cape for the South African summer (Durbach *Kipling's South Africa* 69). *The Times* leader that accompanied the poem called it a "thrilling trumpet-call" but acknowledged that it was "merciless" and tried to temper its message: "Beneath the poetic flight – and, perhaps, we may say, indeed, the rhetorical exaggeration – of this powerful appeal there is an accent of grave sincerity which harmonizes with the feelings that have, silently but strongly, grown up in the minds of the British people during the past two years" (9). "There is much that touches the conscience of us all," asserted *The Times*, "in the stern and stinging rebuke addressed to his 'Islanders'" (9). The newspaper stopped short of endorsing compulsory military service, however, and argued simply for drilling and training in shooting in the schools.

The poem charged the British public with a number of crimes, including being mindless maffickers unworthy of the men fighting for them ("your strong men cheered in their millions while your striplings went to the war"). The upper-class British scorned the army that defended them, the poem asserts:

Because of your witless learning and your beasts of warren and chase,
Ye grudged your sons to their service and your fields for their camping-place.
Ye forced them glean in the highways the straw for the bricks they brought;
Ye forced them follow in byways the craft that ye never taught.
Ye hampered and hindered and crippled; ye thrust out of sight and away
Those that would serve you for honour and those that served you for pay.

Two letters protesting the sentiments in the poem appeared in the very next issue of *The Times*. Herbert Stephen, while agreeing that "compulsory military service would be an excellent thing," nevertheless felt that the poem's rebuke is "so little deserved that it is more likely to do harm than good." Stephen rendered the poem into prose as "That until the South African War began we, the English, were sunk in sloth, and took no pains to secure military efficiency; that we consequently came near to failure in the war, and should have failed if we had not been able, by 'fawning on' the colonies, to get better men than ourselves to fight for us, whereby we were just saved; that we then turned our attention exclusively to cricket and football."[15] The assessment would accord with much in "The Lesson" and "The Absent-Minded Beggar": all Britons need to take responsibility for the defense of the realm and the empire; preparedness, and perhaps a sense of national duty, is sorely lacking amongst the manhood of England. And Kipling did not reply to such critics as Stephen or W. J. Ford, who wrote to *The Times*, "I, for one, wish to protest most strongly against such an expression as 'flannelled fools,' which has been applied by Mr. Kipling in his poem 'The Islanders' to those who happen to play cricket." Ford went on to cite valorous military officers who were cricketers. Seven letters about the poem followed in the next day's paper, most of them taking up the concept of compulsory military service rather than the language of the poem itself, although "A.A." registered a protest at "the tone and the drift" of the poem. Letters about the poem continued, and on 9 January, football fans came to the rescue of the "muddied oafs." The controversy extended through the entire week's letters columns and into the next week's, with *The Times* on 15 January again addressing the poem and the controversy it had stirred and reiterating its support for Kipling. Clearly "The Islanders" had touched a nerve, and a fair proportion of correspondents expressed a feeling of having been betrayed by their pet poet: "I cannot but think that not a few of his genuine admirers, like myself, will feel sadly that this last cannot, in a healthy state of opinion, add to his reputation."[16] But Kipling had never been a fan of organized sport – the biggest fools and villains in his school stories in *Stalky & Co.* are those associated with football and cricket.

English South Africans and Britons concerned with South African affairs expected more of Kipling than poems chiding the British public. The members of the Anglo-African Writers' Club, whom Kipling addressed in May 1898, at the behest of his friend Rider Haggard, wanted the genius of imperialism to be able to create the entire empire in fiction, not just the Indian portions. "Kipling's South African book is yet to come," said the *African Review*, which reported on the speech.

[T]he sooner it comes the better pleased we shall be. He has been to South Africa twice and he must realise – nay, he does realise – that here is a great country to his hand, waiting to be written about as only he can write. It wants to be written about and it needs a strong writer. There is a fine opening for a young man, and Mr. Kipling is fully qualified to take it.

There are a few South African allusions scattered through [Kipling's] volumes, not many, but quite enough to make us so many Oliver Twists, and make us glad that he has recently been up at Johannesburg and Bulawayo, taking voluminous notes in that wonderful mental note-book of his.[17]

The South African book was never to be; as fond as he was of South Africa, Kipling did not produce literature that addressed the people who lived there. Kipling's South African and British public had to settle, for the most part, for some scattered poetry, a bit of non-fiction, and a few short stories.

By 1899 Kipling was synonymous with empire, thanks to his huge sales, including many cheap railway editions of his works, as well as his public visibility in the newspapers. As Robert H. MacDonald points out, Kipling imitators were everywhere, and "[t]his phenomenon ... is more than a tribute to Kipling's widespread fame; it is evidence of the process by which he became a product of his audience" (*Language of Empire* 148). In 1908, the *Canadian Magazine* noted that Kipling appeared when modernity did – mass education, factories, cities (MacDonald *Language* 149). I would argue, however, that Kipling's modern literary celebrity was not simply literary celebrity, arising from such factors alone; it arose also from the commercialization of publishing and the changes in daily journalism in conjunction with the rise of imperialism. Other popular writers benefited from the new ways of publishing and the new working-class access to literature, not the least of them Conan Doyle. But it was Kipling's association with the promotion of the aims of empire that raised him to such celebrity, with its attendant demands. And it was Kipling's responses to those demands that resulted in his name becoming linked in the twentieth century to an embarrassing working-class jingoism that is traced back to just this particular war, with its Mafeking Night, its Absent-Minded Beggar Fund, and its screaming tabloid headlines.

While Kipling was in South Africa, he responded to the requests for him to write about the war by publishing in the *Daily Mail* in April 1900 a series of four impressionistic articles about his experience on a hospital train; this was the closest he came to acting as a war correspondent for a British paper. The articles are moving, occasionally sentimental, and full of Kipling's trademark finely observed detail about the wounded soldiers and their talk ("He argues impersonally on the advantages of retaining the forefinger of the right hand. Not his forefinger by name, but abstract fore-finger.").[18] The articles describe daily life in the hospital train, including grisly detail about wounds, but they only once venture outside the train itself. That occasion is in the first instalment of the series, in which Kipling reminds his readers of who he really is:

Suddenly we overhauled a train-load of horses, Bhownagar's and Jamnagar's gifts to the war; stolid saices and a sowar or two in charge.
  "Whence dost thou come?"
  "From Bombay, with a Sahib." He looked like a Hyderabadi, but he had taken off most of his clothes.
  "Dost thou know the name of this land?"
  "No."
  "Does thou know whither thou goest?"
  "I do not know."
  "What, then, dost thou do?"
  "I go with my Sahib."
  Great is the East, serene and immutable. We left them feeding and watering as the order was.[19]

The encounter is completely spurious, and its account of a loyal Indian servant is the only mention of non-whites in this series of articles about life in a country peopled mainly by Africans. It is as if Kipling is reminding his readers, "I am of India, and those are the people about whom I can write." This imperial encounter may be emblematic – perhaps, for Kipling, the difficulty of the South African situation is its dissimilarity from the Indian. The peoples of South Africa can have no such strong connection to the English, no fierce, unquestioning loyalty. Empire is not immutable; the East is. Kipling could not produce, for the British or South African readers who seemed desperately to want him to, a single, unified empire in which he could be equally at home in Lahore and Johannesburg.

In late March 1900 Kipling traveled up to Bloemfontein to answer a request from the South African Commander-in-Chief, his special friend Lord Roberts. "Bobs" had asked Kipling to put in some editorial time on the recently captured *Friend of the Free State*, now become a troop newspaper renamed the *Bloemfontein Friend*. During his two weeks at the *Friend*, Kipling was under no pressure to please a British public other than his beloved troops. He was content to write in-jokes and to talk soldier-talk, producing some short pieces of fiction and a couple of poems. Despite the fact that in the Boer War he got his only glimpse of hostile military action, Kipling was unable to achieve what the editors of the *Friend* hoped for when they welcomed him to the paper on 21 March:

> To-day we expect to welcome here in our camp the great poet and writer, who has contributed more than anyone perhaps towards the consolidation of the British Empire . . . He will find encamped round the town not only his friend Tommy Atkins, but the Australian, the Canadian, the New Zealander . . . He will see the man of the soil – the South African Britisher – side by side with his fellow colonist from over the seas. In fact, Bloemfontein will present to him the actual physical fulfillment of what must be one of his dearest hopes – the close union of the various parts of the greatest Empire in the world. His visit, therefore, will have in it something of the triumph of the conqueror – a conqueror who with the force of genius has swept away barriers of distance and boundary, and made a fifth of the globe British, not only in title, but in real sentiment.
>
> We . . . feel, all of us [the correspondents], that his brush alone can do complete justice to the wonderful pictures of war which we have been privileged to see . . . [W]e are hopeful that this fresh meeting of Tommy Atkins and perhaps the only man who rightly understands him will be productive of fresh pictures of the British soldier. (*Bloemfontein Friend* 2)

It was a natural aspiration, that the imperial storyteller would see in South Africa the ultimate imperial story. But Kipling did not produce a body of work on South Africa equivalent to *Soldiers Three*, *Plain Tales from the Hills*, or *Barrack-Room Ballads*.

Although Kipling's Boer War writings are not among his most inspired, the stories directed *to* soldiers are the most interesting of the lot. The "Fables for the Staff" are glib object-lesson tales that reinforce the troops' sense of their own good judgment and of the incompetence of certain of their leaders, especially the ever-maligned Intelligence. After watching the Intelligence Officer make "an unnecessary Omelette" out of "a Nestfull of valuable and informing Eggs" laid by a Boer, a Disinterested Observer observes, "Had you approached this matter in another spirit you might have obtained Valuable Information." The Intelligence Officer pooh-poohs the suggestion. "'But am I not an Intelligent Officer?' said the Intelligence Officer. 'Of that there can be no two opinions,' said the Disinterested Observer. Whereupon he was sent down."[20] The sentiment is familiar: the savvy soldier knows better than the pompous officer. And the medium is perfect. Kipling re-adjusted easily to the task of writing fiction to fill a set number of column inches; after all, it was the method with which he began his career, back in his days on *The Civil and Military Gazette* and *The Pioneer*.

KIPLING, AFRICANS, AND AFRIKANERS

The non-British characters who stand out in Kipling's Boer War fiction are never Boers or Africans – an Indian servant narrates "A Sahib's War," an American gun-maker charms the narrator of "The Captive." The poet who praised "Fuzzy-Wuzzy" and Gunga Din and created such memorable characters as Mahbub Ali, the Muslim horse-dealing spy in *Kim*, was unable to create African characters. The most specific references to Africans in Kipling's South African writings appear in "A Sahib's War" and are spoken by Umr Singh, the dignified, wise Sikh servant who accompanies "Kurban Sahib," a British officer in the Indian Army, in search of some fighting in South Africa. Umr Singh's attitude toward Africans is the only one to which we are treated in Kipling's Boer War writings: "Kurban Sahib appointed me to the command (what a command for me!) of certain woolly ones – *Hubshis* – whose touch and shadow are pollution. They were enormous eaters; sleeping on their bellies; laughing without cause; wholly like animals. Some were called Fingoes, and some, I think, Red Kaffirs, but they were all Kaffirs – filth unspeakable" (92). Kipling's use of an Indian mouthpiece for ideas about Africans points to a discomfort with the topic. While Kipling's Indian works certainly acknowledge ambiguities in colonial rule, they also assume a certain recognizable connection between the British and the Indians. This was not the case in the South Africa Kipling knew – imperial rule had been, as Haggard pointed out, fraught with mistakes in the handling of the Boers, and Africans were a constant source of conflict, as the British worked out the extent to which they were willing to support various African grievances and political and economic aspirations. There were no parallels for the Indian situation, and Kipling did not have Haggard's points of reference or sense of the history of the region.

While Africans appear to have had no culture with which Kipling could engage, neither had Afrikaners. The only Boer presence in Kipling's writing is his particularly nasty portraits of Cape Colony Afrikaners in a speech to the Anglo-African Writers' Club and two articles that appeared in *The Times* and were issued as pamphlets for the Imperial South Africa Association. One of the pamphlets, *The Sin of Witchcraft*, opens with the image of a South African statesman who wore a bright flower in his buttonhole on the day of the Queen's death. Kipling's South African poetry and fiction center on the experience of the Englishman in South Africa. The Boer soldier captured by Private Copper in "The Comprehension of Private Copper" is not even an Afrikaner; he is a disaffected English settler. And despite Kipling's professed love for the landscape of South Africa, many of his South African stories could have been set anywhere. Renee Durbach's thorough study of Kipling in South Africa asserts that Kipling "did not have sufficient understanding of or sympathy for either [South Africa's] Boer or its black inhabitants, nor for their past, to be able to draw inspiration from the country" (*Kipling's South Africa* 89) – Kipling could not see South Africa as a country with a history, or histories, as were India and England (or as Haggard was able to do with southern Africa). Durbach notes that "Kipling himself admitted to his young journalist protégé Stephen Black that he had failed to make literature out of South Africa, though it was his view that a man could not write anything of value about a country unless he had been born there" (89). Of the Boer War stories Kipling published in the *Daily Express* in June and July of 1900, Durbach points out, Kipling himself reprinted only one, "The Way that He Took," in a later collection (59).

Stephen Arata notes that Kipling's Indian literature makes few concessions to the English reader, using untranslated phrases and unexplained local references. "Unlike most male romance texts of the fin de siècle, Kipling's fictions tend not to represent the exotic as imaginatively available for the domestic reader. Instead, what his stories repeatedly show are the circumstances under which the exotic might become available, but only for a select coterie of Anglo-Indians" (*Fictions of Loss* 155). Kipling's South African fiction is not aimed at such a coterie and

employs few local references beyond landscape. The only insider references are military ones – it is almost as if the stories could have been set
in an imperial war anywhere.

"The Comprehension of Private Copper" is the closest Kipling
comes to writing about South Africans themselves. The story attempts
to sketch the disgruntled attitude of a British colonial who has gone over
to the Boers after feeling betrayed when the British granted control of
the Orange Free State to the Boers after the first Boer War. While the
story gives the political and economic reasons for the colonial's defec-
tion, it does not succeed in making the character believable; the story
simply makes a case against British leniency with the Boers. In Kipling,
the history of South Africa is simply a history of British-Boer political
squabbling. Durbach implies that Kipling's Indian fiction attributes a
value to Indian civilization, while Kipling's writing on South Africa
finds no comparable civilization. But Kipling's fiction about the Boer
War is not about South Africa or South Africans; it is about war, and,
even then, not about battles but about soldiers.

Edward Said, disputing assessments of Kipling that declare him to be
in touch with a timeless or essential Indianness, says that "we do not
assume that Kipling's late stories about England or his Boer War tales
are about an essential England or an essential South Africa; rather, we
surmise correctly that Kipling was responding to and in effect imaginatively reformulating his sense of these places at particular moments in
their histories" (*Culture* 162). I would argue, however, that in fact Kipling's Boer War tales differ more significantly from his Indian stories
than Said asserts. It is true that Kipling constructs an "immutable"
India even in his South African writing, as he does in his *Daily Mail*
article about the hospital train. Kipling may, as Said says, deliberately
construct an "essential and unchanging" India. But while, essentialist or
no, Kipling's India was a very detailed, evocative *place*, his South Africa
was not. Kipling's South Africa is indeed historically specific, but it is
specific to only the Boer War; Kipling did not imaginatively reformulate
his sense of the land and people of South Africa in his Boer War stories,
for the stories contain almost no sense of South Africa. "A Sahib's War"
or "The Captive" could be taking place anywhere, except that they
include details specific not to South Africa but to the Boer War –
charges of Boer treachery, or stories of high-ranking British pigheaded-
ness. Neither the characters nor the landscapes of the stories are peculiar to South Africa. Unlike the southern African stories of his friend
Haggard, Kipling's South Africa stories attempt to do *imperial* duty, and

they are evidence that imperial stories are impossible. In fact there is no single, identifiable concept marked "empire."

Sara Suleri, in discussing *Kim*, has written, "If one of the manifestations of the anxiety of empire is a repression of the conflictual model even where economic and political conflict is at its most keenly operative, then Kipling's transcriptions of such evasion point to his acute understanding of the ambivalence with which empire declares its unitary powers" (*Rhetoric of English India* 115). *Kim*, Edward Said argued, featured no conflict of loyalties for the title character because it was clear that to be ruled by England was India's destiny. Suleri, however, points us toward Kipling's irony – the basic "anarchic disempowerment" that lies just below the surface of imperial mechanisms of control (115). If we apply Suleri's construction to Kipling's Boer War writings, we can reexamine what has been described as Kipling's crude jingo support for the war.

Kim, which Kipling finished early in the war, is no happy tale of a benevolent colonialism, despite generations of readers' and critics' desires to read it as such. Indeed, Suleri asserts that the novel provides "an ineradicable example of the futility represented by empire" (*Rhetoric* 125). Kipling's deep familiarity with the workings of colonial administration in India allowed for the moral ambiguity Suleri finds in *Kim* and, in fact, for the narrative complexity that all acknowledge in the novel. But Kipling did not have the luxury of creating a *Kim* out of South Africa. The Boer republics at war with Britain – white nations against white nation – bore little relation to the situation with which Kipling had come of age in India. Nevertheless, public understanding of empire called for the erasure of individual political and economic circumstances for the sake of maintaining a vision of One Empire.

In *Kim*, Kipling transcribes an evasion of the conflict model of empire, according to Suleri, because he sees the empire's declaration of "unitary power" as ambivalent, at best. The model of empire Kipling found in South Africa was quite different from that in India – ill-suited to a narrative of loyalty and service to a benevolent ruling power. *Kim* leaves us with a morally suspect British rule, displayed by the very invisibility of the conflicts everyone knew were there.

It is one thing to create a Kim without moral scruples about working in support of the government that holds in thrall the country he loves. But what could be a South African equivalent? How could Kipling's fiction treat the imposition of imperial rule in white republics? And yet Kipling's various publics were calling for just that. The net result – short stories that contain no moral ambiguity and no South Africanness, polemic that rants, and poetry that angered a good percentage of its readers – pleased few. The public that had constructed Kipling as the laureate of empire had failed to understand the effect of a white-on-white war in laying bare the mechanisms of imperialism in such a way as to prevent a morally astute writer such as Kipling from making workable truly imperial art. And yet, as we shall see, Kipling was able to create a *Kim*-like moral ambiguity in certain of his Boer War poems, when what was at stake was more than empire alone.

In his South African writings, Kipling is unable to create even the illusion of a smoothly functioning unitary power because it is impossible to achieve the repression of the economic and political conflict of the region that Suleri sees in *Kim*. Such conflicts rise to the surface in Kipling's Boer War writing. In one case, this makes for rather screeching polemic, when Kipling's Imperial South Africa Association propaganda simply demonizes Cape Colony Afrikaners. In another case, the conflicts take over the fiction, such as when Kipling in "The Comprehension of Private Copper" ventriloquizes his and Haggard's resentment of Colonial Office policy of leniency after the first Boer War.

Conflicts surface in a productive way in Kipling's Boer War writing in his fables for the troops, written for the *Bloemfontein Friend*. Here Kipling is not attempting to create an image of empire; he is simply talking to his troops, addressing issues internal to the army. He does not need to smooth anything over about the army because the ideological stability of the army is never in question, for Kipling or his readers. What get repressed in that genre of writing are the issues of empire itself, the raison d'être for the war. Perhaps the most complex example in Kipling's Boer War writing of the elision of imperial issues for the purposes of producing a coherent narrative is in certain of Kipling's poems, especially those published in *The Times*. In "The Islanders" and "The Lesson," Kipling speaks to Britain about Britain, in relation not to the empire but to the war. The issues behind the war are unimportant to these poems, in which taking the British to task about their support for the army is more important than trying to flatten the entire empire into a unity. Empire lurks behind those poems, but the poems themselves skirt, rather than deliberately repress (as does *Kim*) the moral issues of empire.

The celebration of empire that is most marked in Kipling's Boer War writing is his portrait of the affection between Colonial troops and their British counterparts. "The Parting of the Columns," for example, starts with a news item from "any newspaper, during the South African War," that describes the cheers of British troops for their Colonial brethren returning home. The glory of empire comes in the acknowledgement by the British to the Colonials that "You 'ad no special call to come, and so you doubled out,/And learned us how to camp and cook an' steal a horse and scout" (467). The Australians and New Zealanders and Canadians were recognized as superior in bush-fighting, and one of the aspects of the Boer War that pleased Kipling the most was the imperial loyalty demonstrated by the Colonies in sending so many crack troops to fight with the British.

Despite some of his poetry's depiction of imperial unity by way of fighting together, the most poignant depiction of the importance of empire in Kipling's Boer War poetry is his portrait of a returned working-class soldier whose affection for Britain has been replaced by an affinity for the new colonies in which he has been fighting. Of all Kipling's Boer War writing, perhaps "Chant-Pagan: English Irregular, Discharged" comes closest to doing what Suleri describes *Kim* as doing: repressing political and economic circumstances to produce a rather ambivalent imperial narrative. The imperial solidarity created by the poem, however, is the solidarity of working-class soldiers, Briton and Boer. The returning soldier who narrates "Chant-Pagan" is a working man, changed by the war. After having "been what I've been" and "gone where I've gone," he is no longer content to "roll[ ] 'is lawns for the Squire,/Me!" (459). This soldier, who "lay down an' got up/Three years with the sky for my roof," turns Kipling's Boer War writing into writing about empire. His experience has made the working-class man see "That the sunshine of England is pale,/And the breezes of England are stale,/An' there's something gone small with the lot" (460) for a man who returns with "five bloomin' bars on my chest" (460) only to have to touch his hat to "the parson an' gentry" (459).

Empire has provided an option for this soldier (as well as for the "'Wilful-Missing': Deserters of the Boer War" of the poem of that name [480]). Empire offers opportunities that are denied this working-class soldier back in England, and the narrator of "Chant-Pagan" contemplates "a sun an' a wind,/and some plains and a mountain be'ind,/An' some graves by a barb-wire fence" (460). The scenery of "Chant-Pagan" is the scenery of war, where stars are navigational aids and skies are discussed in terms of heliographs blinking messages. The poem is not a paean to South Africa but to empire as a refuge, as an opportunity for a man whose sacrifices remain unappreciated in his homeland because of his class but whose experience and talents have value in a place "Where there's neither a road nor a tree /But only my Maker an' me." The narrator decides that back in England "it's 'ard to be'ave as they wish/(Too 'ard, an' a little too soon)" (460). The former enemies are now imperial subjects, and there is "a Dutchman I've fought 'oo might give/Me a job were I ever inclined." So it is worth taking a chance on returning to South Africa, for "I think it will kill me or cure,/So I think I will go there and see./Me!" (461). The poem is an imperial poem in the sense that it idealizes the opportunities provided by the empire, but its scope is limited to the character with which Kipling was the most familiar and comfortable in his Boer War writing: the working-class Tommy. Likewise "The Return: All Arms" features a discharged soldier returning to Hackney, a working-class borough of east London: "Peace is declared, an' I return/To 'Ackneystadt, but not the same" (482). This soldier, too, has been altered by his experience: "I started as a average kid,/I finished as a thinkin' man." The poem is more ambivalent than "Chant-Pagan" about criticizing England, providing the back-handed compliment of a chorus that declares, in italics, "*If England was what England seems,/An' not the England of our dreams,/But only putty, brass, and paint,/'ow quick we'd drop 'er!* But she ain't!" (482, 484). England is not what she seems to the returning soldier: "only putty, brass, and paint"; she is more than that – she is part of an empire. The "makin's of a bloomin' soul" (483, 484) felt by the soldier happened in the recognition that he was part of an empire:

> "An' men from both two 'emispheres
>   Discussin' things of every kind;
> So much more near than I had known,
>   So much more great than I 'ad guessed
> An' me, like all the rest, alone
>   But reachin' out to all the rest!"   (483–84)

The poem has little of South Africa in it, but it has much of empire, in this celebration of imperial fellowship. Still, the poem remains doubtful about working-class life in London: "But now, discharged, I fall away/To do with little things again . . ./Gawd, 'oo knows all I cannot say,/Look after me in Thamesfontein!" (484).

Whereas much of Kipling's Boer War poetry focused so specifically on the soldier and technical details of war that it held no larger imperial resonance ("M.I.: Mounted Infantry of the Line," "Boots," "Columns: Mobile Columns of the Boer War"), the poems of returning soldiers, especially "Chant-Pagan," but also including "The Return," celebrate empire in the context of the working-class man who is ill-served by the mother country. Such poems make a far more complex picture of working-class attitudes to empire than the charges of jingoism leveled against both Kipling and the late-Victorian working classes have allowed for.

The laureate of empire struggled under his image, trying in many different genre to provide what was expected of his art but was ultimately impossible – to flatten the whole of the British empire into a unity. Kipling achieved various things in his South African poetry – he made political and military points about British unpreparedness and indifference to the army ("The Lesson," "The Islanders"), and he celebrated Tommies in various categories and states ("M.I.," "The Married Man: Reservist of the Line"). But it was in poems that recognized the importance of class in relation to empire that Kipling was able to make something approaching imperial art out of the Boer War, art that submerged the many differences that made up the empire in exchange for offering an unproblematic idea of empire as a haven for the soldiers celebrated in his other poetry. In "Chant-Pagan" and "The Return," South Africa offers hope and self-awareness to the working-class soldier from England. The South Africa of those poems is not the South Africa of Kipling's other Boer War works – the specific, Boer War South Africa of individual landscape details that serve only to illustrate points about Tommy Atkins. Instead, the South Africa of the returning soldier poems moves into the abstract and becomes Empire – a free, open place without the obstructions of social class. The indigenous people of South Africa do not appear in Kipling's Boer War writing, to be sure, and Kipling is not doing in South Africa what Said charges him with in India, for it is not an idealized, exoticized South Africa for which his narrators are nostalgic. But neither is it simply the experience of war which they miss. Instead, it is an idealized, essential notion of empire that provides these working-class men with what they need. That this empire does not exist is irrelevant; what matters is that Kipling creates that empire, ignores actual political and economic conditions, and provides an abstraction that distracts readers from some of the real issues of imperialism in order to create a space for working-class British men.

LITERARY FIGURES AND THE WAR

In a letter to the *Westminster Gazette* on 24 March 1900, political philosopher Auberon Herbert asked:

Why is it that in all countries, whenever there is war, or a fair chance of making
war, those most excellent gentlemen who instruct the nation by means of the
Press are the most belligerent and bloodthirsty of us all?... We all know that
literary nerves, like musical nerves, are apt to be in a state of hyper-excitation
and imperfect control; and that the literary brain has always a large share of the
feminine element in it – the perceiver, not the doer. The pleasure that our
literary people give us is due to their keen perceptions and finely-shaded
appreciations; and all this means delicately-strung nerves – it may be paren-
thetically said that this is the reason why women have taken so easily their high
place in literature... So perhaps we ought not be surprised, if our literary
friends "see red" more quickly than others, that they give way to certain fine
frenzies, when the blood is stirred by the wild emotions of war, and that they are
the least able among us to resist the influence of the strong wine. (3)

Herbert's conflation of the "Press" with the "literary" is a fascinating
one, as is his association of the literary with the feminine with the jingo. Is
the press to which he refers the newspaper press, in which his own letter
appears, or is it literary publishing? The letter points up the fact that the
two were the same – overheated literary jingoism often appeared first in
the newspapers. Herbert is responding to literary jingoism like that of
Algernon Swinburne, whose Boer War messages of inspiration, all
published in *The Times*, included a call for England "To scourge these
dogs, agape with jaws afoam,/Down out of life" (292). The equation of
such bloodthirstiness with femininity, with "delicately-strung nerves"
links the high emotion of the jingo with the female-associated phenomenon of hysteria, and the connection serves to discredit female authors,
for whom literary fame, because of their supreme sensitivity, comes
"easily." The critique of literary jingoism on such grounds differs from
that mounted by Robert Buchanan's "The Voice of the Hooligan,"
which also links journalism, imperialism, and literature, but which
focuses on jingoism's "vulgarity" and Kipling's correspondence with it:
"Savage animalism and ignorant vainglory being in the ascendant, he is
hailed at every street-corner and crowned by every newspaper" (243).
Kipling represents popular passion and the sentiment of the everyday
jingo, while Swinburne represents the extremes to which the effete
literary man can be pushed by the emotional demands of war.

The celebrity of the Victorian literary figures with whom this book
has dealt was a celebrity that arose in the specific historical conditions of
late-Victorian imperial Britain. The quality and popular press, propaganda, and government publications together established a public discourse of imperialism in which such writers as Kipling, Haggard, Doyle,
and Schreiner had prominent places that were not available earlier in

imperial history. The positions of literary figures within that discourse were part and parcel of the dependence of the ideology of imperialism on the imaginary, even though the primary contributions of these writers to the Boer War were not imaginative literature.

Other critics have explored the psychoanalytic dimensions of imperial literature[21] and even the psychological implications of imperialism itself.[22] This chapter has aimed to explore the position that emerged for authors in an imperial culture that needed such writers to help sustain its sense of imperial mission. The differences between the individual circumstances of Haggard, Kipling, and the writers examined in the previous two chapters are less important than the fact of their privileged positioning within the public discourse of imperialism at the turn of the century. Arthur Conan Doyle's writings on the Boer War prompted John M. Robertson to write, initially in the *New Age*, then reprinted as a pamphlet, *The Truth About the War: An Open Letter to Dr. A. Conan Doyle*. Robertson points to the problematic nature of the authority vested in the literary figure writing on military matters:

> You avow some diffidence as to your fitness for the task, and you well may. Military men have pronounced you incompetent to discuss operations of war; all men know how you have thought a war to be finished in the middle; and any careful reader of your History could see how little trouble you commonly took either to find facts or to weigh them. But in a country which is in large part content to take its sociology from Mr. Kipling, its morals from Mr. Chamberlain, and its code of statesmanship from Lord Milner, you may, I grant, fairly assume that the study of military causation is in the scope of the creator of Brigadier Gerard, and the imbroglio of a long political strife amenable to the methods which constructed Sherlock Holmes. (3)

The credibility of the literary figure as commentator on empire was clearly not universally granted. Nevertheless, press commentators on imperialism throughout the Boer War emphasized the importance of literary figures in bucking up the nation in support of empire, and on that point I want to return to Edward Said's assertion that culture "was mysteriously exempted from analysis whenever the causes, benefits, or evils of imperialism were discussed" (*Culture* 128). From even before the analysis of Hobson, culture, especially popular culture, has been recognized as inseparable from imperialism. In time of war, the connection is strengthened even further, as the controversy over Kipling's "The Islanders" makes plain.

The Boer War was an imperial war with a difference, fought against a white settler population. Because of this, it was difficult to portray the conflict as a step down the road of civilizing the Dark Continent. But the imperial imaginary played a more important role in the Boer War than it had in any earlier imperial conflict, as the newspaper column inches devoted to literary figures reveal. Imagination was essential to the imperial vision, and creators of imaginative literature had an important voice in imperial public discourse – discourse within which the New Journalism reinforced ideology that was so important to the New Imperialism. But there could be no seamless ideology of imperialism for those writers to reinforce, just as there was no single British public for them to address. The coverage of the siege and relief of Mafeking, of the concentration camps scandal, of the debate about the sexual honor of the British soldier, and Olive Schreiner's working out of racial ideology in relation to South Africa are all occasions during which public discourse reveals deep, structural problems with the gender and racial (and sometimes class) ideologies that functioned within the more all-encompassing political and economic program of British imperialism.

Rider Haggard refused to take the logical step of becoming a propagandist for empire during the Boer War; he wrote letters to *The Times*, published a novel, and reissued his old history of the Transvaal before the war began. Haggard recognized a shift in the way empire was perceived by the British public, and even though he had been a colonial administrator, he for the most part kept his views, military and political, to himself. Kipling, on the other hand, obliged the British public's sense of him as the laureate of empire by jumping into the war effort wholeheartedly, first by writing "The Absent-Minded Beggar," then by writing anti-Afrikaner articles for the Imperial South Africa Association, editing a troop newspaper, and writing "foolish yarns about the war which may or may not do some good" (in Pinney *Letters* 23). Kipling's huge popularity made it natural that the colonial public in South Africa should expect him to write of them, but the racial and political circumstances of South Africa, and his own lack of familiarity with the region, meant that Kipling was unable to engage with the colonial project in South Africa in a straightforward way. As Olive Schreiner's and Rider Haggard's writings make clear, Boer War South Africa was a complicated mix of peoples, but it was more Afrikaner than English and more African than Afrikaner. The Africans were not dependably loyal to Britain, the Boers were an independent and threatening political and economic entity, and the fiction that Kipling produced from the war ended up being more about war than about a unified concept of "South Africa" or, in the end, of "empire." Haggard's South African writing focused on the days of southern African exploration and then stopped; Kipling did not pick up where Haggard left off.

The strains on Haggard and Kipling during the Boer War and their inability or refusal to do the ideological work that was expected of them reflect the changing concept of the public in Britain at the turn of the century. The newspaper press's changing place in "public opinion," as readership extended across class and gender lines, was part of the changing publics for journalism, propaganda, and literature about imperialism. Public discourse about the war revealed, in controversy after controversy, that the new crises about gender, sex, race, and class were creating what Alan Sinfield calls "faultlines" in imperial ideology ("Cultural Materialism" 813). Haggard refuses to address the war, Kipling cannot create a unified cultural sense of empire, Arthur Conan Doyle resorts to historical romancing in the guise of history, and Schreiner cannot pull the public together on the anti-war side because she cannot create racial categories about South Africa that can win the sympathy or approval of the British public. The concentration camps controversy, because it was recognized as a large public scandal when it broke, perhaps represents best the kind of faultlines running through a culture of imperialism at the turn of the century: gender, race, class were all read differently by the different sides of the controversy. All three were contested; none was fully doing the job of supporting imperial ideology because the notion of a single public that supported the imperial project was false. There was no single public, independent of such factors as gender and class, and attempts to address British readers as if they were a single public inevitably resulted in failure, whether such attempts were made by *The Times* or by Haggard or Kipling.

Still, Haggard's and Kipling's inabilities to create a unified British imperialist public are not simply the personal failures of individual literary figures. The positions of Haggard and Kipling during the war, together with the controversies in the press about the concentration camps, the Doyle-Stead debates about the sexual honor of the British soldier, and Schreiner's attempts to construct a new South African race, reflect structural instabilities in the culture of imperialism during the Boer War. The racial categories of Boer and Briton and African Black were in flux; gender roles were being rewritten; and the press was courting and creating new and different publics with wildly different relations to government than those upon which earlier concepts of public opinion had been based. This volume has been concerned not with the economic or national-political manifestations of British imperi-

alism but with imperialism in the public sphere, in its cultural manifestations. Of course the cultural expressions of imperialism, in literature or
in the press, do not exist independent of economics and party politics.
But when we trace the workings of gender, racial, and class politics
within the ideology (or, in the case of the concentration camps, the
direct military applications) of imperialism, we see how dependent Boer
War-era imperialism was on these other, constituent ideologies.

The new popular press contributed greatly to the making of the
variety of publics that took shape at the turn of the century, but so did a
wider range of writing, including pamphlets, histories, periodical articles, and poetry. There existed no single concept of the press nor a
single concept of the public but instead an interaction among many
kinds of discourse and the readers and writers of those discourses, as the
New Journalism developed alongside the New Imperialism. The result
was close to consensus on the idea of imperialism but much less hegemony for the concepts of gender and race that worked as part of that
imperialism.

The Boer War, which lost its place in public memory in Britain after
the more sweeping tragedy of the Great War, still has much to teach us
about the workings of imperialism in an empire that was at the turn of
the century struggling with new understandings about race, about the
identity of "the public," and about gender. The erasure of the Boer War
in British history is not paralleled in South Africa, however, where the
war has an entirely different set of political and social associations, and a
study of the significance of the war in the histories of the two countries
awaits another cultural historian. "The last of the gentlemen's wars"
changed the rules of war, confusing the categories of combatant and
noncombatant, and introducing such concepts as the concentration
camp system and the wholesale burning of farms and personal property.
Public discourse in Britain about the Boer War helped to remake the
public image of war itself. All public writing in Britain about the war had
to work with changing notions of gender and race within an ideology of
imperialism. Whether its medium was Blue-book, newspaper, essay, or
poetry, the public discourse on the Boer War examined in this volume
carries a recognition that not even an imperial war could produce what
was being demanded of public officials, military leaders, and literary
figures alike – a single, coherent, workable notion of a British Empire.

Notes

I   THE WAR AT HOME

1 Although British enthusiasm about imperial events had been rising, especially since the media build-up to the death of Gordon, the street scene on Mafeking Night was an entirely new kind of public expression, as many contemporary commentators, such as T. Wemyss Reid in the *Nineteenth Century*, discussed below, and Rudyard Kipling noted (quoted in Pinney *Letters* 18).

2 For an overview of the mid-Victorian periodical press, see Walter Houghton's "Periodical Literature and the Articulate Classes" (3–27).

3 Kipling to William Alexander Fraser, 22 May 1900, in Pinney *Letters* 18.

4 The war is described as such in J. F. C. Fuller's account of his war experience, *The Last of the Gentlemen's Wars* (1937). Fuller's version was published, of course, well after the First World War had forever altered notions of the "gentleman's war."

5 What Antonio Gramsci describes as a "[t]raditional popular conception of the world – what is unimaginatively called 'instinct,' although it too is in fact a primitive and elementary historical acquisition" *Prison Notebooks* 199.

6 As Christopher Lane has noted of the twentieth century, "we can never disband the colonial project without disengaging the imaginary dimension of imperialism" (*Ruling Passion* 228).

7 For an exploration of the myth of the Victorian military hero, see Graham Dawson, *Soldier Heroes*.

8 Ian McAllan, "XXth Century Men/XVIII – Co. Baden-Powell, in Command of Mafeking," 19 October 1899, p. 4.

9 For more information on Lady Sarah at Mafeking, see Gardner *Mafeking*.

10 See, for example, Tim Jeal's *Baden-Powell*, published in the US as *The Boy-Man*.

11 Comaroff *Mafeking Diary* 20. See also Pakenham *Boer War*, chapter 33.

12 "Mafeking Celebrations" 26 May 1900, p. 6.

13 "Mafeking Celebrations" 26 May 1900, p. 6.

14 "Concertina's Deadly Work in the Trenches/Music as an Adjunct to Sharpshooting" (from our war correspondent), 28 March 1900, p. 5.

15 For more on the complicated image of the Jew in relation to imperialism, see Cheyette *Constructions of "The Jew,"* especially 56.

2 THE CONCENTRATION CAMPS CONTROVERSY AND THE PRESS

1 For an example, see parliamentary coverage of 19 February 1901, recounted in this chapter. See also Brown, *Victorian News and Newspapers*, especially chapter seven, "Handling the News," and Koss, *Rise and Fall of the Political Press*, vol. I, 215.

2 William Haslam Mills, in *The Manchester Guardian: A Century of History*, refers to the Boer War ritual of "giving up the *Guardian*," which was "performed with great pomp and circumstance" "in first-class carriages running into Manchester" (130).

3 Lord Milner to Mrs. Ward (copy), 24 June 1901, Chamberlain Papers JC 13/1/153.

4 Lord Milner to Joseph Chamberlain, 24 June 1901, Chamberlain Papers JC 13/1/154.

5 *The Times*, for example, countered its report of Hobhouse's findings with an attack on Hobhouse from "Reverend" Adrian Hofmeyr, who claimed to have visited numerous camps. The *Daily News* ran a letter from "A Journalist," pointing out the "facts concerning Mr. Hofmeyr," which "entirely discredit any evidence whatsoever coming from such a quarter" (p. 3), and the leader page reminded its readers that Hofmeyr had been dismissed from the ministry of the Dutch Reformed Church for "immorality" years before, though he still credited himself with the title of "Reverend" ("Adrian Hofmeyr Again" 27 June 1901, p. 4). Even J. A. Hobson got into the fray, writing in the *Daily News* on 28 June that *The Times* should have known better than to print Hofmeyr's assertions, since Hobson had had a letter printed in that paper in November 1900 "stating the charge to which you make reference" (p. 3). Hobson also noted that in Hofmeyr's book, *The Story of My Captivity*, Hofmeyr "claimed the distinction of being 'a Times correspondent.'"

6 Joseph Chamberlain to Lord Milner (copy), 5 November 1901, Chamberlain Papers JC 13/1/198.

7 Joseph Chamberlain to Lord Milner (copy), 5 November 1901, Chamberlain Papers JC 13/1/198.

8 Lord Milner to Joseph Chamberlain, 17 January 1901, Chamberlain Papers JC 13/1/118; On 7 February 1901, Chamberlain reassured Milner that there would be no "wobble," "provided that our policy is firm, clear, and consistent, and that in carrying it out we do not raise new questions of a deeply controversial character" (13/1/121). The camps would prove to be the most serious threat Chamberlain would encounter during the war.

9 Lord Milner to Joseph Chamberlain, 7 December 1901, Chamberlain Papers JC 13/1/204.

10 Emily Hobhouse to Lord Ripon, 20 July 1901, Ripon Papers, BM Add. MS. 43,638.
11 Lord Ripon to Kate Courtney, 25 July 1901, Ripon Papers, BM Add MS. 43,638, f. 39.
12 *The Times*, hereafter cited as *T*, 18 January 1901, p. 3; *Daily Mail*, hereafter cited as *DM*, 18 January 1901, p. 5.
13 "Parliament," *T* 19 February 1901, p. 6.
14 *DM* 19 February 1901, p. 5.
15 Herbert Gladstone to Campbell-Bannerman, 15 January 1901, Campbell-Bannerman papers, BM Add. MS. 41,216, ff. 69–72.
16 8 December 1900, p. 4, leader; p. 8, letter, signed K. E. Farrer, F. W. Lawrence.
17 "The South Africa Conciliation Committee," *Daily News*, hereafter cited as *DN*, 19 January 1901, p. 7, signed S. H. Swinny, Secretary, South Africa Conciliation Committee.
18 The first such letter appeared on 20 February 1901, p. 3, headed "South African Women and Children's Distress Fund" and signed K. E. Farrer, Hon. Treas., and Fred. W. Lawrence, Hon. Secty.
19 "Proclamation by Lord Kitchener," *T* 28 December 1900, p. 3.
20 "The Alleged Ill-Treatment of Boer Women," *T* 31 December 1900, p. 13.
21 See also, for example, "The Concentration Camps," *T* 3 March 1901, p. 5.
22 "Rosewater War," *DM* 13 April 1901, p. 4; "War in Earnest," 17 April 1901, p. 4; "War in Earnest," 16 May 1901, p. 4.
23 "War in Earnest," *DM* 17 April 1901, p. 4.
24 See, for example, *T* 2 September 1901, 7 September 1901; *DM* 26 July 1901, p. 4.
25 "A 'Vrouwen Congress' in Cape Colony," (from our own correspondent), dateline Paarl, November 10, appeared 6 December 1900, p. 9.
26 "The Outlook in Cape Colony and Natal – The Army and British Colonists," (from our own correspondent) Capetown, dated 28 November, appeared 18 December 1900, p. 9.
27 *T* 7 February 1901, p. 5.
28 For example, see *T* 27 February 1902, p. 9.
29 "Proclamation by Steyn and De Wet," *T* 22 February 1901, p. 5.
30 "The African Prison Camps/Terrible Rate of Mortality/Deaths at the Johannesburg Racecourse/Details for Two Weeks," *DN* 12 June 1901, p. 5. Two days later, 14 June 1901, p. 4, leader: "The 'Pall Mall Gazette' cavils at our figures on the ground that we deduce an annual rate of mortality from a period of epidemic. But there are, unhappily, conditions of life which produce a permanent state of infection, and therefore of epidemic . . ."
31 According to David Ayerst, in *The Manchester Guardian: Biography of a Newspaper*, Arnold learned Dutch during the war in order to provide the *Guardian* with translations of stories from Dutch newspapers from the Boer side. He was a practicing physician in Manchester and had been the medical spokes-

man on a deputation to the Lord Mayor of Manchester to plead for action on the issue of the camps (285).

32 *DM* 14 June 1901, "Some War Topics," p. 4.

33 *T* 18 June 1901, pp. 6–7; *DM* 18 June 1901, "Pro-Boer Fiasco," p. 5.

34 *T* 18 June 1901, pp. 6–7, 9.

35 *T* 18 June 1901, p. 9.

36 *T* 18 June 1901, p. 9.

37 *DM* 18 June 1901, "On a False Scent Again," p. 4.

38 The untitled leader appeared on p. 5.

39 20 June 1901, p. 5.

40 *T* 20 June 1901, "The Refugee Camps," p. 5.

41 *DM* 18 June 1901, "On a False Scent Again," p. 4.

42 *T* 20 June 1901, "The Refugee Camps," p. 5.

43 *T* 18 November 1901, "The Blue-book on the Refugee Camps," p. 8.

44 *T* 23 November 1901, p. 12.

45 *MG* 18 November 1901, leader, p. 4.

46 22 November 1901, p. 5.

47 19 November 1901, p. 7.

48 *DM* 20 January 1902, "Justifying the Camps," p. 5.

49 *T* 27 July 1901, "The Refugee Camps," p. 7; 22 February 1901, p. 11.

50 *T* 13 December 1901, "Austria-Hungary and the War," p. 3.

51 *DM* 18 May 1901, "Blacks as Guards for Boers," p. 5; *DM* 12 December 1901, "Boer Murders of Kaffirs," p. 5. Examples abound of both these kinds of stories during the war.

52 This is a view that had been, as Peter Warwick points out, sustained through historians' neglect. See Warwick, chapter 1, "Myth of a White Man's War," *Black People and the South African War*, and see also Mohlamme, "Black People in the Boer Republics."

53 See Warwick, chapter 6, "The War in the Cape," *Black People and the South African War*, and Pakenham, *Boer War*, pp. 119–20.

54 *T* 5 November 1901, p. 5.

55 For more on sexualized descriptions of African women by European men in this period, see Sander L. Gilman's "Black Bodies, White Bodies," pp. 223–61.

3 GENDER IDEOLOGY AS MILITARY POLICY –
THE CAMPS, CONTINUED

1 Kitchener to Brodrick, Kitchener Papers, PRO 30/57, 22, f. y/9.

2 The anti-war *Manchester Guardian* had calmly pointed this out in early December 1900 but had not protested. "A 'Vrouwen Congress' in Cape Colony," from our own correspondent, dateline Paarl, 10 November 1900, appeared 6 December 1900, p. 9.

3 Kitchener to Brodrick, 7 March 1901, Kitchener Papers, PRO 30/57, 22, f. y/30.

4 "House of Commons," *T*, 26 February 1901, p. 6. The *Daily News* transcription of the exchange differed in subtle ways. It reported that after Brodrick's "They are not prisoners of war," Dillon asked, "Are they prisoners at all? Are they not guarded by sentries with bayonets?" In addition, where *The Times* reported Ellis being "received with loud Ministerial cries of 'Order,'" on his rising to pursue the issue further, the *Daily News* reported "Ministerial cries of 'Oh' and Opposition cheers," p. 2.

5 "Imperial Parliament," *DN* 26 February 1901, p. 2.

6 Brodrick to Kitchener, Kitchener Papers, PRO 30/57, 22, f. Y/64.

7 "News from the Camps in South Africa," p. 10.

8 Leader, 18 June 1901, p. 7.

9 Brodrick to Kitchener, 26 April 1901, Kitchener Papers, PRO 30/57, 22.

10 Brodrick to Kitchener 4 May 1901, Kitchener Papers, PRO 30/57, 22.

11 Kitchener to Brodrick 9 May 1901, Kitchener Papers PRO 30/57, 22.

12 Brodrick to Kitchener, 11 May 1901, Kitchener Papers, PRO 30/57, 22, f. Y/53.

13 This argument is made by Brodrick in Parliament on 25 February 1901, *T* 26 February 1901, p. 6.

14 "House of Commons," *T* 18 June 1901, p. 6.

15 Leader, *T* 18 June 1901, p. 9.

16 See, for example, Etherington, "The Black Rape Scare."

17 A phenomenon discussed in Gloria T. Hull, Patricia Bell Scott, and Barbara Smith, *All the Women Are White, All the Blacks Are Men, But Some of Us Are Brave: An Anthology of Black Women's Studies.*

18 For more narratives by Boer women, see Hobhouse's *War without Glamour.*

19 "The Native Question," 6 August 1901, p. 5. By no means am I denying that Boers were cruel to Africans. British reporting of Boer maltreatment of Africans, however, especially in the halfpennies, which were not known for their negrophilism, usually focused on the fact that the Africans concerned were "loyal coloured subjects" of the Crown.

20 "Woman – The Enemy," 13 August 1901, p. 4.

21 Ripon to Spender, BM Add. MS 43,638, 22 June 1901.

22 "House of Commons," *T* 19 February 1901, p. 7.

23 Letter from Hobhouse to Lady Hobhouse, 26 January 1901, van Reenen *Hobhouse Letters* 53.

24 27 July 1901, p. 4.

25 21 June 1901, p. 10.

26 *Manchester Guardian* 30 October 1901, p. 6.

27 Rowntree said "The Colonel is evidently a humane man, desirous to act for the best on the limited means allowed him" *DN* "A South African Diary – The Boer Women and Children's Camps – Prisoners of War" (By an Englishman in South Africa) R.M.S., off Durban, 7 February, appeared 25 May 1901, p. 5. Hobhouse's view, expressed in a letter from C. Thomas Dyke Acland, was, "Though many officers in charge of the different places are really kind, and do what they can to help, frequently the women are in

want of almost the absolute necessities of life, *DN* "South African Women and Children's Distress Fund," 22 April 1901, letter from C. Thomas Dyke Acland, Chairman, April 20, 1901, quoting "an eye-witness," Hobhouse.

28 *DN* "South African Women and Children's Distress Fund." 22 April 1901, p. 5.

29 Letter from Hobhouse to Lady Hobhouse, 26 January 1901, van Reenen *Hobhouse Letters* 50.

30 In fact, the group was not officially a Royal Commission but a less official Committee. It was referred to in the press as a Commission, however.

31 Barbara Cain, "Millicent Fawcett: The Question of Liberal Feminism," seminar at the Institute of Historical Research, University of London, 5 February 1988.

32 "The Concentration Camps in South Africa," 4 July 1901, p. 2.

33 Fawcett's South African concentration camp diary, *Diary*, Millicent Fawcett Papers 90B/2, dated 20 July 1901.

34 *Diary* 29, Fawcett Papers 90B/2.

35 It is important to note that turn-of-the-century British studies of infant mortality and child welfare in Britain consistently blame poor and working-class mothers for their infants' deaths and bad health, even while the reports list numerous other factors that could be to blame. Anna Davin notes that the Parliamentary Committee investigating physical deterioration in 1904 made fifty-three recommendations about such environmental conditions as overcrowding, smoke, pollution, and insanitary conditions, as well as recommendations about such other aspects of working-class life as unemployment, lack of child care, and working conditions. But, Davin points out, "overwhelmingly, in the discussion which followed publication of the report, most of that range was ignored. The recommendations which were quoted and endorsed were those concerning the instruction of girls and women in cooking, hygiene, and child care" ("Imperialism and Motherhood" 26). It was much easier to blame the women for being ignorant of proper household skills than to address the social and economic conditions at the root of the problem.

36 Mrs. Arthur Lyttleton to Millicent Fawcett, 28 February 1902, Millicent Fawcett Papers, vol. 2C.

37 Leader discussing "philanthropists's" ideas about the goal of the war, *Manchester Guardian* 19 October 1901, p. 7.

38 See, for example, Davin "Imperial Motherhood" 14.

39 "Boer Women in South Africa and Portugal," 25 March 1902, p. 5.

40 Letter to Lady Hobhouse, 2 August 1902, van Reenen *Hobhouse Letters* 256.

41 Letter to Lady Hobhouse, 21 July 1903, van Reenen *Hobhouse Letters* 240.

42 19 October 1901, p. 7.

43 *Report on the Concentration Camps* Fawcett's personal copy, annotated and with photos affixed. This photo appeared on a page inserted between pp. 136 and 137.

4   CANNIBALS OR KNIGHTS – SEXUAL HONOR IN THE
PROPAGANDA OF ARTHUR CONAN DOYLE AND W. T. STEAD

1 Many critics and historians have addressed the question of Victorian medievalism. See, for example, Alice Chandler's *A Dream of Order* and Mark Girouard's *Return to Camelot*.
2 "The Return," cited from *Rudyard Kipling, Complete Verse: Definitive Edition* (New York: Anchor, 1989), p. 482.
3 For a treatment of the significance of Empire for British male sexuality, see Hyam *Empire and Sexuality*.
4 Campbell-Bannerman Papers, British Library Add. MS 41,235, f. 193, 26 January 1900.
5 *War Against War in South Africa*, hereafter cited as *WAW*, 20 October 1899, p. 5.
6 Of course, the corollary to this was that if a man's honor failed, it was because "a woman's hand" had "brace[d] it loosely" (105). Woman's function was not action or intellectual work but "praise." While woman was to be "protected from all danger and temptation" by man, to stay within her sphere, the home, she was also to blame if her man did not remain honorable in his "rough work in open world" (108).
7 *WAW* January 1900, p. 120.
8 *WAW* 8 December 1899, p. 120.
9 "War Letters," *DN* 18 July 1900, p. 3.
10 The line between boy and man proved difficult for both Doyle and Haggard: Doyle's *The Lost World* is dedicated with a verse: "I have wrought my simple plan/If I give one hour of joy/To the boy who's half a man,/Or the man who's half a boy." And Haggard's *King Solomon's Mines* is dedicated "to all the big and little boys who read it."

5   INTERPRETING SOUTH AFRICA TO BRITAIN –
OLIVE SCHREINER, BOERS, AND AFRICANS

1 See, for example, Monsman *Olive Schreiner's Fiction*, Barash *Olive Schreiner Reader*, Showalter *Literature of their Own*, DuPlessis *Writing Beyond the Ending*, Gilbert and Gubar *No Man's Land*.
2 See, for example, McClintock *Imperial Leather*, Walkowitz *City of Dreadful Delight*, and Bland *Banishing the Beast*.
3 Dubow has pointed out that among historians of South Africa, "liberals" have "den[ied] the existence of any intrinsic relationship between capitalism and apartheid" and "have sought to avert largely justified accusations that English speakers – some of whom formed part of an identifiable South African liberal tradition – played an instrumental role in the formation of segregationist ideas earlier this century" (*Scientific Racism* 4). What is ironic about Schreiner is that although she can be seen as part of that liberal tradition because of her links to evolutionist ideas about Africans, she is

nevertheless significant in her early attention to the absolute connection between capitalism and racial segregation. Preben Kaarshom has called Schreiner's Boer War writing "a historically unique mixture of imperialist ideology (e.g. in the form of evolutionism, racism, and eugenicism) and critique of 'commercial imperialism' as it manifests itself in the war" (*Imperialism and Romantic Anti-Capitalism* 24).

4 For work on the racializing of various white European groups in this period, see, for example, Sander Gilman *Difference and Pathology*. Anne McClintock *Imperial Leather* discusses the racializing of the Irish.

5 Schreiner's journalism has received little critical attention. The best work on Schreiner's essays on race and South Africa is Joyce Avrech Berkman's *The Healing Imagination of Olive Schreiner*.

6 Letter from Schreiner to her brother, W. P. Schreiner, December 1896, in Rive *Olive Schreiner Letters* 299.

7 Schreiner once wrote that when she had an attack and thought she was dying, "the one thought that was with me was 'Peter Halket'" (quoted in First and Scott *Olive Schreiner* 231).

8 Letter to Betty Molteno, 30 July 1899, in Rive *Olive Schreiner Letters* 372.

9 See Dubow *Scientific Racism* and Ranger "Race and Tribe in Southern Africa."

10 Anne McClintock describes the Victorian preoccupation with degeneration and its ties to class and ethnicity in Britain (*Imperial Leather* 46–51), and Saul Dubow outlines twentieth-century South African fears about "poor whites" and degeneracy (*Scientific Racism* 166–180). For more on Victorians and degeneration see Daniel Pick *Faces of Degeneration*.

11 Schreiner had been stung by an article in *Ons Land*, the leading Afrikaner newspaper, which objected to her having used as her example for Boer character the "despised white frontiersman," the backward up-country farmer, rather than the educated town-dweller. Schreiner wrote to her brother Will, then Attorney General of the Cape Colony,

I have just got the copy of *Ons Land* you sent me. The leader fills me with astonishment and I may add pain. How any human creature could so misread such an article ["The Boer"] is difficult for me to understand. I don't think I have ever felt so deeply wounded by any criticism which has been made in the fifteen years I have been writing. It is as though you came to a man's help when a big man was trying to get him down, and he planted you a blow between the eyes! (22 April 1896, in Rive *Olive Schreiner Letters* 273)

Schreiner's defense of the Boer was unpopular in a Britain gearing up for a war over South Africa, and the lack of Afrikaner support for her seemed to leave her without a constituency. She wrote to a friend, "I *did* expect all the English papers to attack me and say I was playing into the hand of the Dutchman, but that the Dutch papers should attack me about it seems to me impossible" (Letter to Mary Sauer, 25 April 1896, in Rive *Olive Schreiner Letters* 274).

12 Schreiner expresses a similar sentiment in her essay, "The Englishman,"

which Cronwright-Schreiner does not date, and which never appeared in print until the 1923 collection.

13 For the influence of Spencer on Schreiner, see, for example, Berkman *Healing Imagination*.

14 See, for example, Greta Jones' discussion of *Social Darwinism and English Thought: The Interaction Between Biological and Social Theory*, Douglas Lorimer's *Colour, Class and the Victorians* and "Theoretical Racism in Late-Victorian Anthropology, 1870–1900," and Nancy Stepan's *The Idea of Race in Science: Great Britain 1800–1960*.

15 See Dubow *Scientific Racism*.

16 For an examination of the ways Britons categorized Africans by racial type throughout the late nineteenth century, see Ranger "Race and Tribe in Southern Africa."

17 Schreiner found herself unable to remain long in London and continually returned to South Africa, especially to the karroo landscape she found so inspirational.

18 Other white writers concerned with the "native question" likewise deplored miscegenation. Schreiner was unusual in her focus on white men's sexual exploitation of black women rather than the spectre of black men raping white women. See, for example, M. J. Farrelly, an advocate of the Supreme Court of Cape Colony, in "Negrophilism in South Africa" in 1902. For more on the uses of the image of black men raping white women see my chapters three and four, as well as Jenny Sharpe *Allegories of Empire* and Brantlinger *Rule of Darkness*.

19 For a thorough discussion of Schreiner as "unique in the comprehensiveness of her critique of social Darwinism," see Berkman, *The Healing Imagination of Olive Schreiner*, chapter three.

6 THE IMPERIAL IMAGINARY – THE PRESS, EMPIRE, AND THE LITERARY FIGURE

1 For a discussion of the divergence of "Literature" from "journalism" at the end of the nineteenth century, see Laurel Brake (*Subjugated Knowledges*), to whom I am indebted for conversations on the richness of the Victorian periodical press.

2 For Swinburne, see Beerbohm ("No. 2 The Pines" 235), and for Ouida see Bigland (*Ouida* 223–36).

3 Many recent studies have examined Haggard's imperial fiction. See, for example, Brantlinger *Rule of Darkness*, Chrisman "Imperial Unconscious?", Gilbert and Gubar *No Man's Land*, Katz *Rider Haggard*, Lane *Ruling Passion*, Low *White Skins/Black Masks*, McClintock *Imperial Leather*. Few have even mentioned his non-fictional contributions to public debate on South Africa.

4 Much valuable work has been done on imperialism and adventure novels; see, for example, Castle *Britannia's Children*, Brantlinger *Rule of Darkness*, Bristow *Empire Boys*, and Green *Dreams of Adventure*.

5 *Times* 26 October 1882 "Colonists and the Mother Country," p. 3.
6 "Mr. Rudyard Kipling at the Anglo African Writers' Club / His Views on South Africa," *African Review* 21 May 1898, p. 312.
7 "The South African Crisis – An Appeal," 1 July 1899, p. 16.
8 "Commandant-General Joubert and Mr. H. Rider Haggard," 8 September 1899, p. 8.
9 "Recent History in the Transvaal," *South African*, 5 October 1882, p. 3.
10 "The South African Crisis – An Appeal," p. 16.
11 "Commandant-General Joubert and Mr. H. Rider Haggard" 8 September 1899, p. 8.
12 *The Times* 1 July 1899 "The South African Crisis – An Appeal," p. 16.
13 These historical conditions of course include the changes in the publishing industry explored by Norman Feltes in *Modes of Production of Victorian Novels* and *Literary Capital and the Late Victorian Novel*, such as new marketing techniques, the formation of authors' associations and authors' use of literary agents, and changes in international copyright law. Feltes points out, in *Literary Capital*, that by Kipling's heyday in the 1890s, "the ideologies of 'literary value' encompassed not only the traditional but the very recent, not only the exceptional but the 'personal' association, not only the 'best' but the accessible or attainable" (63).
14 *Rudyard Kipling, Complete Verse, Definitive Edition* (NY: Anchor, 1989), 327. Unless otherwise cited, all subsequent references to Kipling poetry will be to this edition.
15 *The Times* 6 January 1902, p. 4.
16 15 January 1902, p. 12.
17 "Rudyard Kipling and South Africa," *African Review*, 21 May 1898, p. 313.
18 "With Number Three/No. IV. – By Rudyard Kipling," 25 April 1900, p. 4.
19 "With Number Three – By Rudyard Kipling," 21 April 1900, p. 4.
20 "Fables for the Staff/The Elephant and the Lark's Nest," *Bloemfontein Friend* 26 March 1900, p. 2. From Kipling's personal copy of the newspaper, File 565, British Library.
21 See, for example, Gilbert and Gubar *No Man's Land*, Low *White Skins/Black Masks*, and McClintock *Imperial Leather*.
22 See, for example, Hyam *Empire and Sexuality* and, to an extent, Lane *Ruling Passion*.

Works cited

Allett, John. *New Liberalism: The Political Economy of J. A. Hobson.* University of Toronto Press, 1981.

Amery, L. S. *The Times History of the South African War.* London: *The Times*, 1903.

Arata, Stephen. *Fictions of Loss in the Victorian Fin de Siècle.* Cambridge University Press, 1996.

Ayerst, David. *The Manchester Guardian: Biography of a Newspaper.* Ithaca, N.Y.: Cornell University Press, 1971.

Barash, Carol. *An Olive Schreiner Reader: Writings on Women and South Africa.* London: Pandora, 1987.

Beerbohm, Max. "No. 2 The Pines." In Clyde K. Hyder (ed.), *Swinburne: The Critical Heritage.* London: Routledge, 1970. 233–49.

Beeton, Ridley. *Facets of Olive Schreiner: A Manuscript Sourcebook.* Human Sciences Research Council Publication Series No. 81. Cape Town: Donker, 1987.

Bennett, Tony. "Introduction: Popular Culture and the 'Turn to Gramsci.'" In Tony Bennett, Colin Mercer, and Janet Woollacott (eds.), *Popular Culture and Social Relations.* Milton Keynes, England: Open University Press, 1978.

Berkman, Joyce Avrech. *The Healing Imagination of Olive Schreiner: Beyond South African Colonialism.* Amherst: University of Massachusetts Press, 1989.

Olive Schreiner: Feminism on the Frontier. Monographs in Women's Studies. St. Albans, Vt.: Eden, 1979.

Bigland, Eileen. *Ouida: The Passionate Victorian.* London: Jarrolds, 1950.

Birbalsingh, Frank. "An Interview with Richard Rive." *Southern African Review of Books* 3(3/4) (February/May 1990): 38–39.

Birkenhead, Lord. *Rudyard Kipling.* New York: Random House, 1978.

Bland, Lucy. *Banishing the Beast.* London: Penguin, 1996.

Bolt, Christine. *Victorian Attitudes to Race.* London: Routledge, 1971.

Boggs, Carl. *The Two Revolutions: Antonio Gramsci and the Dilemmas of Western Marxism.* Boston: South End Press, 1984.

Boyce, George. "The Fourth Estate: The Reappraisal of a Concept." In George Boyce, James Curran, and Pauline Wingate (eds.), *Newspaper History from the Seventeenth Century to the Present Day.* Beverly Hills: Sage, 1978. 19–40.

Boyce, George, Curran, James, and Wingate, Pauline (eds.). *Newspaper History from the Seventeenth Century to the Present Day*. Beverly Hills: Sage, 1978.

Brake, Laurel. *Subjugated Knowledges: Journalism, Gender, and Literature*. Macmillan: London, 1994.

Brake, Laurel, Jones, Aled, and Madden, Lionel (eds.). *Investigating Victorian Journalism*. London: Macmillan, 1990.

Brantlinger, Patrick. *Crusoe's Footprint: Cultural Studies in Britain and America*. New York: Routledge, 1990.

    Rule of Darkness: British Literature and Imperialism 1830–1914. Ithaca: Cornell University Press, 1988.

Bristow, Joseph. *Empire Boys: Adventures in a Man's World*. London: Unwin Hyman, 1991.

Brown, Lucy. *Victorian News and Newspapers*. Oxford: Clarendon, 1985.

Buchanan, Robert. "The Voice of the Hooligan." In Roger Lancelyn Green (ed.), *Kipling: The Critical Heritage*. London: Routledge, 1971. 233–49.

Buchanan-Gould, Vera. *Not Without Honour: The Life and Writings of Olive Schreiner*. London: National Book Association, 1948.

Burdett, Carolyn. *The Hidden Motives of Olive Schreiner*. London: Macmillan, forthcoming.

Butler, Judith. "Contingent Foundations: Feminism and the Question of 'Postmodernism.'" In Judith Butler and Joan W. Scott (eds.), *Feminists Theorize the Political*. New York: Routledge, 1992. 3–21.

Carby, Hazel V. "'On the Threshold of Woman's Era': Lynching, Empire, and Sexuality in Black Feminist Theory." In Henry Louis Gates, Jr. (ed.), *"Race," Writing, and Difference*. University of Chicago Press, 1986. 301–28.

Carr, John Dickson. *The Life of Sir Arthur Conan Doyle*. London: John Murray, 1949.

Castle, Kathryn. *Britannia's Children*. Manchester University Press, 1996.

Cecil, Violet. "Female Emigration II: The Needs of South Africa." *Nineteenth Century* 51 (April 1902): 683–92.

Centre for Contemporary Cultural Studies. *The Empire Strikes Back: Race and Racism in 70s Britain*. London: Hutchinson, 1982.

Chandler, Alice. *A Dream of Order: The Medieval Idea in Nineteenth-Century English Literature*. Lincoln: University of Nebraska Press, 1970.

Cheyette, Bryan. *Constructions of "The Jew" in English Literature and Society: Racial Representations, 1875–1945*. Cambridge University Press, 1993.

Chrisman, Laura. "The Imperial Unconscious? Representations of Imperial Discourse." *Critical Quarterly* 32(3) (Autumn 1990): 38–58.

Clarke, Tom. *My Northcliffe Diary*. London: Victor Gollancz, 1931.

Clayton, Cherry, (ed.) *Olive Schreiner*. Southern Africa Literature Series No. 4. Johannesburg: McGraw, 1983.

Comaroff, John. "Prologue." In Sol T. Plaatje, *Mafeking Diary: A Black Man's View of a White Man's War*. John Comaroff (ed.) with Brian Willan and Andrew Reed. Cambridge: Meridor Books, 1990. 15–22.

Cronwright-Schreiner, S. C. *The Letters of Olive Schreiner 1876–1920*. 1924. Pioneers of the Women's Movement Series. Westport, Conn.: Hyperion, 1976.

The Life of Olive Schreiner. Boston: Little, 1924.

Curran, James. "The Press as an Agency of Social Control: An Historical Perspective." In George Boyce, James Curran, and Pauline Wingate (eds.), *Newspaper History from the Seventeenth Century to the Present Day*. Beverly Hills: Sage, 1978. 51–75.

Curtin, Philip. *The Image of Africa: British Ideas and Action, 1780–1850*. Madison: University of Wisconsin Press, 1964.

Darragh, J. T. "The Native Problem in South Africa." *Contemporary Review* 81 (January 1902): 87–102.

Davey, Arthur. *The British Pro-Boers 1877–1902*. Cape Town: Tafelberg, 1978.

David, Deirdre. *Rule Britannia: Women, Empire, and Victorian Writing*. Ithaca: Cornell University Press, 1995.

Davidoff, Leonore, and Hall, Catherine. *Family Fortunes: Men and Women of the English Middle Class, 1780–1850*. University of Chicago Press, 1987.

Davin, Anna. "Imperialism and Motherhood." *History Workshop* 6 (Spring 1978): 9–65.

Dawson, Carl, and Pfordresher, John. *Matthew Arnold, Prose Writings: The Critical Heritage*. London: Routledge, 1979.

Dawson, Graham. *Soldier Heroes: British Adventure, Empire and the Imagining of Masculinities*. London: Routledge, 1994.

Doyle, Adrian Conan (ed.). *Sir Arthur Conan Doyle Centenary, 1859–1959*. London: John Murray, 1959.

Doyle, Arthur Conan. "The Doctors of Hoyland." In *Round the Red Lamp*. London: Methuen, 1894. 294–315.

The Great Boer War. 1900. Anglo-Boer War Reprint Library Vol. 1. Cape Town: C. Struik, 1976.

The Great Boer War. Complete Edition. London: Smith, Elder, 1902.

"An Incursion into Diplomacy." *Cornhill Magazine* 58 (June 1906): 744–54.

The Lost World. Oxford University Press, 1995.

Memories and Adventures. 1924. London: Greenhill, 1988.

Micah Clarke. London: Longmans, 1889.

The White Company. London: Smith, Elder, 1891.

The War in South Africa, Its Cause and Conduct. New York: McClure, Phillips, 1902.

The War in South Africa, Its Cause and Conduct. New Edition. London: Smith, Elder, 1902.

Dubow, Saul. *Scientific Racism in Modern South Africa*. Cambridge University Press, 1995.

DuPlessis, Rachel Blau. *Writing Beyond the Ending: Narrative Strategies of Twentieth-century Women Writers*. Bloomington: Indiana University Press, 1985.

Durbach, Renee. *Kipling's South Africa*. Plumstead, South Africa: Chameleon, 1988.

Eby, Cecil Degrotte. *The Road to Armageddon: The Martial Spirit in English Popular Literature*. Durham, N.C.: Duke University Press, 1988.

Eley, Geoff. "Nations, Publics, and Political Cultures: Placing Habermas in the Nineteenth Century." In Nicholas B. Dirks, Geoff Eley, and Sherry B. Ortner (eds.), *Culture/Power/History: A Reader in Contemporary Social Theory*. Princeton University Press, 1994.

Ellis, Peter Berresford. *H. Rider Haggard, a Voice from the Infinite*. London: Routledge, 1978.

Elshtain, Jean Bethke. *Women and War*. New York: Basic Books, 1987.

Ensor, R. C. K. *England, 1870–1914*. Oxford: Clarendon, 1936.

Etherington, Norman. "The Black Rape Scare of the 1870s." *Journal of Southern African Studies* 15 (October 1988): 36–53.

Rider Haggard. Boston: Twayne, 1984.

Farrelly, M. J. "Negrophilism in South Africa." *Fortnightly Review* 78 (1902): 301–08.

Fawcett, Millicent Garrett. *What I Remember*. New York: Putnam, 1925.

Report on the Concentration Camps in South Africa by the Committee of Ladies Appointed by the Secretary of State for War; Containing Reports on the Camps in Natal, the Orange River Colony, and the Transvaal. London: HMSO 1202, 1902, Cd. 893.

Feltes, N. N. *Literary Capital and the Late Victorian Novel*. Madison: University of Wisconsin Press, 1993.

First, Ruth, and Scott, Ann. *Olive Schreiner*. New York: Schocken, 1980.

Olive Schreiner. London: Women's Press, 1989.

Friedmann, Marion V. *Olive Schreiner: A Study in Latent Meanings*. Johannesburg: Witwatersrand University Press, 1955.

Fuller, J. F. C. *The Last of the Gentlemen's Wars: A Subaltern's Journal of the War in South Africa 1899–1902*. London: Faber, 1937.

Gagnier, Regenia. *Subjectivities: A History of Self-Representation in Britain, 1832–1920*. New York: Oxford University Press, 1991.

Gardner, Brian. *Mafeking: A Victorian Legend*. New York: Harcourt, 1966.

Garrett, Edmund F. "The Inevitable in South Africa." *Contemporary Review* 77 (October 1899): 457–81.

Garrison, William Lloyd. "Preface." *Narrative of the Life of Frederick Douglass, an American Slave, Written by Himself*. New York: Signet, 1968.

Gates, Henry Louis, Jr. "Introduction: Writing 'Race' and the Difference It Makes." *"Race," Writing, and Difference*. University of Chicago Press, 1986. 1–20.

Gibson, John Michael, and Green, Roger Lancelyn (comp.). *The Unknown Conan Doyle: Letters to the Press*. London: Secker and Warburg, 1986.

Gilbert, Sandra M., and Gubar, Susan. *No Man's Land: The Place of the Woman Writer in the Twentieth Century. Vol. 2: Sexchanges*. New Haven: Yale University Press, 1988.

Gilman, Sander. "Black Bodies, White Bodies: Toward an Iconography of Female Sexuality in Late Nineteenth-Century Art, Medicine, and Literature." In Henry Louis Gates, Jr. (ed.), *"Race," Writing, and Difference*. University of Chicago Press, 1986. 223–61.

Difference and Pathology. Ithaca: Cornell University Press, 1985.

Girouard, Mark. *The Return to Camelot: Chivalry and the English Gentleman.* New Haven: Yale University Press, 1981.

Gordimer, Nadine. "Introduction." In Ruth First and Ann Scott, *Olive Schreiner.* London: The Women's Press, 1989.

Gramsci, Antonio. *Selections from Prison Notebooks.* London: Lawrence and Wishart, 1986.

Green, Martin. *Dreams of Adventure, Deeds of Empire.* London: Routledge, 1980.

Green, Roger Lancelyn. *Kipling: The Critical Heritage.* London: Routledge, 1971.

Gunn, J. A. W. *Beyond Liberty and Property: The Process of Self-Recognition in Eighteenth-Century Political Thought.* Kingston, Canada: McGill-Queen's University Press, 1983.

Haggard, H. Rider. *King Solomon's Mines.* 1885. Oxford University Press, 1991.
The Days of My Life: An Autobiography. London: Longmans, 1926.
The Last Boer War. London: Kegan Paul, Trench, Trübner, & Co., 1900.
Swallow, A Tale of the Great Trek. London: Longman, 1899.
Cetywayo and His White Neighbours: Or, Remarks on Recent Events in Zululand, Natal and Transvaal. London: Trübner, 1882.

Hall, Catherine. "Competing Masculinities: Thomas Carlyle, John Stuart Mill, and the Case of Governor Eyre." *White, Male, and Middle-Class: Explorations in Feminism and History.* London: Routledge, 1992. 255–95.

Hall, Stuart. "Race, Articulation, and Societies Structured in Dominance." In UNESCO, *Sociological Theories: Race and Colonialism.* Paris: UNESCO, 1980. 305–46.

Hall, Stuart, and Schwartz, Bill. "The Crisis in Liberalism." In Stuart Hall, *The Hard Road to Renewal: Thatcherism and the Crisis of the Left.* London: Verso, 1988.

Hamilton, J. Angus. *The Siege of Mafeking.* London: Methuen, 1900.

Harris, Michael, and Lee, Alan (eds.). *The Press in English Society from the 17th to 19th Centuries.* Rutherford, N.J.: Fairleigh Dickinson University Press, 1986.

Headlam, Cecil (ed.). *The Milner Papers.* London: Cassell, 1931–1933.

Hennessy, Rosemary, and Mohan, Rajeswari. "The Construction of Woman in Three Popular Texts of Empire: Towards a Critique of Materialist Feminism." *Textual Practice* 3(3)(Winter 1989): 323–59.

Herd, Harold. *The March of Journalism: The Story of the British Press from 1622 to the Present Day.* London: Allen, 1952.

Hobhouse, Emily. *The Brunt of the War and Where It Fell.* London: Methuen, 1902.
Report of a Visit to the Camps of Women and Children in the Cape and Orange River Colonies. London: Friars, [1902].
War Without Glamour: Women's War Experiences Written by Themselves, 1899–1902. Bloemfontein: Nasionale Pers Beperk, 1924.

Hobsbawm, Eric. *Nations and Nationalism Since 1780: Programme, Myth, Reality.* Cambridge University Press, 1991.

Hobson, J. A. *Confessions of an Economic Heretic: The Autobiography of J. A. Hobson.* 1938. Hamden, Conn: Anchor, 1976.

The Evolution of Modern Capitalism: A Study of Machine Production. New York: Scribner's, 1902.

Imperialism: A Study. New York: Pott, 1902.

The Psychology of Jingoism. London: Richards, 1901.

The War in South Africa: Its Causes and Effects. New York: Macmillan, 1900.

Hofmeyr, Adrian. *The Story of My Captivity During the Transvaal War 1899–1900.* London: Arnold, 1900.

Houghton, Walter. *The Victorian Frame of Mind, 1830–1870.* New Haven: Yale University Press, 1957.

"Periodical Literature and the Articulate Classes." *The Victorian Periodical Press: Samplings and Soundings.* Leicester University Press, 1982. 3–27.

Huebner, Count. "Appendix." In Arthur Conan Doyle, *The War in South Africa: Its Cause and Conduct.* Bernhard Tauchnitz: Leipzig, 1902. 270–71.

Hull, Gloria, Scott, Patricia, and Smith, Barbara (eds.). *All the Women Are White, All the Blacks Are Men, But Some of Us Are Brave: An Anthology of Black Women's Studies.* Old Westbury, N.Y.: Feminist Press, 1982.

Husband, Charles. "Introduction: 'Race,' the Continuity of a Concept." *"Race" in Britain: Continuity and Change.* London: Hutchinson, 1982. 11–23.

Hyam, Ronald. *Empire and Sexuality.* Manchester University Press, 1991.

Hyder, Clyde K. (ed.). *Swinburne: The Critical Heritage.* London: Routledge, 1970.

Jaffe, Jacqueline. *Arthur Conan Doyle.* Twayne's English Author Series. Boston: Twayne, 1987.

Jeal, Tim. *Baden-Powell.* London: Pimlico, 1991.

Jones, Greta. *Social Darwinism and English Thought: The Interaction Between Biological and Social Theory.* Sussex: Harvester, 1980.

Jordan, Winthrop. *White over Black: American Attitudes Toward the Negro, 1550–1812.* Chapel Hill: University of North Carolina Press, 1968.

Judd, Denis. *The Boer War.* London: Hart-Davis, 1977.

Kaarsholm, Preben. *Imperialism and Romantic Anti-Capitalism: Four Papers on Culture and Ideology c. 1900.* Kultur og Samfund 1/83, Institut VI, Roskilde Universitetscenter, 1983.

Katz, Wendy. *Rider Haggard and the Fiction of Empire: A Critical Study of British Imperial Fiction.* Cambridge University Press, 1987.

Kipling, Rudyard. *The Complete Verse. Definitive Edition.* New York: Anchor, 1989.

The Sin of Witchcraft. London: Imperial South Africa Association, 1899.

Something of Myself: For My Friends Known and Unknown. London: Penguin, 1987.

The Writings in Prose and Verse of Rudyard Kipling. New York: Scribner, 1899, 1907–1926.

Kitchin, F. Harcourt. *The London "Times" Under the Managership of Moberly Bell: An Unofficial Narrative.* New York: Putnam, 1925.

Koss, Stephen. *The Rise and Fall of the Political Press in Britain. Vol. 1, The Nineteenth Century.* London: Hamilton, 1981.

Koss, Stephen (ed.). *The Pro-Boers: The Anatomy of an Antiwar Movement.* Chicago: University of Chicago Press, 1973.

Kruger, Rayne. *Good-bye Dolly Gray: The Story of the Boer War.* Philadelphia: Lippincott, 1960.

Lake, Brian. *British Newspapers: A History and Guide for Collectors.* London: Sheppard Press, 1984.

Lane, Christopher. *The Ruling Passion: British Colonial Allegory and the Paradox of Homosexual Desire.* Durham, N.C.: Duke University Press, 1995.

Lawrence, Errol. "Just Plain Common Sense: The Roots of Racism." In Centre for Contemporary Cultural Studies (ed.), *The Empire Strikes Back: Race and Racism in 70s Britain.* London: Hutchinson, 1982. 47–94.

Le Bon, Gustave. *The Psychology of Peoples.* New York: Macmillan, 1898.

Lee, Alan J. *Origins of the Popular Press 1855–1914.* London: Croom Helm, 1976.

Lellenberg, Jon L. (ed.). *The Quest for Sir Arthur Conan Doyle: Thirteen Biographers in Search of a Life.* Carbondale: Southern Illinois University Press, 1987.

Lenin, V. I. *Imperialism: The Highest Stage of Capitalism.* 1916. Peking: Foreign Languages Press, 1975.

Lenta, Margaret. "Racism, Sexism, and Olive Schreiner's Fiction." *Theoria* 70 (October 1987): 15–30.

Lippmann, Walter. *Public Opinion.* New York: Macmillan, 1965.

Lorimer, Douglas A. *Colour, Class, and the Victorians.* Leicester University Press, 1978.

"Theoretical Racism in Late-Victorian Anthropology, 1870–1900." *Victorian Studies* 31(3) (Spring 1988): 405–30.

Low, Gail Ching-Liang. *White Skins/Black Masks: Representation and Colonialism.* London: Routledge, 1996.

MacDonald, Robert H. *The Language of Empire: Myths and Metaphors of Popular Imperialism, 1880–1918.* Manchester University Press, 1994.

Macdonell, John. "The Question of the Native Races in South Africa." *Nineteenth Century and After* 49 (February 1901): 367–76.

MacKenzie, John M. *Propaganda and Empire: The Manipulation of British Public Opinion, 1880–1960.* Manchester University Press, 1984.

MacKenzie, John M. (ed.). *Imperialism and Popular Culture.* Manchester University Press, 1986.

McClelland, J. S. *The Crowd and the Mob: From Plato to Canetti.* London: Unwin Hyman, 1989.

McClintock, Anne. *Imperial Leather: Race, Gender and Sexuality in the Colonial Contest.* New York: Routledge, 1995.

Mills, William Haslam. *The Manchester Guardian: A Century of History.* London: Chatto and Windus, 1921.

Moers, Ellen. *Literary Women.* Garden City, N.Y.: Doubleday, 1976.

Mohlamme, Jacob Saul. "Black People in the Boer Republics During and in the Aftermath of the South African War of 1899–1902." Ph.D. Diss. University of Wisconsin-Madison, 1985.

Monsman, Gerald. *Olive Schreiner's Fiction: Landscape and Power.* New Brunswick, N.J.: Rutgers University Press, 1991.

Neilly, J. Emerson. *Besieged with B.-P.: Complete Record of the Siege and Relief of Mafeking.* London: Pearson, 1900.

Odendaal, Andre. *Vukani Bantu! The Beginnings of Black Protest Politics in South Africa to 1912.* Cape Town: David Philip, 1984.

Pakenham, Thomas. *The Boer War.* New York: Random House, 1979.

Palmer, Michael. "The British Press and International News, 1851–99: Of Agencies and Newspapers." In George Boyce, James Curran, and Pauline Wingate (eds.), *Newspaper History from the Seventeenth Century to the Present Day.* Beverly Hills: Sage, 1978. 205–19.

Parry, Ann. *The Poetry of Rudyard Kipling: Rousing the Nation.* Buckingham: Open University Press, 1992.

Phillips, Richard. *Mapping Men and Empire.* London: Routledge, 1997.

Pick, Daniel. *Faces of Degeneration: A European Disorder, c. 1848–c.1918.* Cambridge University Press, 1989.

Pinney, Thomas (ed.). *The Letters of Rudyard Kipling, Vol. III, 1900–1910.* University of Iowa Press, 1996.

Plaatje, Sol. T. *Mafeking Diary: A Black Man's View of a White Man's War.* Cambridge, England: Meridor, 1990.

Porter, A. N. *The Origins of the South African War: Joseph Chamberlain and the Diplomacy of Imperialism, 1895–99.* New York: St. Martin's, 1980.

Porter, Bernard. *Critics of Empire: British Radical Attitudes to Colonialism in Africa 1895–1914.* London: Macmillan, 1968.

Poovey, Mary. "The Abortion Question and the Death of Man." In Judith Butler and Joan W. Scott (eds.), *Feminists Theorize the Political.* New York: Routledge, 1992. 239–56.

Uneven Developments: The Ideological Work of Gender in Mid-Victorian England. University of Chicago Press, 1988.

Price, Richard. *An Imperial War and the British Working Class: Working-Class Attitudes and Reactions to the Boer War, 1899–1902.* Studies in Social History. London: Routledge, 1972.

Pykett, Lyn. "Reading the Periodical Press: Text and Context." In Laurel Brake, Aled Jones, and Lionel Madden (eds.), *Investigating Victorian Journalism.* London: Macmillan, 1990. 3–18.

Ranger, T. O. "Race and Tribe in Southern Africa: European Ideas and African Acceptance." In Robert Ross (ed.), *Racism and Colonialism.* The Hague: Martinus Nijhoff, 1982. 121–42.

Read, Donald. *The Age of Urban Democracy: England 1868–1914.* Rev. edn. London: Longmans, 1994.

Rive, Richard (ed.). *Olive Schreiner Letters 1871–1899.* Cape Town: David Philip, 1987.

Robertson, John M. *The Truth About the War: An Open Letter to Dr. A. Conan Doyle.* London: New Age Press, 1902.

Ross, Edward. *Diary of the Siege of Mafeking October 1899 to May 1900.* Ed. Brian P.

Willan. Cape Town: Van Riebeeck Society, 1980.

Ruskin, John. "Of Queen's Gardens." *Sesame and Lilies*. 1865. London: George Allen, 1902. 87–143.

Said, Edward. *Culture and Imperialism*. London: Chatto, 1993.

Schottler, Peter. "Historians and Discourse Analysis." *History Workshop Journal* 27 (Spring 1989): 37–65.

Schreiner, Olive. *An English-South African's View of the Situation*. London: Hodder and Stoughton, 1899.

Closer Union: A Letter on the South African Union and the Principles of Government. London: Fiefield, 1909.

Woman and Labour. London: Unwin, 1911.

From Man to Man. 1927. Chicago: Cassandra-Academy, 1977.

The Story of an African Farm. 1883. New York: Schocken, 1976.

Thoughts on South Africa. 1923. Johannesburg: Africana Book Society, Africana Reprint Library Vol. X, 1976.

Trooper Peter Halket of Mashonaland. 1897. Johannesburg: Donker, 1974.

Schreiner, Olive, and Cronwright-Schreiner, C. S. (sic). *The Political Situation*. London: Unwin, 1896.

Scott, Joan Wallach. *Gender and the Politics of History*. New York: Columbia University Press, 1988.

Sedgwick, Eve Kosofsky. *Between Men: English Literature and Male Homosocial Desire*. New York: Columbia University Press, 1985.

Sharpe, Jenny. *Allegories of Empire*. Minneapolis: University of Minnesota Press, 1993.

Shattock, Joanne, and Wolff, Michael. "Introduction." *The Victorian Periodical Press: Samplings and Soundings*. Leicester University Press, 1982. xiii–xix.

Showalter, Elaine. *A Literature of their Own: British Women Novelists from Bronte to Lessing*. Princeton University Press, 1977.

Simons, Jack, and Simons, Ray. *Class and Colour in South Africa 1850–1950*. London: International Defence and Aid Fund for Southern Africa, 1983.

Sinfield, Alan. "Cultural Materialism, *Othello*, and the Politics of Plausibility." In Julie Rivkin and Michael Ryan (eds.), *Literary Theory: An Anthology*. Malden, Mass.: Blackwell, 1998. 804–26.

Smith, Iain. *The Origins of the South African War, 1899–1902*. Origins of Modern Wars. London: Longman, 1996.

Solomos, John, Findlay, Bob, Jones, Simon, and Gilroy, Paul. "The Organic Crisis of British Capitalism and Race: The Experience of the Seventies." In Centre for Contemporary Cultural Studies, *The Empire Strikes Back: Race and Racism in 70s Britain*. London: Hutchinson, 1982. 9–46.

Spies, S. B. *Methods of Barbarism? Roberts and Kitchener and Civilians in the Boer Republics, January 1900–May 1902*. Cape Town: Human and Rousseau, 1977.

The Origins of the Anglo-Boer War. The Archive Series. London: Arnold, 1972.

Spivak, Gayatri Chakravorty. *In Other Worlds: Essays in Cultural Politics*. New York: Methuen, 1987.

Stead, W. T. *Shall I Slay My Brother Boer?* London: Review of Reviews, 1899.
  The Truth about the War. London: Review of Reviews, 1900.
  How Not to Make Peace. London: Review of Reviews, 1900.
  Methods of Barbarism. London: Review of Reviews, 1901.
Stead, W. T. (ed.). *War Against War in South Africa.* 20 October 1899–26 January
  1900. London: Review of Reviews (BL P.P. 3610.f.).
Stepan, Nancy. *The Idea of Race in Science: Great Britain 1800–1960.* London:
  Macmillan, 1982.
Stirling, Monica. *The Fine and the Wicked: The Life and Times of Ouida.* London:
  Victor Gollancz, 1957.
Stokes, Eric. "Kipling's Imperialism." In John Gross (ed.), *Rudyard Kipling: The
  Man, His Work, and His World.* London: Weidenfield and Nicolson, 1972.
  90–8.
Storey, Graham. *Reuters: The Story of a Century of News Gathering.* New York:
  Crown, 1951.
Suleri, Sara. *The Rhetoric of English India.* University of Chicago Press, 1992.
Sussman, Herbert. *Victorian Masculinities.* Cambridge University Press, 1994.
Swinburne, Algernon. *The Complete Works of Algernon Charles Swinburne Vol. VI.*
  Bonchurch edition. Ed. Edmund Gosse and Thomas James Wise. Lon-
  don: Heinemann, 1925.
Symons, Julian. *Conan Doyle: Portrait of an Artist.* New York: Mysterious Press,
  1979.
Thompson, Leonard. *The Political Mythology of Apartheid.* New Haven: Yale
  University Press, 1985.
Thornton, A. P. *The Imperial Idea and Its Enemies: A Study in British Power.* London:
  Macmillan, 1959.
UNESCO. *Sociological Theories: Race and Colonialism.* Paris: UNESCO, 1980.
van den Boogaart, Ernst. "Colour Prejudice and the Yardstick of Civility: The
  Initial Dutch Confrontation with Black Africans, 1590–1635." In Robert
  Ross (ed.), *Racism and Colonialism.* The Hague: Martinus Nijhoff, 1982.
  33–54.
van Reenen, Rykie (ed.). *Emily Hobhouse's Boer War Letters.* Cape Town: Human
  and Rousseau, 1984.
Van Wyk Smith, M. *Drummer Hodge: The Poetry of the Anglo-Boer War (1899–1902).*
  Oxford: Clarendon, 1978.
Wahrman, Dror. *Imagining the Middle Class: The Political Representation of Class in
  Britain, c. 1780–1840.* Cambridge University Press, 1995.
Walkowitz, Judith. *City of Dreadful Delight: Narratives of Sexual Danger in Late
  Victorian London.* University of Chicago Press, 1992.
  Prostitution and Victorian Society: Women, Class, and the State. New York: Cam-
  bridge University Press, 1980.
Wallace, Edgar. *The Four Just Men.* New York: Dover, 1984.
Walvin, James. *Black and White: A Study of the Negro in English Society 1555–1945.*
  London: Allen Lane, 1973.

Warwick, Peter. *Black People and the South African War, 1899–1902.* African Studies Series No. 40. Cambridge University Press, 1983.

Warwick, Peter (general ed.), Warwick, Peter and Spies, S. B. (advisory ed.). *The South African War: The Anglo-Boer War 1899–1902.* London: Longmans, 1980.

Willan, Brian. *Sol Plaatje, African Nationalist 1876–1932.* London: Heinemann, 1984.

Williams, Raymond. *Problems in Materialism and Culture.* London: Verso, 1980.

"The Press and Popular Culture: An Historical Perspective." In George Boyce, James Curran, and Pauline Wingate (eds.), *Newspaper History from the Seventeenth Century to the Present Day.* Beverly Hills: Sage, 1978. 41–50.

Wilson, Angus. *The Strange Ride of Rudyard Kipling: His Life and Works.* London: Secker and Warburg, 1977.

Wilson, C. Usher. "A Situation in South Africa: A Voice from the Cape Colony." *Nineteenth Century* 46 (November 1899): 521–26.

Winks, Robin (ed.). *The Historiography of the British Empire-Commonwealth; Trends, Interpretations, and Resources.* Durham, N.C.: Duke University Press, 1966.

Wirgman, A. Theodore. "The Boers and the Native Question." *Nineteenth Century* 47 (April 1900): 593–602.

Woods, Katharine Pearson. "The Evolution of an Artist." *Bookman* 9 (June 1899): 350–52.

Woods, Oliver and Bishop, James. *The Story of the Times.* London: Michael Joseph, 1983.

Woolf, Virginia. *Three Guineas.* London: Hogarth, 1938.

Worcester, Robert M. *British Public Opinion: A Guide to the History and Methodology of Public Opinion Polling.* Oxford: Basil Blackwell, 1991.

NEWSPAPERS AND PERIODICALS

Daily Mail
Daily News
Manchester Guardian
The Times
The Bloemfontein Friend
Westminster Gazette

ARCHIVES AND PRIVATE PAPERS

Sir Henry Campbell-Bannerman Papers, British Library
Joseph Chamberlain Papers, University of Birmingham
Kate Courtney Papers, London School of Economics
Millicent Fawcett Papers, Fawcett Library
Herbert Gladstone Papers, British Library
Kitchener Papers, Public Record Office, Kew
Kitchener-Marker Correspondence, British Library

Milner Papers, New College, Bodleian Library, Oxford
Solomon T. Plaatje Papers, University of London, School of Oriental and African Studies
Ripon Papers, British Library
Olive Schreiner Papers, Microfilm, University of York Southern African Studies Archives
War Office records, Public Record Office, Kew
Colonial Office records, Public Record Office, Kew

Index

CAMBRIDGE STUDIES IN NINETEENTH-CENTURY
LITERATURE AND CULTURE

GENERAL EDITOR
GILLIAN BEER, *University of Cambridge*

Titles published